Universality
The Blueprint for
Soccer's New Era

How Germany and Pep Guardiola are showing us the Future Football Game

by Matthew Whitehouse

BENNION KEARNY

Published by Bennion Kearny Limited
6 Woodside
Churnet View Road
Oakamoor
ST10 3AE

www.BennionKearny.com

For Richard, the bravest man I know.

My friend always.

Acknowledgements

I have been discussing the idea of universality for some time with many coaches and thinkers of the game. It has been a great project to work on, seeking to analyse the game's trends and deciphering these changes and developments. There is no doubt that great coaches of the game have been key to my understanding and development as a thinker and coach in the game of football. However, the key people are those closest to me who have allowed me to share and develop my ideas.

I wish to thank Devine Caddick for all the times we discuss the game. Without question this the one person who I share my thoughts with most on the game. Our time together is precious. I also wish to thank Paul Evans and Don Gethfield for all those hours after training when we have discussed ideas about coaching and the evolution of the game. These have been invaluable as well as enjoyable. Above all I wish to thank Jade for her patience and willingness to put up with the amount of time she has put into watching and discussing football with me.

Thanks go to this11.com for allowing me to use their diagrams for the team line-ups. And squawka.com for allowing me to use their own diagrams. Finally, I wish to thank my publisher Bennion Kearny for their support and insight into this second project - with their help we have developed a collection of thoughts and ideas on the game into a coherent and detailed book.

About the Author

Matthew Whitehouse is a professional football coach who has worked across the globe. A UEFA 'A' licenced coach with a Master's degree in Sports Coaching specialising in skill acquisition and motor skill learning. He has extensive experience both academically and practically on coaching and youth development.

Matthew is also a prominent and influential writer, author of *The Way Forward: Solutions to England's Football Failings*, and is the editor of the award winning *The Whitehouse Address* blog.

Table of Contents

Introduction

Part I | The Rise and Fall of Nations   **6**

Chapter 1: The Summer of 2003   7

Chapter 2: England's Dominant Era   10

Chapter 3: España   23

Chapter 4: The German Model   36

Part II | 21st Century Evolution   **52**

Chapter 5: Tactical Evolution   53

Chapter 6: Pressing   73

Chapter 7: Team-building   87

Chapter 8: Keeper Sweeper   95

Chapter 9: Modern Libero   102

Chapter 10: The Wing Back   106

Chapter 11: The 'Water Carrier'   112

Chapter 12: The Complete Midfielder   120

Chapter 13: The Trequartista   131

Chapter 14: The Inside Forward   142

Chapter 15: The Dying Breed   147

Part III | The Future Game   **155**

Chapter 16: Visionaries   156

Chapter 17: The Architect   169

Chapter 18: Universality   181

Bibliography   193

"In football the result is an imposter.
There's something greater than the result, more lasting - a legacy."
Xavi Hernandez

Introduction

"The game has become faster, more technical, and will continue to do so." Arsène Wenger

Football is a fascinating game. It has the ability to excite, frustrate and captivate billions of people across the world. It's a game which generates a passion that is unrivalled by many other sports. And as the game grows richer, it has become not only a spectator sport but a business too. Therefore, 'success' is more important than ever before. And those who seek to prepare for the future have a greater chance of success. Future success will come from philosophies, finances, players, and coaching.

The modern game is very different to what it was a decade ago and the future game will be markedly different. The game is always changing, it is always in flux. Players, coaches, teams and nations are constantly evolving in order to stay ahead of the others and be successful. Those who were dominant before, have been replaced by others, and those who lead - in the present - will find their position under threat in the future. As many countries and clubs have learnt - standing still means going backwards; it is important to always be adapting, evolving and anticipating the future.

Those who wish to be successful in the future need to anticipate what the game will be like and put in place methods and styles which will help produce players and teams who can succeed in the coming years. To look at what the future of football requires we must look at what is happening in the elite areas of the game.

The modern game has evolved, in the way it has, because of the money which now dominates its elite levels. Vast wages, agents, and extortionate transfer fees have made the game at the highest level an almost fantasy world. As the game has become richer, it has attracted the interest of rich businessmen, oligarchs, and sheikhs to invest in football clubs. This substantial financial investment has helped sides like Chelsea, Manchester City and Paris Saint-Germain to challenge football's elite of Real Madrid, Milan, Bayern Munich, Barcelona, Juventus and Manchester United.

Yet, in recent times, sides like Borussia Dortmund and Arsenal have shown that ingenuity in coaching and development can lead to sustainable growth and management that can still challenge the top sides. In fact, Germany as a nation has excelled through new ideas and an evolution of their coaching methods and philosophies.

This investment in youth development and coaching has seen Germany become World Cup champions and this was also seen with Spain, whose national side and domestic clubs have seemingly dominated football since 2008. Both counties invested in quality coaching and a philosophy, which followed the Dutch style of player development - allied with their own cultural backgrounds and modern tactical creativity.

Other nations have followed suit, most notably Belgium which, in recent years, has emerged as a developer of high quality talent, producing players equipped for the modern game. A nation such as Belgium has shown that an investment in youth development, alongside the implementation of a philosophy that suits the modern game, is a path to success.

Although finance has become a massive part of modern football, there is no doubting that the 'game' itself is still the single most important element to success. Therefore, in this book we will be looking at the game, its recent evolution, and where it is heading.

Football's evolution

Contemporary football has been derived from the past (obviously), and the new generation of coaches who have come into the sport. Modern day coaches have used the previous methods and styles of greats like Rinus Michels, Johan Cruyff, Arrigo Sacchi, Fabio Capello, and Alex Ferguson; men who have influenced numerous players and coaches. In turn, superb sides of the past have strongly influenced the game: Hungary with Franc Puskas in the 1950's, Brazil with the talents of Pelé, Carlos Alberto, Rivelino and Jairzinho, and Holland with Cruyff and Neeskens in the 1970's. Diego Maradona inspired a whole nation with his skill and flair. These sides and players mesmerised and inspired fans both then and now.

As great as those players, coaches, and sides of the past were, there is no doubt that, in today's game, coaching has become more technical, more precise, and those who understand the game and *all* that is required – technical, tactical, psychological and more - are best equipped to succeed.

What the top players and teams show us, nowadays, is how players at the elite levels have become expert technicians, with speed and precision increasing at a rapid pace. Pass completion and the importance of possession has seen players seeking (and able) to reach 90% pass accuracy rates on a consistent basis. More passes are being attempted and completed at a higher percentage than ever before. The speed of the game has increased with players in possession of the ball for an average of 2 seconds whilst in an average English Premier League match - 80 % of passes are played with one or two touches. This means actions need to happen in split-seconds and, importantly, decisions need to happen even quicker. The game has become much more technical and tactical as well physically and mentally demanding.

And it is not just when in possession that teams have become more progressive. In fact, it may be when out of possession that teams have become noticeably more complex and smarter. Possession-based football has forced coaches to produce smarter defensive tactics.

Because of the creativity of many top sides, allowing space behind the defence is a risk, so sides drop deeper, and allow the opposition to come onto them. They draw the opposition in, and then hit them on the counter with ruthless precision. Jose Mourinho has built his sides' successes on defence, whether at Porto, Chelsea, Inter or Madrid. All his sides are always organised, compact, and extremely ruthless on the counter. Present day sides like Atlético Madrid and Dortmund are similar in their style.

We only have to look at the importance that sides have put on defensive 'pressing', whether Barcelona's high pressing transition game or German football's *gegenpressing* method as proof that the modern game requires a complete (team-based) defensive foundation and understanding. The truth is that if you are not defensively aware and organised then you are not going to be able to compete in Europe, yet alone win there.

It is possible that it was the change to the offside rule that brought about this shift in defending. Changes to the offside law in 2005, where only players who were in a position to impact upon the opponent or ball would be deemed offside, have meant that the classic 'offside trap' of previous decades became much harder to implement. As Jonathan Wilson stated, *"against savvy opponents, who contrive to keep the ball away from those who have wandered offside, the offside trap has been rendered ineffective."* He added, *"The modern offside law remains unappreciated, but it has generated a climate in which some of the most beautiful football ever played has been produced."* This change has revolutionised the way teams defend and set up, because it has allowed teams to be more creative when they attack.

A new era

As the elite game continues to develop along its present lines, the teaching and coaching of our players must evolve with it. We must aspire to lead the game in the development of our players by looking forward and anticipating upcoming advancements.

Spain have shown us the way forward in recent years, and it appeared that their 'blueprint' was to be the one for football's future. And yet, we now see the emergence and rise of Bayern Munich and German football. We see what kind of player they are developing, and what style they are seeking to implement. A new force has come to dominate football.

It is evident that we are now entering a new era for football. One can argue that this new era has been a decade in the making. What this book will do is seek to explore how we have got to the present day, what the modern game involves, and seek to develop a blueprint of what the future game will require. In order to anticipate the future, however, we must look to learn from the past…

Part I | The Rise and Fall of Nations

Chapter 1: The Summer of 2003

"He is the biggest talent I have seen in football. The greatest. Ronaldinho, when he arrived, changed the history of this club." Ex-Barcelona goalkeeper Victor Valdes

In the summer of 2003, Chelsea FC was purchased by the billionaire Roman Abramovich. The Russian oligarch had a vision of dominating Europe and would embark on a summer of lavish spending in order to build a side capable of competing with the top sides across Europe. It sent shockwaves across football.

Abramovich had fallen in love with football when he visited Old Trafford to see Manchester United play Real Madrid in the quarter finals of the Champions League the previous April. Madrid were 3-1 up from the first leg and although United would win their home tie 4-3 - it was not enough to put them through. That game would see Ronaldo, the Brazilian forward, score a superb hat-trick for Madrid.

It was a game which would make anyone fall in love with football. It possessed flair and skill, it was fast and exciting, and it was entertaining. Abramovich was inspired and eagerly sought to buy a football club. Initially he wanted Manchester United but was advised to purchase Chelsea instead. That summer he purchased the London club and, in doing so, created a new superpower in world football.

The summer of 2003 was a time of great change in world football, overall. Manchester United appeared set for a new era of their own. After being knocked out of the Champions League (by Real Madrid) Alex Ferguson felt that he needed to take the team in a fresh direction. He wanted something new, something more… *modern.* Young exciting players like Ronaldinho and Arjen Robben were targeted, players who could deliver a new style for United.

In Spain, Barcelona were also looking for a fresh start after a few years of mediocre performances in La Liga and Europe. It had been a difficult few years for the Catalan side who had seen Valencia and Real Madrid become the two main clubs battling it out for Spain's top prizes. Joan Laporta, running for the club's presidency, promised to make Barcelona a force once again. As part of his campaign he even promised to sign David Beckham. It would turn out that the Beckham saga was significant, not only because of where various players ended up, but because of what Beckham, as a player, represented.

Beckham was significant for many clubs. United appeared set on a new course *without* him, and Barcelona and Madrid sought him to help initiate new eras of their own. Although Laporta would become president of Barca, Beckham would ultimately move to Real Madrid under a deal which involved the exit of Claude Makélélé (who moved to Chelsea, in order to make way for a new 'Galactico').

This deal can be seen as one of the biggest mistakes in Madrid's history. They replaced their superb defensive midfielder with a right midfielder. They gave up a player who was a key part of Madrid's success under Vicente del Bosque from 2000-2003, winning the league twice and the Champions League in 2002 (incredibly del Bosque would be sacked after the 02/03 season – another reason for Madrid's era of decadence). It is no surprise that without Makélélé and del Bosque, Madrid went downhill quickly while Chelsea would become one of Europe's elite.

Manchester United had anticipated replacing Beckham with more dynamic players in Ronaldinho and Robben. However, Barcelona would snatch the Brazilian away from them for £25m and Ferguson would lose out on Robben who opted to move to Chelsea instead. United had lost their two main targets and now had to look elsewhere. They would take a £12m gamble on a young Portuguese winger called Cristiano Ronaldo.

Although something of a surprise signing, Ferguson was confident he had found a gem of a player. He said, *"He is one of the most exciting young players I've ever seen."* Perhaps Ferguson was just attempting to soften the blows of losing Ronaldinho and Robben; no-one, not even Ferguson, could have seen what this young Portuguese winger would become in the following years.

Perhaps you are wondering why we are beginning our journey by looking at this moment in football history. The reason is that these transfers had vast implications for both the clubs involved and football as a whole. These players - Ronaldinho, Robben, and Cristiano Ronaldo - highlighted the start of a new era for football. The 'dribbler' had returned to the game.

The time of the 'classic' winger, players like Beckham, appeared to be dying in the early 2000's. Whilst individuals like Figo and Nedved had charmed football fans and pundits at the turn of the century, these young players pointed to the *future*. The game was changing and these players represented the start of something new and exciting.

Ronaldinho, in particular, was the type of player which the 90's had seemingly left behind; a man who opened the footballing world's eyes to a style of football which appeared to have been lost. He brought something special to Barca; his flair, speed, and skill put Barcelona back on the map as one of football's finest sides. It is not too far-fetched to say that the Brazilian was responsible for a major part of Barcelona's success over the past decade.

How ironic, therefore, that he was the second choice option after Beckham, a player who represented the 'old school' style of play of the 90's. Imagine if Barcelona had landed Beckham and United had got Ronaldinho… would not the landscape of football be different now?

Football's future changed dramatically in the summer of 2003. And as we will see, these signings made vast differences to the fortunes of Europe's top clubs. Yet, before these players made their significant impacts, let us first look at the French revolution which was in the midst of dominating English football. In those early years of the 2000's, under the Frenchman Arsène Wenger, Arsenal were becoming the strongest side in Europe and laying down their own blueprint of the future game.

Chapter 2: England's Dominant Era

"Arsène's a miracle worker. He's revolutionised the club. He's turned players into world-class players. Since he has been here, we have seen football from another planet." Former Arsenal Vice-Chairman David Dein

A decade ago, in 2004, Arsenal had just won the Premier League title without losing any of their 38 games, winning 26 and drawing 12 times. That achievement would have them named the *'Invincibles'*, a team which was recently voted the best side in Premier League history. It is important for us to look at how Arsenal got to this level and why they failed to challenge for the title again afterwards.

It all started in 1995 when David Dein, Arsenal's vice-chairman, flew out to Italy in order to sign one of Europe's best talents, returning with a 'true international superstar' in Dennis Bergkamp. Arsenal had bought the Dutch International for £7.5 million from Inter Milan. It was seen as a coup for the London club, and it was a sign of their ambitions to become one of Europe's top sides.

However, in his first season people were doubting Bergkamp's quality. Under the management of Bruce Rioch, and the style of the English game, Bergkamp appeared to struggle. Although he returned a goal every three games in his first season, it was clear that he was not making the impact expected of him.

Perhaps it was the restriction of playing in a functional 4-4-2, typical of the British game at that time? Perhaps those around him didn't know the runs and movement he liked to make? Or perhaps Bergkamp was actually struggling to find personal form after two difficult seasons in Serie A where he found the style of football not to his liking? Yet, England would be the perfect fit for him, under the right manager.

Had Bergkamp continued to play under a British manager it could have ruined the Dutch playmaker's career. Luckily, Dein decided to recruit a visionary and modern coach who could take the talents of Bergkamp and propel Arsenal to great heights.

The arrival of Arsène Wenger was fortuitous for Bergkamp in the same way that Bergkamp's presence was for Wenger. Bergkamp became the key, the maestro, the man who pulled the strings. In turn, he was to play alongside one of the best defences in England (perhaps Europe) in David Seaman, Tony Adams, Steve Bould, Lee Dixon and Nigel Winterburn.

A French revolution

In the period between 1997 and 2001 Wenger brought in other key players like Marc Overmars and Freddie Ljungberg as well as the French connection of Patrick Vieira, Emmanuel Petit, Robert Pires, Nicolas Anelka, Thierry Henry, and Sylvain Wiltord. The coach, along with these players, would revolutionise the club as well as English football.

The recruitment of the French players was something different for England. To see such a number of foreign players come into the league had never happened before. It was revolution for the league as much as for Arsenal. The French national side were without doubt the best side in international football at the time, winning both the World Cup in 1998 and the European Championships in 2000 and Wenger would use his connections, and knowledge of the French league and players, to build his foreign force in English football.

Arsenal's success was thus built on the quality and (importantly) the mentality of this group of players. The English contingent embodied the history and values of Arsenal Football Club, while the French incumbents were top quality players who were winners on the world stage. Wenger had assembled a high quality, balanced, modern, dynamic, and athletic side.

After Premier League and FA Cup success in the late 1990's Wenger knew his job was to evolve the side, specifically the defence. Between 2001 and the 2004 he brought in Jens Lehmann in goal, Sol Campbell from rivals Spurs, Lauren from Mallorca, and Ashley Cole emerged from the club's academy. Kolo Toure was bought from Ivorian side ASEC Mimosas for a mere £150k, a deal which turned out to be great value (and a sign of Wenger's future transfer philosophy). The attack became focused on the trio of Thierry Henry, Robert Pires and Bergkamp.

As mentioned above, during the 2003-04 season the team would win the league for the third time under Wenger and, incredibly, go unbeaten in all 38 games. They did this whilst playing some of the best football ever seen in England. In fact, the club also had their best chance to win the Champions League during that season. They were arguably the best side in the competition yet in the quarter final (against Chelsea) Arsenal would be eliminated in the second leg, at home, losing 2-1.

It was a performance which characterised Wenger's philosophy and the Arsenal team. The first half was seen by some to be the best football played by Wenger's side. The speed of play was sublime and Arsenal should have been leading by more than a single goal. Yet Chelsea's coach, Claudio Ranieri, would make a key tactical switch in the second half which would change the balance of the game.

He would replace the central midfielder Scott Parker for the fast and tricky winger Jesper Gronkjaer to put more pressure on Arsenal by offering more impetus in attack, which would force their full backs back. As Phillipe Auclair observed, *"The shrewdness of the Italian manager had altered the physiognomy of the game as a whole.*" It was an indication as to why Arsenal and Wenger have not won the Champions League. Free-flowing attacking football is scintillating to watch yet smart tactics produce more success. The fact that Jose Mourinho would win the Champions League that very season, with Porto, indicated that the future of football was becoming ever more tactical.

Arsenal's Invincibles 2003/04. Some would say it was a 4-4-2, others would see a 4-2-3-1. Importantly it had quality throughout, with a beautiful 'balance' throughout.

In 2004/2005 Arsenal's era of dominance would begin to unravel. It was Arsenal's centenary year yet Jose Mourinho, now Chelsea's new coach - the self-proclaimed 'Special One' - would make sure that Arsenal did not celebrate it with a title. Arsenal finished 12 points behind Chelsea, with Manchester United third. Although the team would enjoy FA Cup success over Manchester United, the gap between them and the League winners was worryingly large.

During the previous summer the team had lost some key 'leaders' in Martin Keown and Ray Parlour, the last of the George Graham era to leave. Wiltord and Edu would also leave that season. Arsenal had lost a significant amount of experience and 'winners'. Added to the departures was the pursuit of Patrick Vieira by Real Madrid. Although Vieira chose to stay at Arsenal the saga had clearly affected the team's harmony, and his mentality.

A philosophical change

Vieira would leave for Juventus the following summer, and it was a huge loss for the side as the Frenchman had been such a key player and leader. Arsenal struggled in the league and barely scraped fourth place to gain Champions League football, finishing 24 points behind the winners Chelsea. However, against all the odds, Wenger would take his team to the Champions League final, overcoming Real Madrid and Juventus along the way. His young, inexperienced, and some would say rather mediocre, side were 90 minutes from European success. They just had to overcome Ronaldinho's Barcelona.

Wenger had adopted a 4-5-1 formation in Europe, different to the 4-2-3-1 style he preferred in England. And perhaps they could have won it had Henry taken his chances or had Lehmann not been sent off for taking out Samuel Eto'o. They would even lead 1-0 at half time with 10 men, yet whether it was their legs or their mentality towards the end, they would end up losing 2-1. It was clear that the gap between Arsenal and the best was widening. But, aside from personnel changes, what else might have been causing this?

Some will point to the financial issues which affected Wenger when the Arsenal board decided to move from Highbury to the new Emirates stadium. This put significant financial constraints on the club. Wenger would know that he would struggle to compete with the money which Europe's elite, yet alone Chelsea and Manchester United, were able to pay for players. But perhaps the problem which many have neglected is that Wenger attempted to *change* his approach at Arsenal. One should actually identify two 'eras' at Arsenal under Wenger; one being French, the other Spanish.

Between 2004 and 2008 Arsène Wenger went about dismantling his *Invincibles* team. Out went Keown, Parlour, Vieira, Pires, Cole, Edu, Henry, Campbell, Ljungberg and Lehmann in the space of four seasons. The end to the exodus was Gilberto Silva who left in 2008.

Many, at the time, believed Wenger was a 'genius' as the conviction was that 'he knew the right time to let players go'. And perhaps things would not have been as catastrophic had his approach to the 'modern game' not been so flawed. Evolution is important in football but what came in to replace this winning group of players became the reason for Arsenal's failings.

France's dominance from 1998-2000 was built on strength, physicality, and (of course) technical skill. However, at the 2002 World Cup France were nothing short of awful; Zidane was injured before the start and Henry was struggling to impose himself on the national side. The loss of leaders in Laurent Blanc and Didier Deschamps had taken away the discipline and leadership which characterised the team's success in 1998 and 2000. A perceived arrogance had apparently taken hold too. French football was in turmoil. The French period of supremacy was coming to an end.

Arsène Wenger, being a man who likes to stay ahead of the game, envisaged a growing need for technicians. From 2004 he set out to revolutionize his club in this new image and style. Perhaps he had always looked at developing more of possession-based side over a faster-paced attacking side. It was clear that Wenger felt football was moving away from the 'type' of player that he had built his success on previously; he moved away from size and power and turned his focus to the slighter, more technical player. Since the *Invincibles* season Arsenal started to integrate players like Jose Antonio Reyes, Cesc Fàbregas, Mathieu Flamini, and Alexander Hleb into the side.

If this was Wenger's belief - that the Spanish type of player was the future - then he was both right and wrong. The Spanish model of development, notably being put in place by Barcelona more so than others, was already over a decade old, having been set up around 1990 by Johan Cruyff. For Arsenal to overhaul their previous French/African type of player and style was risky, dangerous, and ultimately flawed.

In Wenger's attempts to replicate the Spanish model Arsenal lost their power, strength and... *dominance*. The mid-2000's midfield moved from one of might and power (along with skill and quality) with Vieira, Petit, Edu and Gilberto Silva to players more slight and technical in Reyes, Flamini, Fàbregas, Hleb, Rosicky, Denilson, Fran Merida and Alex Song. Young, impressionable, and 'technically good' players yes, yet Arsenal who once overpowered sides with physical dominance were now being overpowered themselves. The *change* was not conducive for success.

There is no doubt that the change in player size has had a major impact on Arsenal's success. Arsenal went from possessing World Cup winners and world class genius to using small inexperienced 'kids'. Although Wenger saw a new style of football coming into being - he forgot some crucial things.

Firstly, his side's French style was perfect for the Premier League; his players were tall, strong, and powerful. The 'French era' did not possess just brutes, of course, and Arsenal played some great football, but they had the key to success: experience and 'balance'. In their unbeaten season Arsenal conceded only 26 goals which pointed to their strong defensive setup. They possessed quality, skill, flair and, importantly, intimidation. The squad had an intensity and dominance which was feared by many.

And for some reason, call it ideology or misguided vision, Wenger threw it all away. Arsenal became timid, small, and vulnerable; where they were once strong and fearsome, they were now weak. Wenger had a winning formula at Arsenal and yet his change in philosophy cost the club success. His team could have dominated Europe for the past decade if he had not changed (or should that be 'embraced') his new philosophy.

The Special One

Compare the above to when Jose Mourinho arrived at Chelsea in 2004. We will be looking at lot more at Mourinho later on, so this section is just a pointer to the influence and impact he had on the English league.

In the summer of 2004 Mourinho arrived at Chelsea after winning the Champions League with Porto. He inherited a team who had proven their ability to be a top side the previous year but Mourinho would take them to another level. Perhaps Mourinho understood and learnt from Wenger's success. He built his side on an *English core* of John Terry and Frank Lampard (in a similar vein to what Wenger initially did) and made sure he had a strong, dominant spine in his side. Ricardo Carvalho was brought in from Porto, along with the Czech goalkeeper Petr Čech who was signed from Rennes. Mourinho now had one of the best defences in the Premier League.

In his midfield, Mourinho possessed the strength and defensive force of Claude Makélélé, adding even more physicality, athleticism and skill in 2005/06 with the signing of Ghanaian midfielder Michael Essien. Up front he enhanced the skills of the Ivorian Didier Drogba and turned him in to one of the best forwards to play in England. These players could be said to be Arsenal 'type' players of the 1998-2004 vintage. With the arrival of the quick Dutch winger Arjen Robben from PSV, Mourinho would have the resources and balance which he required to implement his 4-3-3 formation to dominate the English Premier League for two years running from 2004-2006.

Chelsea's 2005/06 Premier League winning team.
Mourinho's 4-3-3 proved incredibly effective and dominant throughout
the season and helped Chelsea to back-to-back titles.

Mourinho's understanding of the league was the key in catapulting Chelsea to the top of the tree. Yes, finances played a part, but it was up to the coach what type of player to purchase. He would put together a team which possessed athleticism, strength, and an ability to dominate. Back-to-back league titles for Chelsea highlighted the rise of a new force in England and across Europe.

Perhaps Mourinho could have won a Champions League had it not been for Liverpool and a rather dubious goal which was given in the 2004/2005 semi-final. The following season Chelsea would be knocked out by the rising force in European football, Barcelona, in the knockout stages. In Mourinho's final year at Chelsea he would take the club to the semi-finals, again, only to lose to Liverpool, again. This time losing on penalties to Rafa Benitez's side.

Whilst Mourinho was not able to take Chelsea to European success - he did show what was required to succeed in England. He had brought a new tactical element, a more European approach to controlling games (something which was not all that common in England at that time). This was the modern coach, and what the game required. A lesson Alex Ferguson had learned at the turn of the century at Manchester United.

Ferguson's European vision

With the influx of foreign coaches like Wenger, Mourinho, and Benitez, English football evolved; it became more European in its style and success was built on new ideas and methods. Although Manchester United were England's biggest side, this new influx appeared, seemingly, to be leaving the club behind the rest. United had started to trail behind Arsenal and Chelsea between 2003 and 2005, with many in the media believing Ferguson's dominant days were behind him.

However Alex Ferguson was developing a new plan, a new vision of making United Europe's top side again. His plan involved developing his side to become capable of competing in the 21st century. United would become more European, moving away from how they played in the 90's.

After the treble success in 1999, Manchester United appeared set for a period of supremacy . However the following seasons would actually throw up more questions than answers for Ferguson. With Arsenal serious contenders to United, and Real Madrid asserting themselves at the top of European football, it was clear to Ferguson that United needed something new.

One of the major criticisms of Ferguson has been his failings in Europe; he had reached just one final by 2000 which seemed a poor return for the dominance that United enjoyed in England. It was clear that the coaching of Brian Kidd and Steve McLaren, although successful domestically, meant that United lacked the edge and understanding of the European game. Ferguson sought out a coach who could take United into the 21st century.

In 2002, Alex Ferguson made a bold and visionary decision to bring in Carlos Queiroz, as his assistant, to replace Steve McLaren. It was a masterstroke in terms of modernising Manchester United for European competition. Queiroz had previously been coaching the national sides of the UAE and South Africa and Ferguson brought him in to further the work of McLaren. He did an excellent job in his first year and United took the title back to Old Trafford in the 02/03 season, snatching it from Arsenal.

As we saw in Chapter 1, United would subsequently embark on a new approach, in 2003, into how they played the game. Out went the classic winger, David Beckham, and in came Cristiano Ronaldo (after failed attempts to sign Ronaldinho and Robben). These targets indicated that the classic United style of play was about to change; they looked to favour dribblers over crossers.

United's new era

In the summer of 2003 Queiroz left Manchester United and became the manager at Real Madrid. His time there was not a positive one, and he returned as Ferguson's assistant the following summer, just as Wayne Rooney was being signed from Everton.

Had Queiroz not returned, the career of Cristiano Ronaldo may have been different to the one we know now. Ronaldo's first season at Old Trafford was a difficult one; a boy who appeared to be very skilful yet very selfish with the ball, seemingly happier to beat a player than make good decisions for the team. He was ridiculed by fans across the country. After the productive quality of Beckham many were led to question the logic of United's acquisition and their vision for the future. With the return of Queiroz, however, Ronaldo had a man who could teach and educate him to further his game, and develop him into one of the world's best.

Although Manchester United won no trophies the following season, they were developing a new style, and Ferguson appeared willing to show patience in order to build and develop their excellent youth players in Ronaldo and Rooney. United were building an exciting attacking style yet, in order to achieve success, they needed 'balance'.

In November 2005 United made their most decisive move. They released Roy Keane from the club, with Queiroz rumoured to be one of the main drivers behind team captain Keane's departure. According to Keane, he did not like the tactics that Queiroz employed, and he did not like the way Queiroz was given so much responsibility (as if he was manager of the club).

There was a clear indication that the old school United mentality was being phased out with David Beckham, Phil Neville, Nicky Butt and now Roy Keane moved on. Ferguson was willing to trust the vision of Queiroz and create a side capable of not just dominating England, but Europe.

Defensive improvements arrived with the signings of Edwin van der Sar in 2005 and Nemanja Vidic and Patrice Evra in 2006. These players brought stability to what was, at times, a leaky defence. Michael Carrick arrived in 2006 to fill the void left by Roy Keane and it was clear that both Ferguson and Queiroz felt Carrick was an instrumental addition to their new style.

As United sought to play a fluid, attacking four, in a 4-2-3-1 formation, they needed a player who could supply balls to the attacking quartet. In his first season Carrick played 46 games; he was the missing piece in the development of this new generation.

Queiroz's transformation of the side was complete in the summer of 2006 when Ruud van Nistelrooy was moved on, with apparent issues between him and Ronaldo, whose late and staggered delivery meant van Nistelrooy was not receiving the right service for his type of runs in the area. Ferguson had a choice and chose Ronaldo. That following season United not only won the league, but did it in style. Ronaldo scored 23 goals in all competitions, almost as many as he had done over the previous three seasons combined.

United's evolution pointed towards a new type of forward. Ronaldo was now the goal scorer, yet his position was on the right wing. This style of play was markedly different to United's wide play tactic of crossing and finishing. Ronaldo was now instructed to stay wide and drive inside, with the single mentality of scoring goals.

It showed how far United had come in terms of their progressive style, their winger was now their forward, and the side was created to get the best from Ronaldo. Often the ball would be played down the left, it would then be switched long to Ronaldo who would be hugging the right touchline, his immaculate touch and then speed and skill would scare full backs, and his ability to drive and shoot at speed with power and precision meant he was the most frightening player in the world. Pure perfection and all credit to Queiroz in making this possible.

Queiroz clearly saw the way football was developing and the use of 'inverted wingers', those who cut inside not out, and who sought to score not provide. This was what Ronaldo was groomed to be.

United won the title three times in a row from 2006 to 2009 and it was apparent that Ferguson's own vision to develop the side and create a truly modern European team was vindicated. Queiroz was the architect; he solidified the defence and created an attacking foursome which was fluid, creative, and ruthless. It was clear that Queiroz had succeeded in transforming the side from a rigid 4-4-2 into one which was now *fluid* and *flexible*.

United vs Chelsea in the 2008 Champions League final.
At times a 4-2-3-1, other times a 4-3-3 and, when needed, a fluid 4-2-4.
Ferguson and Queiroz had seemingly found the modern formula.

The creator leaves and old ways return

In 2008, amid rumours of an opening for the position of Portuguese National Coach, Alex Ferguson started to push for Queiroz to become his successor as manager at Old Trafford, and he sought to discourage potential suitors from courting Queiroz. However, speculation over the summer of 2008 continued to link Queiroz with Portugal (following the departure of Luiz Felipe Scolari) and in July

2008, Manchester United agreed to release Queiroz from his contract and he was appointed manager of the Portuguese national team.

This was a major loss for United and Ferguson. Ferguson clearly was grooming Queiroz as his replacement; he had handed over much responsibility and had allowed Queiroz to develop the style of the side. Ferguson should have done more to keep Queiroz, perhaps even stepping aside to allow him to manage the club. Queiroz's departure would mean a gradual decline in style, quality, and success.

United were unable to keep Queiroz for the 08/09 season yet they did keep Ronaldo, and they almost won the Champions League again, losing to Barcelona in the final in Rome. Yet losing Ronaldo and Tevez (the following summer) meant the team which Queiroz had perfected was no longer. His departure was a damaging blow which many fail to comprehend.

Ronaldo, a player who had become world class, was always going to be difficult to replace, and the signings of Antonio Valencia and Michael Owen showed a regression back to the old ways. Both players suited the style of the 1990's more than the modern game. Valencia was a classic 'out and out' winger and Owen was more of a poacher than a modern forward.

After Queiroz left United, they lost their throne as Europe's kings. A club which, for several years, appeared to be leading the world of football in a tactical revolution regressed back to their old ways; reverting back to a 4-4-1-1 which offered little creativity or variety.

England's dominance ends

It was quite a period for English football. Between 2005 and 2012 English clubs had been represented in the Champions League final for seven out of the eight seasons, winning the trophy three times. It was a statement of how strong the Premier League was.

Unlike Spain and Italy who were only represented in finals by Barcelona and Milan respectively, England would see all four of their big clubs reach one final or more. United and Arsenal, along with Chelsea and Liverpool, became four of the most dominant sides across the continent. This was a glorious period for English football as it was clear that the league possessed the strongest teams with some of the best players and coaches.

And yet, in 2012, Liverpool were no longer contenders for the Champions League, Manchester United and the *nouveau riche* Manchester City failed to get out of their groups, Arsenal were taught a lesson by an average Milan side, and although Chelsea went on to win it, the manner in which they did so showed an admittance that they weren't as good as others. A 'defend at all costs' mentality was their only way of overcoming sides like Barca and Bayern.

Now, of course, it feels weird to think of England's demise when Chelsea conquered Europe in just 2012. And the year before that, United were in the final. Yet the manner in how both sides won and lost their respective games highlights where English sides had gone in terms of quality.

This past decade has seen the English style move from dominance to relative ineffectiveness. In the mid-2000's the power, speed, and intensity of the games were too much for many sides across Europe. English sides simply overpowered many 'foreign' sides and it gave English sides a belief that they were superior to the rest. It led the media to portray English sides as Europe's strongest; they continually made out the English league as the best. It also made English sides lazy.

The truth is that the power and strength which made England so dominant for the past decade has been replaced by a more technical and tactical game. The changes in modern football have seemingly surprised many English sides. Whilst the game has changed, many English clubs hung on to the previous decade's style with a desire to retain their power.

Power seemingly started seeping out of teams after the 2009 final between Manchester United and Chelsea. An exodus of talent from the league did not help. Ronaldo and Tevez (and of course Queiroz) left Manchester United. Liverpool did not just lose Xabi Alonso and Javier Mascherano from their side, but also Rafa Benitez (replaced by Roy Hodgson). Benitez's tactical knowledge had been a big reason for Liverpool's success in Europe.

The same is true of Jose Mourinho. He made Chelsea a big player not just domestically but in Europe. Of course he had money to buy talent, yet he possessed great coaching talent. His ability to bring a team together, to motivate and inspire them, was key to his success. Importantly, he had a great tactical brain.

The truth is, England's dominance was really built on the quality of *foreign imports*, both players and managers. As they left, the quality seemingly dropped also.

Football works like this… where cycles of success and dominance come and go. Is it possible that the dominance of the 2000's restricted the top English teams from adapting and evolving their tactics and their personnel? As the game developed with new coaching methods and tactics - was English football left behind? Had English football been found out? Was their period of dominance over? The answers were yes.

The door was opened for other leagues and sides to dominate European football. And in the 2009 Champions League final Barcelona, under Pep Guardiola, opened the eyes of many to the future of football. A new force had arisen. Spanish football would overthrow the Premier League, yet perhaps no-one could imagine how dominant or revolutionary it would be…

Chapter 3: España

"We go out from the first moment looking for the ball and looking to put pressure on the opposition. If you are not going to pass the ball then why play the game? That is not football in my opinion." Xavi Hernandez

The Galacticos

At the turn of the 21st century Spanish football offered consistent challengers for the Champions League with Real Madrid or Valencia reaching the final, four out of five times from 1998 to 2002. Madrid, in particular, looked on course to dominate Europe for years to come.

Florentino Perez, a Spanish businessman, took over as Madrid's president in 2000, and he inherited a team that had just won two Champions Leagues (in 1998 and 2000). Perez had won the presidency by his insistence on bringing Luis Figo to the club from arch-rivals Barcelona. He promised that, as president, he would embark on his 'Galactico' project, which for many meant buying the best and biggest names in world football. However, the term was also meant to describe the policy of signing big superstars for large transfer fees while promoting the best players from the club's youth system (although things never quite worked out this way). This project would see lavish money spent on players like Figo, Zidane, Ronaldo, and David Beckham.

The potential in bringing all these players together appeared huge yet the reality was somewhat different. At first it seemed a success, another Champions League win in 2002 confirmed Madrid as Europe's top side. Yet the Galactico project would, ultimately, prove to be something of an anti-climax. Madrid's president would end up destroying a winning team and ultimately put Madrid on course for a decade of disappointment.

Vicente del Bosque was fired in 2003 after winning the league and after Champions League success just the season before. Perez wanted a 'shake up'. Perez also decided to let Claude Makélélé leave (refusing him the contract he wished for) and replaced him with David Beckham. Perez clearly did not 'know' football, he only knew 'flair' and this quote confirms as much: *"We will not miss Makélélé. His technique is average, he lacks the speed and skill to take the ball past opponents, and 90% of his distribution either goes backwards or sideways."*

Real Madrid's 'balanced' 2002 Champions League final winning side.

With Makélélé in the team, the side had 'balance' and it was successful. Selling Makélélé ruined that balance. In the following years more 'Galacticos' arrived in the form of Michael Owen and Robinho yet Madrid were not able to replicate their previous triumphs. It didn't work as planned for Perez and the success of Madrid – and their potential dominance - at the turn of the century was lost.

Florentino Perez resigned in 2006, stating the club needed a 'new direction'. A lack of vision, philosophy, and culture had defined Madrid during his tenure. Madrid appeared to move from coach to coach without any kind of strategy (we will look at his return, later on, and how a new approach made Madrid one of Europe's best sides and finally brought the coveted tenth European crown in 2014). This period seemingly opened the door for Barcelona to become Spain's best side. Yet perhaps no-one could have anticipated how great they would turn out to be.

Brazilian influence

In 2012 Spain rewrote the history books by winning their third major tournament in a row, confirming their dominance in international football. Since 2008 Spain have won the European Championships twice and the World Cup, and their youth sides are winning tournaments too; the under 21's (2011 and 2013) and under-19's (2011) were both successful in the European Championships. It has been a glorious period for Spanish football.

Since their Euro triumph in 1964, Spain was always a nation that under-achieved; always possessing good players, yet never able to perform with consistency or with the mental strength required to win a major tournament. Yet, in 2008, something changed. Success arrived, and from that - winning became a habit.

There have been many reasons offered as to why Spain and Barcelona have dominated world football over the past several years. They have included the impact of Cruyff at Barcelona in the early 1990's with his transformation of the club (and ultimately the nation) into the Dutch philosophy in terms of style and youth development. This led to, or coincided with, improvements in coaching from the Spanish FA. Some even believe that the removal of Raúl from the Spanish national side was a factor. Or could the key to the glittering success of Spanish football be down to one man? A Brazilian who arrived at Camp Nou in the summer of 2003…

When Barcelona missed out on Beckham the new president, Joan Laporta, had to produce a big name to appease the fans who voted him in. Barcelona decided to snatch Ronaldinho from under Manchester United's nose for a fee of £25m while, at the same time, hiring Frank Rijkaard as the new coach. With the arrival of a new President, a new young manager, and a marquee signing, the club appeared set on a new course - a course which perhaps even the board and fans did not expect and one which laid the foundations for the dominance of Barcelona and Spain today.

The first season under Rijkaard saw the side finish second behind Rafa Benitez's Valencia. It was not an easy season since and in January 2004 the side were mid-table. The pressure on the new coach was very high. Rijkaard decided to bring in a more combative midfielder to help the side and loaned Edgar Davids (an Ajax youth graduate) from Juventus. Davids became vital and he helped stabilize the side and propel them up the league. This gave Rijkaard more time and importantly helped Ronaldinho's integration.

It was in the 2004/05 season, however, when Ronaldinho put Barcelona back on the map. Major changes happened that year; out went Luis Enrique, Marc Overmars,

Patrick Kluivert, Edgar Davids and Phillip Cocu and in came Samuel Eto'o, Deco, and Ludovic Giuly for a combined total of £55m. The changes ended a six year wait to top La Liga.

The performances of Ronaldinho and Eto'o earned them both places in FIFA's World XI and Ronaldinho was named FIFA World Player of the Year for 2005. In the 2005/2006 season Barcelona would win the league again and overcome Arsenal in Paris to win the Champions League. The side, which three years previously had finished *sixth* in La Liga (2003), were now European Champions and playing the best football in the world, possessing the best player in the world.

The Champions League success would be Rijkaard's and Ronaldinho's pinnacle during their careers at Camp Nou as the following season Barcelona lost out to Fabio Capello's Madrid (on the head-to-head record) and would be knocked out by Liverpool in the first knockout round of the Champions League. Rijkaard and Ronaldinho's final season at the club would lead to reports of a lack of discipline in the squad. Even the arrival of Thierry Henry did not help the club who would go on to come third in the league.

At the end of the 2007/2008 season - Barcelona were a team lacking ideas, motivation, and belief. A third place league finish (18 points behind the winners Madrid) would indicate how the side which won the Champions League in 2006 were now a shadow of their former selves. Changes needed to be made, Rijkaard was shown the door and a new man was brought in.

Spain's final hurdle

While Barcelona were in some sort of turmoil the Spanish national team were travelling to Switzerland and Austria for the European Championships. Under the leadership of Luis Aragonés, Spain played some excellent attacking football playing a 4-3-3 and tasted success in a major tournament for the first time since 1964. The team which had always underachieved had finally overcome their mental deficiencies and impressed the world with their technical brilliance.

Aragonés' decision to focus the team around the talents of Xavi Hernandez and play a possession-based style was key. Aragonés saw the talent in his side yet understood their vulnerabilities with height and strength. Therefore he played a style which brought the best out of players like Xavi, Iniesta, and David Silva. Wenger had been right, the Spanish type player and philosophy *was* the next step in football's evolution. Yet the difference was that Aragonés, and then Guardiola, would turn this into *great* success.

A key element for success is having experience of winning. Was the 2008 triumph thanks to the influence of Ronaldinho? Is it possible that Spain's success arrived on the back of Barcelona's triumphs, especially their success in the Champions League in 2006? National team players like Valdes, Puyol, Xavi and Iniesta were experiencing success and the national team profited from it. For these Spanish players, the era of Ronaldinho developed their games and, importantly, instilled a belief in their abilities to win; Ronaldinho was integral to pushing Spanish football over the final hurdle.

Back at Barcelona, Pep Guardiola took over from Frank Rijkaard in 2008 and was fortunate to inherit a beautiful mix of talent and hunger, with players like Iniesta, Messi and Bojan ready to step into the shoes of Ronaldinho and Deco. Yet what he did with the squad, and club as a whole, was thanks to his education as a player and his talents as a coach.

Cruyff's protégé

Pep Guardiola was the man who the board believed could galvanize Barcelona. A great player for Barcelona in the 90's, yet with limited coaching experience (having only spent a season coaching the 'B' side) Guardiola's appointment at Barcelona was seen by many as folly. Here was a man with no experience in management, coaching one of the best sides in the world. However, his education under Cruyff and Louis van Gaal, as well as his experiences in Italy and Mexico, meant he was more qualified for the role than many would realise.

In his first meeting with the squad, the players' doubts would be squashed. Xavi recalled, *"Instantly I could sense a different atmosphere, new standards. Standards had slipped. A kilo here or there, a few minutes late did not matter. Now everything mattered, Pep was on top of everything like a hawk."*

He won the confidence and respect of the players with his approach. Unity was the first thing he sought. At 37 he appeared too young, yet he told the players that, *"If you think I'm going to be soft on you, an easy touch, simply because I'm only 37 then you are wrong. My pride and ambition are enormous, and let's be clear, you're going to work hard."*

Guardiola intended to bring glory back to the Camp Nou, and to do it with the quality that was expected of the great club. He began by moving out disruptive or dysfunctional players like Ronaldinho, Deco, Zambrotta, Edmilson and Giovanni dos Santos who were all deemed surplus to the plans of the new boss. In came *his* players: Dani Alves, Seydou Keita, Alexander Hleb, and Gerard Pique (the former La Masia graduate). He also promoted players who he worked with in the Barca B side which had won Spain's third tier; Sergio Busquets, Pedro, and Jeffren Suarez.

Incredibly during the summer of 2008 Xavi Hernandez was considered, by some, to be surplus to requirements, with a move to Bayern Munich looking probable. Yet Guardiola had different ideas, stating that, like Aragonés, Xavi would be the *key* to his team. He saw himself in Xavi, the fulcrum for his *Totalfootball* tactic to work; he required a coach on the pitch and Xavi was the ideal choice. Xavi's performances at

Euro 2008 and onwards had shown how such a player, when used correctly, can control and dominate a game like no other midfielder.

The philosophy that Cruyff had introduced to Barcelona was implemented by Guardiola, an emphasis on what the player can do with the ball, an emphasis on technical ability, creativity, and intelligence. At other clubs and youth academies, individuals like Messi, Xavi, and Iniesta would perhaps have been deemed 'too small and frail', yet at Barcelona, with their philosophy on developing *footballers* (and not just physical athletes) these players helped make the club the best team in the world.

The biggest tactical decision made by the new coach was to implement a high pressing defensive game when his team lost possession of the ball. In his opinion 'pressuring high limits the amount of running players must do'. Not only does this tactic stop the opposition creating a goal scoring opportunity but, of course, when you win back the ball high up the pitch you are closer to goal. It makes sense and has been deployed by many teams in the past. Yet it requires a lot of energy and team cohesion, as well as strict tactical discipline – which we are finding to be very important in the pursuit of success! Thierry Henry had remarked that he never worked as hard than when he was at Barca under Guardiola.

Barcelona also embarked on their infamous possession-based approach to football.

"The mistake many made was concluding that a commitment to creative possession football inherently means turning your back on hard work and discipline, on pragmatism and competitiveness; that the aesthetic is by definition incompatible with the effective. Guardiola is every bit as meticulous as, say, Rafa Benítez; every bit as much of a control freak; every bit as pragmatic. And he is every bit as determined to win." Sid Lowe *The Guardian*.

It was hard not to fall in love with Barcelona, or at the least respect them for their quality and achievements during the Guardiola era. Their treble success in the first season highlighted the special achievement Guardiola had produced. The 6-2 demolition of Real Madrid at the Bernabeu that season was a sign of how far the side had come under Guardiola.

The following season saw the side win the league again, yet fail at the semi-final stage of the Champions League, with the signing of Zlatan Ibrahimovic seen as a negative influence on the team's balance and harmony. Ibrahimovic would leave and be replaced by David Villa in the 2010/11 season, when the side recaptured their balance and quality. In fact they were truly excellent; in terms of technical and tactical mastery, the team played like one whole organism knowing each other's movements and playing with fluency. It was mesmerising. The 5-0 defeat of Real Madrid at Camp Nou, and 3-1 defeat of Manchester United in the Champions League final were spectacular. Yet the following season the team started to lose its magic again.

"The greatest team ever" Barcelona's starting XI versus Manchester United in the 2011 Champions League final. As close to perfection as possible?

Striving for perfection

In the 2011/12 season things started to look a little wrong. There were rumours that Guardiola wanted to quit after his Champions League success in 2011 yet he could not resist the attempt to win back-to-back European Cups - as some of the great sides of previous decades had. In that final season Guardiola sought to change the formation and introduce Cruyff's dream 3-4-3 formation. He also showed a desperation to bring back another La Masia graduate - Cesc Fàbregas. And with these changes and adaptations, Barcelona lost something.

Universality

As the 2011/12 season progressed, people started questioning the tactics deployed by Guardiola. He attempted to take Barcelona to another level, and aimed to achieve what Michels and Cruyff had wished for decades previously, the *pinnacle* of total football, the 3-4-3. Michels had called the formation *"spectacular but risky"*. Yes, there were times when the formation produced amazing results, 5-0 against Villareal for instance but it also resulted in disappointing outcomes as well. Too many draws, and perhaps a stubbornness and restrictiveness in playing the Barca 'way'.

Guardiola's dream appeared to be a team of midfielders who would take possession football to another level. Yet, at the same time, they seemed to lose the chemistry, fluency, and balance which made them so majestic in the 2010/11 season. The new approach consisted of too much possession and not enough penetration. The tiki-taka style became stale and as teams figured Barca's style out, Barca simply kept the ball more and more.

The Dutch philosophy introduced by Michels and Cruyff was to dominate and play attacking football. This tiki-taka football was not what Cruyff imagined. Had it become possession for possession's sake?

So what changed? Firstly, the formation - the ultimate dream of the 3-4-3 was not as beneficial to the side as hoped. Guardiola sought to continually evolve his Barcelona side and he did so through the Totalfootball philosophy of Michels and Cruyff. Through injury (Puyol) and perhaps lack of focus (Pique) Guardiola started to bring in more midfielders to his defensive line. Players like Busquets and Mascherano, regarded as holding midfielders, were being played in the back line. It was Guardiola's way of overloading the midfield even more while giving licence to players like Dani Alves to play high and wide in an attacking winger role.

In fairness to Guardiola it was hard to ever say he played a 4-3-3 with Alves in the side, a player who like to attack and push very high up the pitch. It would always become a back three in this instance. But there was a sense that, in his last season, Guardiola was seeking something more, something different from his players and tactics. Was it too much? Had he pushed the boundaries too far after three years? Was he guilty of trying to be too smart or was he seeking to make Barca the most complete side in football history? The fact his final season ended with just the Copa Del Rey (playing the 4-3-3 which was so dominant before) highlighted the truth that he had taken Barca as far as he could.

Yet it wasn't just tactics. The team appeared to have lost its focus. Guardiola had talked about cycles, about how teams need to keep changing. A common idea in football is that teams and coaches have three year cycles. This was Barca's fourth under Guardiola and there had been little transition. The lesson appeared to be that coaches had to move on in order to maintain standards and keep players focused. It was possible that *Guardiola's* cycle had come to an end.

As touched on, previously, Barca's defence was in serious need of investment and strengthening. Although Barcelona had been blessed with attacking individuals, they had built their success on defensive solidity through players like Puyol, Abidal, Valdes, Alves, Pique, and with midfield players like Busquets and Xavi. In 2011/12, except for perhaps Busquets, each player mentioned in this defensive list experienced a loss of form. Whether through the natural decline of age, or injury, or the difficulty of balancing a celebrity lifestyle with a football career - the truth is that Barcelona's defence suffered.

The failure to evolve and add new pieces to the degraded defence was an indictment of Barca's philosophy and their beliefs. A cynic, however, may argue that Guardiola left because his players had stopped listening to him. The intensity and constant need with which he wanted them to work and press had lost its impact. Could it be that they had achieved so much in those previous years that some had lost their drive to continue it?

Perhaps the most famed aspect of Barca's play during Guardiola's era was their high pressing game. For most periods of the Guardiola years - whenever the team lost the ball everyone knew that they had to press and seek to win it back within five seconds. The team's ability to press and deny counter attacking opportunities was a major part of their success.

In Guardiola's last season there were signs that Barcelona had stopped pressing high up the pitch. Or at least were becoming less effective at it. Whether through fatigue or a lack of focus Barcelona dropped their work rate and high pressing game. They became slower and less effective defensively which exposed them and their defensive frailties more.

It was understandable because, since 2008, the majority of the squad (being mostly Spanish) had not properly taken a break. Due to international tournaments, and the lack of a meaningful preseason the players were simply exhausted. It is perhaps why they kept possession for longer… in order to 'rest on the ball'.

At the end of the 2011/2012 season it was deemed 'the end of an era' for Barcelona. Guardiola (who was essential to the success of the side) could take no more. He had put enormous pressure on himself to make his work a success and had achieved more than many coaches in his four years. He knew it was time for him to move on and allow a new man to push the club forward.

The Messi problem

Let us look at the relationship between Guardiola and Messi as it is important when we consider the importance of 'balance' when achieving success. It was evident that Guardiola's work, and relationship, with Lionel Messi further demonstrated his talents as a man-manager. When Guardiola took over, Messi showed the potential of being something special yet he wasn't, by any means, the end product we know today. Guardiola was perfect to help Messi become the player he became.

Guardiola's first decision would influence how Messi would view him. That summer Messi was desperate to go to the Olympics to win gold for his country, however the board at Barcelona was adamant that he was needed for their Champions League qualifier. Guardiola made sure Messi went to represent his country, having won gold himself with Spain in 1992.

Messi would go and win the gold with Argentina, Barca would qualify for the Champions League, and a bond would be forged. Guardiola won over the Argentinian and created a relationship which gave Messi the willingness, belief, and desire to become the best and take Barcelona to glory. Another coach may have failed Messi and we may never have seen such quality.

Now there is no doubt that Messi has been the world's best player these past four years; he has been the Champions League top scorer from 2009 to 2013 and has won the trophy twice, scoring in both finals. His progression as the world's best goal scorer is evident from Guardiola's first season; 38 goals in 08/09, 47 the season after, 53 the next, 73 after.

Guardiola learnt early on that Messi was special and would be central to his success. He learnt also that Messi needed to be pleased. His comment, "*If Leo smiles, everything is easier*" was a dangerous message. As Guardiola admitted in Guillem Balague's book, *Guardiola: Another Way to Win,* he was having to please Messi, often at the expense of the team. Yet Guardiola knew how great Messi was and knew that if he could not find an answer in a game - Messi would likely find it instead. Ultimately, however, it became a case of putting too much onto Messi.

In the Champions League semi-final against Chelsea in 2012 Barcelona proved that they had become too reliant on Messi. In that game there was a clear sense that the team and coach were hoping for Messi to come up with some kind of magic, on which he did not deliver. The pressure on him showed as he missed a penalty in the second half. As the game went on Chelsea suffocated his space and restricted his influence. In fact, throughout the season as a whole, it was clear that Barca had become too Messi reliant.

The idea of having a 'go to guy' is not uncommon; indeed to be a world class winning side you will (more often than not) need world class talents. Yet when that player becomes too important, when the focus and *balance* of the team becomes unhealthy, this is when success can turn to failure. A successful winning side cannot be just about one player - it often makes the team one dimensional, predictable, and easier to play against. It is important, almost essential, to have a strong team with supporting players in the side to provide dynamism and variation.

For Messi to be at his most effective it is important to have players around him who not only support him but who *benefit* the team. Forwards like Villa and Pedro who expose the space Messi leaves behind when he drops deeper. Options for players like Busquets, Xavi, and Alves to find, not just Messi. In 2010/11 the balance was perfect, Villa, Messi, and Pedro with Iniesta and Xavi behind. That balance was lost and Barca suffered because of it.

In Guardiola's first season he had Eto'o, Henry, and Messi. The goals were shared almost equally; 36, 26 and 38 respectively. Notably, Bojan and Xavi scored 10 goals too. They won an unprecedented treble that season. When Eto'o left, and Ibrahimovic arrived in the 2009/10 season, the goals were becoming more disproportionate; Messi scored 47, Ibrahimovic 21, Pedro 23 and Bojan 12. They won the league yet could not reach the European final that year. The Ibrahimovic experiment was deemed a failure due to the conflict between Messi and Ibrahimovic wanting to play the same role. Guardiola chose Messi and burnt bridges with Ibrahimovic.

As mentioned above, David Villa was brought in, in the summer of 2010, and the team found balance again. The front three of Messi, Villa and Pedro were sublime in the 2010/11 season. Barcelona had found an even stronger balance in their 4-3-3; the midfield of Busquets, Xavi, and Iniesta were tactically and technically perfect and the front three offered penetration and movement which was at times unplayable. Messi played as the 10 and created opportunities for both Villa and Pedro who came from wide to inside. At other times he played as the 9 and was the centre forward. Messi scored 53 that season, Villa 23, and Pedro 22.

In the 2012/2013 season only Messi scored over 20 goals. Fàbregas, Xavi, Alexis and Pedro all reached the mid-teens, Villa only reached 9 due to his injury in December. As referenced previously, Messi scored 73 goals. The impressiveness of Messi's achievements was startling and one cannot take away from what he did. However, as the team became more and more 'Messi-centralised', its balance and therefore effectiveness was lost. Messi *was* Barcelona. His development had taken him to becoming the focal point of *everything*.

The Mourinho effect

It is important to look at what was happening at Real Madrid as Barcelona were making their ascent and becoming the world's best side. After treble success with Inter Milan in 2010, when Mourinho defeated Barcelona in the semi-final and whose celebration at Camp Nou would make him a villain to Barca fans, Florentino Perez could not resist luring the 'Special One' to the Bernabéu to take on Barcelona.

The season before, Florentino Perez had returned as president of Madrid. He continued his Galacticos strategy and spent lavish sums of money on Cristiano

Ronaldo, Kaka, Karim Benzema and Xabi Alonso, spending that totalled almost £200m in his first summer back. However under their coach, Manuel Pellegrini, they could not take the title and although Pellegrini achieved the highest points total for a second-placed side in La Liga history he was moved on and Jose Mourinho arrived.

With the talents which Madrid now had, and a coach who was regarded as the best in the world, it seemed Madrid could challenge Barcelona's dominance. However, in Mourinho's first encounter against Guardiola's side - Barca would destroy Madrid 5-0, the Portuguese's biggest loss as a coach. This result made him re-evaluate his approach and the following two-and-a-half years would see Mourinho attempt to defeat Barca with tactics, mind games, and theatrics.

El Clásico became the greatest spectacle in world football. Madrid versus Barca, Mourinho versus Guardiola, Ronaldo versus Messi. It would become the battle of the two best sides in world football, possessing many of the world's best players, and the two best coaches. La Liga had, without doubt, become the best league in Europe.

Mourinho would try to counter the style of Barca and yet it seemed whatever he did Barca would still come out on top. The rivalry arguably made Barcelona a better side, it made Guardiola better by pushing him tactically, and brought out the best in Messi. The rivalry took Barca to a new level. However, the mind games from Mourinho finally took their toll on Guardiola and Barca. Madrid would go on to win the league in 2011/12 and the stress of the job finally overcame Guardiola, who would resign that summer.

Perez had sought to make Madrid Spain's best team once more yet what he wanted most of all was for Mourinho to win Madrid's tenth Champions League, *La Decima*. Mourinho would reach three Champions League semi-finals in his three years at Madrid yet fell short each time. It appeared La Decima was not meant to be for Madrid and Perez. That was until Carlo Ancelotti arrived in the summer of 2013 (more later).

The end of an era

As football has shown, periods of dominance must inevitability come to an end. No side has dominated football and captivated fans across the world like Barcelona did under Guardiola. The world of football may not get to see this brilliance again, but football is a better place because of what they achieved. Teams have improved in order to emulate and compete with Guardiola's side. Barcelona's style has inspired young children to play the game and coaches to use a style which professes skill over physicality.

No other national side has excelled and prospered in the 'modern game' more than Spain. The style of play has dominated world football both at club and international levels and made the physical dominance of the mid 2000's look laboured and brutish. Barcelona and Spain have proved that guile, craft, and intelligence can overcome physicality.

The development of players like Xavi, Iniesta, and Messi has changed the dynamics of football and made nations and youth academies re-evaluate how they develop and scout for young players.

Without doubt Spanish football has proven to be ahead of the rest in terms of what the present game requires, yet is this is what the future game requires? Are we now at the end of Spain's cycle? Have other nations caught up with their technical and tactical brilliance? More teams and nations across Europe are showing signs of developing towards the demands of the modern game and Spain's dominance has been put under threat.

The Germans appear to be Spain's biggest rival, with perhaps new tactical ideas (as well as players) that have the potential to dominate world football. Like Spain their success has come from long term planning and development. And like Spain they appear to have the blueprint for the future game.

Chapter 4: The German Model

"We upped the ante and worked harder, and this is the result. It's quite possible that a new era in Europe, under Bayern, might have begun." Jupp Heynckes

The blossoming of Germany

So far, since the turn of the century, we have seen how Real Madrid lost their potential to be a modern day dynasty, how England's top Premier League sides were continually challenging for Europe's biggest prize, and how Spain become the world's best national side built off the success of Barcelona. A decade is a long time in football and while England and Spain were dominating, another nation was gradually building the foundations for their future. Those seeds blossomed into something *very* special.

At the 2000 European Championships Germany failed dramatically with a squad which was, quite frankly, inept. Problems clearly needed to be addressed and it was decided that *big* changes were needed. The German FA looked at why their team failed and believed there were not enough *young players* with the necessary qualities to make the German national team great. So what did they do?

An increased investment in youth development involving a new philosophy focusing on developing technically excellent players as well as investment in coaching and improvement in facilities, was what they did. The German FA instructed German club sides that more work needed to be done in developing youth. Everyone was informed that Germany must produce better quality players.

Over the following years German football would implement new youth guidelines and seek to make necessary improvements across the whole country. 121 national talent centres were built in order to help 10 to 17-year-olds with technical coaching. Each centre would employ two full-time coaches. It was a large, but necessary, investment. Secondly all 36 professional clubs in Bundesliga and Bundesliga 2 were instructed to build youth academies.

Perhaps the most significant change was insisting that, in these new academies, at least 12 players in each intake had to be eligible to play for Germany. The statistics had shown, previously, that the Bundesliga was suffering from a lack of domestic players. In fact, in 2003/04, Germany had 44% foreign players playing in the Bundesliga. Today it is down to 38%, which means the Bundesliga has 62% of players - playing each week - able to play for the national team. What the German model enables is for home grown youth to play more, enabling more players to gain the necessary experience to improve.

Based on this we have seen, in recent years, the emergence of a new breed of player and new style of football from Germany. Mixed with the efficiency and organisational qualities for which they are famed, German youth development has been busy working away on developing players, coaches and teams built for the top levels of the game. From a plan laid down a decade ago we are now seeing the emergence of talents in players like Mesut Özil, Thomas Müller, Julien Draxler, Mario Götze, Toni Kroos and Andre Schürrle.

Performing at the top stage

This development of talent had seen many tip Germany's top club sides and their national side for big things. This was the case in 2012. In the build up to the 2012 Champions League final it appeared that Bayern Munich and Germany were set to not only win but dominate European and world football. With Bayern as the clear favourites against a Chelsea side that was evidently in the twilight of their dominant years it appeared a formality for Bayern to lift the trophy in their own stadium. And with the European Championships looming in the summer it was Germany who were regarded as the favourites.

The brand of football Germany was playing was a more direct attacking style than Spain's possession-based approach. It was perceived by many to be the 'style for success', as many had flagged-up how the 'tiki-taka' style of Barcelona (and Spain) had gone too far in terms of possession. The Barcelona model of play had seemingly revolutionised the game, and had changed ideas on how the game can be played. Yet there were many who believed a direct style was to be more effective in the modern game.

German football believed in this transition-based style of play (as was seen in the 2010 World Cup where Germany scored the most goals in the tournament with 16). They would lose 1-0 to Spain in the semi-final from a corner kick. It was a game which could have gone either way.

Two years later it appeared that German football was on the verge of dominating football. And yet... Bayern would choke in the final and lose on penalties and Germany would be knocked out by Italy in the semi-final losing 2-1. It was supposed to be the year that Germany moved to the top of football; instead it raised questions about their mentality.

Bayern had reached the Champions League final in 2010 but would lose to Jose Mourinho's Inter Milan side. It was a disappointment but the signs were that Bayern (like the German national team) were building for something special. 2012 was therefore a greater blow and many wondered if they could recover.

Yet perhaps it was the story of Dortmund, who had won back-to-back Bundesliga titles in 2011 and 2012, that pointed to the way forward for Germany and for success in the modern game. Before we look at what both sides achieved in the 2012/13 season, let's look at how Dortmund achieved their success.

Successful sustainability

In the past decade the English Premier League has seen the emergence of billionaire owners which, in turn, has affected the mentality in English football. Money has always played a part in football, particularly its success, yet with the excessive 'financial doping' of the league, success appears *only* possible with vast amounts of money. The corresponding success that sides like Chelsea and Manchester City have achieved because of their money has painted a bleak picture of the future of football.

The antithesis of these sides has been Borussia Dortmund. As mentioned, Dortmund won back-to-back German titles in 2011 and 2012 and reached the 2013 Champions League final. They have achieved their success with a net spend close to *zero*. The rise of Dortmund, out of the flames of financial ruin to Champions League runners up, is a story which not only inspires but which is also a model that can be replicated by many sides across the world.

In the mid 90's Dortmund enjoyed their greatest successes, winning the Bundesliga in '95 and '96 and the Champions League in 1997. Dortmund, with European player of the year Matthias Sammer, as well as Andreas Möller and Karl-Heinz Riedle overcame the talent of a Juventus side blessed with Didier Deschamps, Zinedine Zidane and Alessandro Del Piero.

However, the following two seasons meant their glory was short lived. A fourth place finish the following season was nothing compared to the capitulation that followed in 1999-2000 when they avoided relegation by only five points. It emerged that problems had surfaced through the poor management of finances, whilst a change of manager had rocked the club and affected results.

Management decided to take drastic action and Dortmund became the first, and only, publicly traded club on the German stock market in October 2000. This generated money which enabled the purchases of Marcio Amoroso, Jan Koller, Ewerthon, and the creative Tomas Rosicky. Dortmund became a force once again.

However problems surfaced once more, with further financial mismanagement between 2000 and 2003. The club had spent beyond their means on foreign imports, and heavy debts of £125 million led to the sale of their ground when they failed to advance in the 2003 Champions League (amazingly they had budgeted for Champions League football without the guarantee of actually being in the competition). This put the club on the brink of bankruptcy in 2005. The ambition for success had come at a cost and one of the biggest teams in Europe was on the verge of financial collapse.

Between 2005 and 2008 the club embarked on a mass clear-out in order to balance the books. It led to a time of mid-table finishes. When Thomas Doll, the coach in 2007-08, led the side to a 13th place finish, their worst position in 20 years, it appeared that the 'might' of Dortmund was never to be again. That is until some inspired management decisions revolutionised the club.

Year zero

In the summer of 2008 a new management team came in with the intention of slashing costs and boosting commercial activity. After Doll they knew that they needed a coach who could inspire the club and fans and make Dortmund a 'respectable' club again.

They chose Jürgen Klopp, the highly-rated young manager who had just led Mainz into the Bundesliga for the first time in their history. Klopp was regarded in Germany as a progressive, disciplined coach and was hired on an initial two-year deal with the remit to make Dortmund 'respectable' once again. He was told that he would have to follow a sustainable model which would not burden the club with debts.

Klopp therefore set out with the intention of signing cheap young players as well as embracing the club's youth academy. He sought to build a side of hungry, young players whose value would gradually improve. A business model for growth and sustainability without doubt; but one that could achieve success? Today, the arrival of Klopp and new model is termed "Year Zero".

The impact was almost immediate with the club winning the DFB Supercup in Klopp's first competitive game. They finished the season in 6th place, much improved on 13th and lost only five of their 34 league games. Klopp understood the importance of building defensive foundations and his side boasted the best defence in the league.

The team's defensive might was built on the impressive Neven Subotic, the Serbian defender signed from Klopp's former club Mainz for a bargain €4.6m, and Mats Hummels, the talented German youngster who was deemed not good enough when at Bayern. Hummels joined on an initial loan deal from Bayern, before signing permanently at the end of the season. Their partnership was, and has been, the foundation for Dortmund's success and shows that with the right manager, spending money is not the answer to every problem.

Klopp and his team had to be shrewd because of their restricted budget and more precise in their scouting. With their in-depth scouting network they worked from a template in order to recruit players based on their attributes more than reputation. Their best 'find' was Shinji Kagawa. Kagawa was playing in the J-league Second Division and was bought for just £300,000. It was to prove a very astute piece of business for the club. Added to this, the club's recruitment of Polish players such as Robert Lewandowski, Lukasz Piszczek and Jakub Błaszczykowski have all proven fruitful and benefited the side.

These recruits have become high quality players because of the work of the coach. Klopp has shown he is able to get the best out of players who were either unknown or not highly regarded; his trust in players and his ability to develop them has seen the improvement of individuals like Kagawa and Lewandowski from unknowns into world class players. Klopp's coaching ability and talent should not be underestimated.

In just three years Klopp had taken the club from 13th to Bundesliga champions. With debt-reduction being Dortmund's main aim, Klopp had to buy carefully and the championship-winning squad of 2010-11 cost less than £5m to assemble. There was something about this Dortmund team which indicated this was not just a one off, a new force had awoken in Germany.

Conquering Europe

European competition was Dortmund's next step. In the 2011/12 season Dortmund really struggled in the Champions League; quite simply they were too naïve, and tactically and mentally immature for the competition. They could not deal with the extra travel and Klopp admitted that some players were simply overwhelmed by the competition.

Balancing the Champions League and Bundesliga was difficult for the Dortmund players and coach and it showed with mixed results in both. When the burden of the Champions League was removed, the side went on an unbeaten run which lasted for the remainder of the season and which propelled them to the top of the league.

Yet in 2012/13 Klopp's Dortmund were arguably the team of the season in Europe, their style of play both in attack and defence was scintillating and they deserved to reach the Champion's League final. Dortmund's level of play and intensity, along with their technical and tactical quality, in all their group games was sublime. They looked focused, driven, organised and completely together in their performances. In the space of a year they had gone from a side looking out of their depth, to a side that looked capable of winning the competition.

They had replaced the loss of Kagawa (to Manchester United) with Marco Reus, a previous Dortmund academy player (who was released at 16 years old from Borussia Mönchengladbach). His arrival, as well as the growing improvements of midfielders Sven Bender and Ilkay Gündoğan and the burgeoning talent of young academy product Mario Götze would make Dortmund a genuine force in Europe. Yet above all it would be their defensive quality which would propel them to success.

While Barcelona and Spain had shown the value in a possession-based game, coaches were looking for ways to counter this tactic. This led to the increase in deep defensive blocks in order to try to counter, and deal with, possession-based styles. Yet Dortmund were looking for a new style of their own.

While many sides were defending 'for their life' in their own box, Dortmund were developing a defensive style which was more proactive. This defensive strategy was different to Barca's high pressing style. In fact it has proved to be a style which has the potential to become the default for many sides and a strategy for the future game.

Klopp developed 'counter-pressing' with his side (in German it is called 'gegenpressing') and it has become a tactic which has taken Dortmund and German football to the top levels of the game. This tactic would work in the framework of the 4-2-3-1 and would work as follows.

Klopp would work on the defensive organisation of his side to nullify space behind the defence, draw the opposition into the mid-third, and then pounce to seek to win the ball and counter. In dropping their forwards off to a point 10 yards ahead of the halfway line, there was a lack of space for the opposition to penetrate through (and behind). This transitional defensive tactic has become invaluable for sides seeking to limit opposition teams' attacks and exposing them on the break.

In their group game against Manchester City, and the 4-1 semi-final demolition of Real Madrid, they gave a first class performance of how to play in Europe, in terms of both attacking and defending. It was the exact balance required of technical quality, work rate, and the implementation of tactics and strategy for success at such a level.

What Klopp has achieved makes many people hopeful for the future of football. A manager who has shown that, through strong leadership and principles, through nurturing and developing players, and importantly building a united and committed team, you can defeat sides that have simply had money injected into them to become successful.

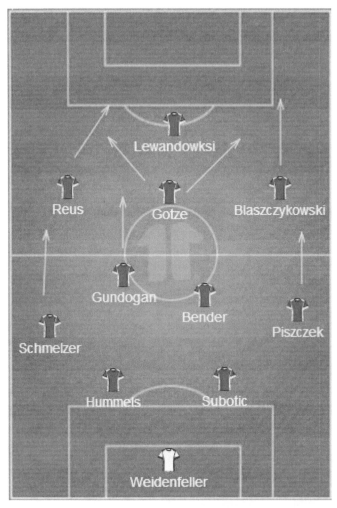

Dortmund's XI versus Jose Mourinho's Real Madrid in the first leg of the 2011/12 Champions League semi-final. Lewandowski would score all four goals in a 4-1 win.

The might of Bavaria

Dortmund won the hearts of many fans with their style of play yet it is Bayern Munich who have risen to the very top of European football. And their rise and status would appear likely only to get stronger in the coming years.

In the semi-final of the Champions League, in April 2013, Bayern would be drawn against Barcelona. It would be seen as their biggest test so far after knocking out Arsenal and Juventus previously. This was supposed to be their toughest test yet, but Bayern Munich made it their most dominant and convincing performance.

Barcelona, who since 2009 had conquered world football so spectacularly, were to be the gauge of Bayern's rise to the top of Europe.

It was as comprehensive a beating as when Fabio Capello's Milan defeated Johan Cruyff's Dream Team in 1994. That final effectively ended the era of that Barcelona team and of Cruyff's time as Barca's coach. It was 4-0 that night, the same result as at the Allianz in April 2013. Barca's keeper Victor Valdes admitted, *"We have been defeated by a great team."*

It was perhaps fitting that both Bayern and Dortmund overcame La Liga's Madrid and Barcelona. Here were the best four sides in Europe going against each other and the Bundesliga would come out 11-1 winners overall.

In the game against Barcelona it was evident that Bayern could deal with the threat that the Catalan club provided. The issue with Barca had been their ability to play only 'one way', which (although proven to be dominant and successful) was clearly becoming more predictable and 'easier' to play against as coaches analysed Barca's style and found ways to counter it.

The Achilles heel to Barca had been sides that possessed strength, height, defensive organisation, and the ability to counter at speed. This is why Chelsea have always been a thorn in Barca's side and why Jose Mourinho sought to play this way to counter them when he was at Madrid. Yet Bayern nullified and punished Barca more than any other team in recent years.

They were simply awesome in both legs, nullifying Barca's ability to penetrate. Bayern played an aggressive pressing game which even Barca struggled to deal with; they also showed a ruthlessness on the counter attack, organization and dominance on set pieces. Yet this was no surprise, Bayern's coach Jupp Heynckes and their president - Uli Hoeness - had been building the squad for this level of performance. Maybe defeat in the 2012 final was the catalyst needed to develop the 'right' mindset?

Laying the foundations

Perhaps you can go back to 1998 when Ottmar Hitzfeld took over as coach of the club and made Bayern one of Europe's top sides. After six years with Dortmund he was recruited by Germany's biggest side. They wanted a coach who would take them to the top of Europe. It should have happened in 1999, yet Bayern would throw the win away in the final minutes to Manchester United. It was cruel yet Hitzfeld would win the clubs first Champions League in 25 years, in 2001, defeating Valencia. Between 1998 and 2001 Hitzfeld would dominate the Bundesliga winning it for three years in a row. Hitzfeld had put Bayern back to the top.

However, he would leave in 2004 due to a poor run of form, and Felix Magath would take charge. During Magath's time Bayern moved from the Olympic stadium into their new state-of-the-art Allianz Arena. It was a time when the 'new' Bayern would be born. Hitzfeld returned to help the club after Magath failed to get the team into the Champions League. Although it was a short term loss – the club may have benefited overall.

In 2007 the club made drastic changes to the squad bringing in players Franck Ribéry, Miroslav Klose, and Luca Toni – changes which helped propel Bayern back to the top of German football. Jürgen Klinsmann came in to succeed Hitzfeld - after he had stabilised the club once again - yet he only lasted a matter of months before he was fired. His coaching methods and style were criticised by many players. Jupp Heynckes was brought in as caretaker manager for the remainder of the season and helped Bayern achieve a second place finish.

The summer of 2009 saw the arrival of ex-Ajax and Barcelona coach Louis van Gaal alongside the big money signings of Arjen Robben and Mario Gomez. The team was being built to dominate European football and van Gaal came close to winning a first year treble, but ultimately lost 3-1 to Mourinho's Inter in the Champions League final.

In van Gaal, Bayern were taught and coached in the Dutch attacking philosophy which produced attacking flair and creativity as well as tactical organisation. However the following season Bayern exited the Champions League in the knockout stages and van Gaal, who was supposed to leave at the end of the season, was relieved of his duties early. Bayern's management was worried that the side would not qualify for the Champions League.

Jupp Heynckes would return again, this time inheriting a side much better than the one he took caretaker ownership of in 2009. In Heynckes, Bayern had a man who was disciplined and organised in his approach and who made the side much more defensively minded. This Bayern side had invested in some world class players and were fluent in attacking football - what was needed was a defensively minded coach who could make the side a defensive powerhouse also.

Around Christmas 2011 Heynckes was under a lot of pressure from the media and there were reports of unrest with certain players. He managed to salvage the season and took Bayern to the Champions League final, which would be played at the Allianz Arena, their home. Bayern appeared obsessed with winning the Champions League in their own stadium yet choked, in the final, to Chelsea. Whether it was an issue of pressure, mindset, or fate for Chelsea to win the Champions League - Bayern would end their season coming second in the league, cup, and Europe. It was a big test for the club, coach, and players. The signs were evident that they could be a great side yet did they have the mentality to achieve it?

The most complete team ever

In the 2012/13 season Bayern became an ever better side, more *complete* than perhaps any side seen in recent years. After years of building the foundations in terms of the stadium which meant increased revenues, and bringing in world class players, the squad were as close to perfect as possible. Bayern looked like a team capable of doing anything necessary in terms of tactics, style, and approach to counter the opposition.

Many teams have certain styles of playing and will continue to play that way to break teams down. Some play direct football, some play counter attacking football, others use the wings and seek to cross, and others play a shorter passing game seeking to control the game. Conceivably *that* Bayern side could play any style required to suit the game and overcome the opposition. By keeping the majority of the team together, they developed into a complete unit which appeared to have mastered *all* facets of the game both in and out of possession.

Perhaps in a similar way to Arsenal in the early 2000's, their style of play involved skill and creativity as well as physicality and aerial dominance. The difference with Arsenal was that they had been developed tactically and psychologically better than Wenger achieved. The different coaches Bayern had used over the years had brought new ideas and styles. Each new coach added something to the team and gave them a new dimension. In turn, players adapted and evolved - facilitating the *variety* in Bayern's approach and style.

And in the summer of 2012 Bayern arguably made their best capture. Matthias Sammer was brought in as Bayern's sporting director. The ex-Dortmund defender came from the German FA and was put on the management board responsible for the playing staff. Sammer was a major coup for Bayern: his esteemed ability to develop talent and his knowledge as a player, coach, and manager made him a key asset for Bayern's evolution; it was clear that his arrival instilled the mentality Bayern required to go to the next level. He was a great asset for the club and for Heynckes.

Although the value of coaching and tactics is important, you cannot ignore how the quality of the player is essential. And in this respect Bayern possessed some of the best players in world football. World class players like Franck Ribéry, Arjen Robben and Mario Gomez arrived to aid the attack. In turn, the investment in defence was pivotal, notably the acquisition of Germany's No.1 Manuel Neuer, the closest successor to Oliver Kahn German football has seen. This intense and smart investment meant Bayern didn't just add quality, but *world class* quality.

The additions made by Heynckes in the summer of 2012 helped perfect the team. The speedy and skilful centre-back Dante was bought to add more dynamism in their defence. In midfield £40m was spent on Javi Martinez to give Bayern a similar player to that of Sergio Busquets at Barca. Martinez added more control, poise and steel in Bayern's midfield which enabled Bastian Schweinsteiger, the converted right midfielder (van Gaal should be commended for seeing Schweinsteiger as a controlling central midfielder, and moving him to that role during his reign at Bayern) to control games with his composure and passing quality.

And although Bayern spent vast amounts on some real quality, their desire and ability to *develop* their own talent cannot be ignored. Players like Holger Badstuber, David Alaba, Bastian Schweinsteiger, Philipp Lahm, Toni Kroos and Thomas Müller have all come from Bayern's youth system. In this respect it is a compliment to the club and their ability to develop and nurture talent that they have been willing to build a team based on home grown talent and then surround them with world class talent from elsewhere. Maybe it is the key to their success? Players who know the club's values more than many others.

Bayern utilised the value of various coaches and philosophies to help develop an all-round team. A blend of academy players with world class quality enabled them to build a team which was genuinely top notch in every position. Both in and out of possession the team knew its roles and executed them to perfection as a complete team. That Bayern side were as complete a team as has been seen in the present game. Yet the club wanted more. They wanted to develop a *legacy*.

Gegenpressing

A key tactical development which helped Bayern move to a new level came from their rivals Dortmund. Jupp Heynckes replicated Dortmund's counter-pressing, with the gegenpressing method, in the 2012/13 season with Bayern.

In the semi-final against Barcelona Heynckes said Bayern were *"tactically brilliant"*, in the way that they played against Arsenal and Juventus earlier in the competition. In turn, using gegenpressing, Bayern nullified Barca's possession-based game and punished them ruthlessly on the counter attack. They would win 7-0 on aggregate.

Bayern taught Europe a valuable lesson. Learn how to defend and you learn to control games. Philipp Lahm has called their approach *"aggressive pressure"* and this idea has become a key facet in the modern game. Of course, it is not too different to how Sacchi's Milan defended: a whole unit working together to apply pressure on the opposition, knowing the triggers of when and where to press.

Adding this new defensive pressing strategy meant Bayern refined the 4-2-3-1 formation further and their treble success in 2013 was much deserved.

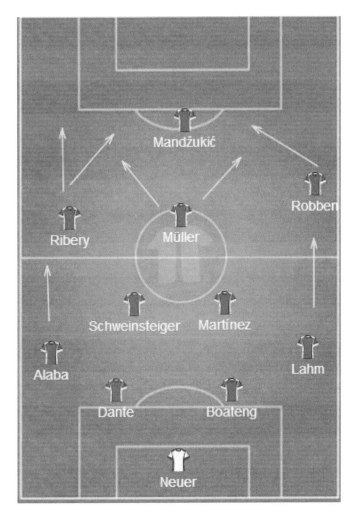

Bayern's 'complete' team. The XI which defeated Dortmund in the 2012 Champions League final.

The signing of the Croatian Mario Mandžukić enabled Bayern to enhance not only their attack but also their defensive game. Although Mario Gomez scored over 40 goals in the 2011/12 season, Mandžukić improved the side and restricted Gomez's role to being a substitute.

Mandžukić was more important to Bayern than Mario Gomez because he offered, in a similar way to Robert Lewandowski at Dortmund, the ability and dynamism to press when *out of possession*. The modern game requires forwards to work hard when defending and Mandžukić's ability to press the centre backs and also press the defensive midfield enabled Bayern to close space and restrict the opposition's time.

As well as this, Mandžukić's ability to play as a central number nine, effectively a target man for others to play off, or as a more roaming forward who pulls wide and creates space for others in central areas helped take Bayern's game to a new level.

And of course a strong defence enables moments of transition when the team win possession. Bayern's 'counter-pressing' ability with the speed and drive of players like Franck Ribéry, Arjen Robben and Thomas Müller created many transitional opportunities and made Bayern one of the best counter attacking sides in Europe. Gegenpressing had proven not only to help the defensive strength of the side but also to help create goal scoring opportunities. It was no surprise that both Bayern and Dortmund reached the Champions League final in 2013. It was the final of 4-2-3-1, of *gegenpressing*.

Leading football's 'new era'

The past decade had shown how variable football can be, how dominant sides and nations can fall off the top and be replaced. Football is a changing game such that anticipating where football is heading (and importantly what is required) is the key for prolonged success and dominance. Bayern sought to achieve this when, in January 2013, it was announced that Pep Guardiola would be taking over from Heynckes the following season.

It was seen as another step in the club's growth . Heynckes was not happy with the announcement, disappointed that he wouldn't be able to continue the project, yet the club felt it needed a change and that Guardiola (regarded as the world's best coach) was too enticing not to secure. Perhaps the board had noted the lesson of Barca and their inability or refusal to adapt and evolve? The Bayern board decided they wouldn't allow this to happen to them. The hope was that Guardiola, seen as the most progressive coach and thinker in the game, would help the club become even greater, and would enable them to build a *legacy* in terms of success and style.

Bayern offered a perfect opportunity for Guardiola. They possessed everything which he desires; a great playing staff with a focus on home grown talent, a stable and well-structured club, and a club with a rich history and prestige. Guardiola had the choice of any club and chose very wisely. There were some lucrative offers, notably from Chelsea, yet he wanted a project that would capture him. He found that at Bayern.

A clash of styles

In the 2013/14 season Guardiola would transform Bayern, he would move the club's style very much away from the German philosophy and the one which

Heynckes had dominated Europe with the year before. Guardiola brought 'tiki-taka' to Bayern. Whereas the 2012 Champions League final was a battle between two sides playing a 4-2-3-1 using gegenpressing - Bayern were now different a proposition.

This battle between possession-based 'tiki-taka' and counter attacking 'counter-pressing' football could be seen in the 2013 German Super Cup tie between Dortmund and Bayern Munich. This Super Cup match was in contrast to the Champions League final between the two just months earlier because the arrival of Guardiola meant that a greater 'Barcelona' style was expected and that is what the game produced.

Guardiola's team was more patient in their build up and dominated possession against Dortmund. Yet they would be punished four times by Dortmund's excellent counter-pressing method, with Dortmund running out 4-2 winners. It was a lesson for Guardiola and other coaches across Europe on how to exploit the Barca model of play.

However, as the 2013/14 season progressed it appeared that perhaps counter-pressing wasn't going to be as dominant as thought. It was certainly becoming more popular than the 'Barca way', so much so that coaches like Brendan Rodgers at Liverpool embraced counter attacking football, a move which propelled Liverpool to becoming title challengers in the Premier League.

However, in Germany, by the end of the 2013/2014 season it was evident that Bayern and their new style was the prevailing way of playing. Bayern had set a new record, winning the Bundesliga in the earliest time ever. They were dominating everyone around them. Guardiola had proven his quality once again.

The first league meeting between Dortmund and Bayern would be significant, not just for the title (and their rivalry) but because of what Guardiola showed that day. In what was perhaps the most eagerly anticipated match of the season across Europe, Bayern played Dortmund on November 23rd 2013. The game itself highlighted the growing gap between Germany's top two sides.

Recent history would not have predicted the scoreline yet as the game went on, and changes were made, the gulf in depth and quality became clear. A 3-0 win confirmed that Bayern were the best team in Europe.

It was not the most enticing or exciting of games in the first 60 minutes, it was understandably cagey, cautious and scrappy. It was quite rigid and subdued from Bayern and although Dortmund created some chances they were not clear cut. And then came the tactical changes. Guardiola would succeed in two ways; through innovation and through quality. To have the ability to bring on players of Thiago Alcantara and Mario Götze's class highlighted the embarrassment of riches which Bayern and Guardiola possessed. Yet it was what they did and what Bayern altered which was significant.

Before the introduction of Götze, Bayern were using Mandžukić as their 'target man' forward. As impressive as Mandžukić was during the 2012/13 season, Bayern no longer offered the same environment or style under which he prospered previously. Under Guardiola he looked slow and predictable, he made Bayern look rigid. He is what Mario Gomez had shown to be for the German national side. And in the same way as Germany's national coach Joachim Löw sought to mould his national team into a more fluid and interchangeable system, this is precisely what Bayern were also moving towards.

A fluid front four, a combination of Robben, Müller, Kroos and Götze would expose Dortmund's defence and turn the game. They interchanged between the two wide roles and the 10 and 9 positions. Guardiola played not a false nine but a rotating one. This is even harder to deal with as players are pulling the defence laterally and vertically. The space created between and behind the units became hard for Dortmund's defence. Dortmund's defensive pairing were quite simply pulled apart by the movement and intelligence of Bayern in the final 30 minutes when Bayern would score three times to win 3-0.

The use of a fluid front four, involving positional interchange looked to be the vision of Guardiola. And Götze was the key piece to Guardiola's system. When he came on Bayern looked sharper, dynamic, and became much harder to track and mark. This is what changed the game.

The tactical changes of players and style shifted the match. They gave a glimpse of what the future holds for this Bayern side. It was a statement by Bayern (and possibly an admission from Dortmund) that the gap between the two sides was getting wider. All across the team Bayern were stronger.

Although Guardiola had inherited a great side, the work he had done with them in one season was marvellous. What he had achieved with his Bayern side over a season was an indication of where he was looking to take the team in terms of philosophy and style.

And yet many will point to the defeat to Real Madrid in the Champions League where he was overcome in the semi-final by Carlo Ancelotti's side (who would ultimately win the Champions League and bring Florentino Perez and the Madrid fans *La Decima*). Madrid played a counter-pressing style similar to Dortmund which simply overwhelmed Bayern's players.

The semi-final with Real Madrid highlighted the fact that Guardiola's work was not complete. In both games Bayern were found wanting, they had a lot of the ball but failed to do a lot with it. Real on the other hand were ruthless in transition and in this battle of tiki-taka and counter-pressing Guardiola would lose out. An aggregate score of 5-0 was a shocking result, yet perhaps it was the *manner* of the performance from the players which was the most disconcerting thing.

The team looked dejected, they looked low on confidence and belief, not something you would expect from a Guardiola side. Something was not right and Madrid punished them. Was this enough to say tiki-taka was dead? Of course not. But it did point to the fact that this project was still developing.

Guardiola's use of Mario Mandžukić in both games highlighted his lack of confidence in his own system, showing something of a philosophical dilemma between his way and the Bayern of the previous season. Not surprisingly Bayern were poorer for this decision, they looked as though they lacked ideas and a clear strategy.

Guardiola had seemingly lost the team in these two games and his reputation was damaged. Just when Guardiola's modern form of 'tiki-taka' appeared to be as dominant as Barca's had been, counter-pressing blew the team and style away. And although Guardiola had been beaten badly his philosophy and vision should not be discarded. In fact football's evolution appears to be being led by Guardiola himself. As we will see in the next part of the book, the evolution of the game is moving towards one of universality.

Part II | 21st Century Evolution

Chapter 5: Tactical Evolution

"Almost every tactical innovation of the past five years can be seen as developments from a 4-2-3-1." Jonathan Wilson

Italy's decade of dominance

Italian football was to play a big part in the 1990's, and it was Arrigo Sacchi's Milan that started Italy's period of supremacy with back-to-back European success in 1989 and 1990. Sacchi had developed a very fluid 4-4-2 system in the late 80's-early 1990's with his AC Milan side. With the Dutch trio of Ruud Gullit, Marco van Basten and Frank Rijkaard, Milan became one of the great sides in football history. The fact that Sacchi developed his philosophy from Dutch football was revolutionary for Italian soccer which had, basically, become a 3-5-2 nation. 4-4-2 pressing was not Italian football, yet Sacchi would show everyone how effective it could be.

Sacchi's Milan was built on some very basic principles, most notably a high 'team pressing' style in the mould of Rinus Michels' *Totalfootball*. Sacchi would instruct his side to push high up the pitch, looking to win the ball back quickly, trying to force the opposition into mistakes. To ensure they didn't leave gaps, the players were told to leave no more than seven metres between the lines of attack, midfield, and defence, with no more than a total of 25 metres between the team.

Sacchi also used zonal marking (which was in contrast to what the majority of Italian football was doing). The use of man marking with a sweeper was prominent across Italian football at that time, a strategy which meant the opposition would dictate where the defending team would be positioned. However with zonal marking, the defending team took control, looking to manipulate where the attacking side went. Sacchi's success with Milan revolutionised this defensive tactic. It took a few years but eventually everyone, in Italy, changed how they defended. Nowadays, it is extremely rare to see teams man mark.

Sacchi's Milan side which beat Benfica in the 1990 European Cup final

Sacchi would move on from Milan to manage the national team, missing out on winning the World Cup in 1994 against Brazil on penalties. His successor at Milan was Fabio Capello, who would take the 4-4-2 and make it into more of a diamond using players such as Demetrio Albertini and later Marcel Desailly as holding midfielders. This would give the team more licence to attack with its extra defensive support. Milan would prove to be Europe's best side, and between 1992 and 1994 the club would go on a 58 game unbeaten run in the league, earning the title *The Invincibles*.

Capello would also reach three consecutive European Cup finals from 1993 to 1995 yet they could not replicate Sacchi's back-to-back success. In 1993 they would lose to Didier Deschamps and Marcel Desailly's Marseille (who, as mentioned, Milan would sign the following summer). The following year they would come up against Johan Cruyff's Barcelona. Cruyff was making history with Barcelona at the time. The protégé of Rinus Michels was now manager of the Catalan club playing his Dutch 4-3-3 formation, and he had brought Barca their first European Cup success in 1992.

In the 1994 final, against Milan, Cruyff had players like Romario, Stoichkov, Michael Laudrup and Ronald Koeman to call on, a team which was called the 'Dream Team'. Many wrote off Milan but they would defeat Cruyff's Barcelona 4-0 with a ruthless performance ostensibly putting an end to the 'Dream Team'. The Dutch-Italian side had defeated the Dutch-Spanish side.

The next season Milan would reach the final once again, coming up against Louis van Gaal's Ajax, a team that was playing the purest form of *Totalfootball* at the time (playing between a 4-3-3 and 3-4-3). Milan would lose 1-0 to a Patrick Kluivert goal. The success was a sign of van Gaal's quality as a coach as well as Ajax's ability to develop and produce quality young players including Clarence Seedorf, Edgar Davids and Marc Overmars. With Frank Rijkaard returning from Milan to help bring leadership to the group, and with the Finnish playmaker Jari Litmanen in the side, van Gaal had brought Ajax back to the top of Europe.

The following season (continuing the Holland vs Italy rivalry) Ajax would come up against another Italian giant in Juventus, the 'Old Lady' of Italian football. Van Gaal had a chance, like Capello, to win the tournament back-to-back yet Ajax would lose on penalties to Marcello Lippi's side. The game was a battle between the Dutch 4-3-3 and Italian 4-4-2 diamond formations. It appeared that this was the tactical battle of the 90's, between two different football cultures but it was Germany, however, who was to show that another formation could prove a success.

3-5-2 vs 4-4-2

The following season - 1997 - the Old Lady would reach the final again, this time coming up against Matthias Sammer's Borussia Dortmund. This would pit the Italian diamond against the German sweeper system, the 3-5-2. With the signing of Zinedine Zidane it seemed back-to-back success was a formality for Juve, however Dortmund would stifle the French playmaker with an excellent man-marking job by the Scot Paul Lambert and Dortmund would run out 3-1 winners.

That summer Germany would also win the European Championships in England using the same system of 3-5-2, defeating the Czech Republic 2-1 after extra time. It now appeared as though the 3-5-2 was new way to succeed!

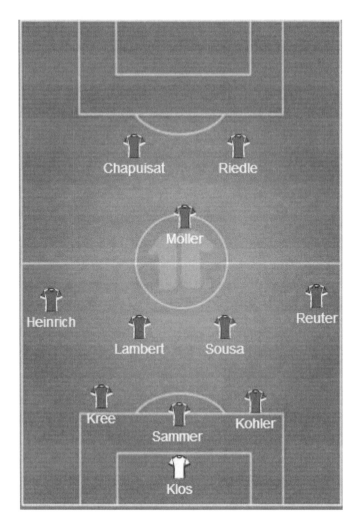

Dortmund's 3-5-2 which defeated Juve in the 1997 Champions League final

However, it would be Juve who would return to the Champions League final in 1998; their opponents this time - Real Madrid. Lippi, perhaps seeing what German football had achieved the previous year altered his formation to a three-at-the-back system. Juve would use wing backs with two 'holding' midfielders in Didier Deschamps and Edgar Davids, with Zidane in the 10 role. Yet, in this battle, it would be Madrid's 4-4-2 diamond which would win out.

Juve had reached three finals in a row yet would only win one, perhaps a reason why this Juve side (perhaps unfairly) is not regarded more highly in the pantheon of football's greatest sides.

1999 would see Manchester United somehow overcome Juventus in the semi-final to prevent a fourth final in a row for the Old Lady. It would see United face Bayern in a game which was dominated by Bayern using a 3-5-2 sweeper system with Lothar Matthäus playing the libero role. Sir Alex Ferguson used a classic English 4-4-2, with two strikers in Dwight Yorke and Andy Cole and traditional wingers in Jesper Blomqvist and Ryan Giggs with Nicky Butt and David Beckham playing in the centre (as Paul Scholes and Roy Keane were suspended). As is the case with the 4-4-2 the midfield was overrun for much of the game.

For United to have come out of the final with a win was very surprising when you watch the game. Two late corners snatched success from Bayern. It was a lesson in perseverance, belief, and determination from Ferguson's side; traits which characterised his reign at the club and a key reason for the side's success. It wasn't a tactical success, but a mental one. Yet the game was in no way an endorsement of the English 4-4-2 in Europe.

The 2000 Champions League would see an all-Spanish final with Real Madrid facing the up-and-coming Valencia who were benefitting from the Argentinian imports of Kily Gonzalez and Claudio Lopez. Under coach Héctor Cúper, Valencia would use a 4-4-2 diamond to bring out the talents of the team. Madrid's coach, Vicente del Bosque, would set out his Madrid side in a 3-5-2 with the attacking wing backs of Roberto Carlos and Michel Salgado. Madrid would dominate the game and run out 3-0 winners. At the turn of the century it looked as though a three at the back system was the way forward for the 21st century!

The battle between the 3-5-2 and 4-4-2 diamond would continue in 2001 when Bayern Munich faced Cúper's Valencia. Otmar Hitzfeld continued with the classic German formation and this time would be successful, yet only after penalties. In fact it would be a 'game of penalties'; two penalties in normal time took the game to extra time and then it was decided by a penalty shoot-out.

In 2002 del Bosque would return Real Madrid to the final again, this time facing Bayer Leverkusen. However Bayer would move away from a three at the back system and use a four at the back formation, setting up in a 4-1-3-2 style, highlighting the beginning of a change in German philosophy. Remember this was post Euro 2000 which was seen as a disaster for German football. Philosophical changes were starting to be seen. Bayer's setup sought to dominate the central areas yet this game was about the quality of the Galacticos of Madrid. The most expensive-ever-signing Zidane would be the star of the game, scoring an exquisite volley to win the game for Madrid 2-1.

Football appeared to be moving towards a back four system. Germany had determined their more traditional system redundant for the new century. Yet before three at the back was consigned to the history books it would be Brazil, at the 2002 World Cup under Luiz Felipe Scolari, who would win using a three at the back system.

Universality

Scolari had taken over the national team only 12 months earlier and, at the time, Brazil had their worst-ever qualifying campaign for the tournament. When Scolari took over, Brazil was actually sitting outside the qualification places. Under him Brazil *narrowly* qualified. Yet at the World Cup they came alive using a 3-4-1-2 formation. This was a side which possessed the attacking trio of Ronaldo, Rivaldo, and Ronaldinho, as formidable an attacking force as had been seen at the World Cup.

Scolari used a sweeper system with Edmilson playing as a ball-playing libero, given licence to drive out into midfield with the ball. This gave Cafu and Carlos, as wing backs, the freedom to maraud forwards and do what they did best – attack! It was a system which used the talents of the team perfectly and perhaps it was a shame that this system looked to become a dying breed.

The end of a back three? Brazil's 2002 World Cup winning 3-4-2-1 formation.
It was a formation which got the best out of its parts, something many coaches often struggle to do.

As successful as the 4-4-2 and 3-5-2 had proven to be, football was about to embrace the 4-2-3-1 - a formation which would dominate the following decade. It would be France who would show where the game was heading.

France lead the way

At the 1998 World Cup, which France hosted, there was much expectation on them to win the tournament. However, they had competition from the holders – Brazil –

to contend with. They would meet in the final, in Paris, where both sides would use holding midfielders in a formation. France would play a 4-3-2-1 formation with Deschamps, Emmanuel Petit and Christian Karembeu supporting their defence from the attacking threats of Ronaldo, Bebeto, Rivaldo and Leonardo, with Dunga and Cesar Sampaio in the holding roles for Brazil. France would run out 3-0 winners with Brazil suffering from issues surrounding Ronaldo. Zidane would be crowned the player of the tournament, scoring two goals in the final - cementing his place as one of the great playmakers of the time.

France's successful side that defeated Brazil 3-0 in the 1998 World Cup final.

At Euro 2000 France had the chance to win another international tournament. Coming up against Dino Zoff's Italy which was using a three at the back system (3-

5-2, moving away from Sacchi's 4-4-2 and back to what they were used to) France would alter their set up in the 4-2-3-1, with Deschamps and Patrick Vieira in the holding roles. Italy were minutes from winning yet a late Sylvain Wiltord goal would send the game to extra time, where David Trezeguet would score the 'golden goal' to clinch success for France. It was a cruel blow for Italy yet the success of France would lead to them being held up as a blueprint for a new generation of coaches.

The 4-2-3-1 was being embraced in England yet many saw it as a 4-4-2. Arsène Wenger had arrived in 1996 to English football and had built his success on the import of French talent into the Premier League. Playing a 'fluid' 4-4-2 Wenger utilised a style more akin to a 4-2-3-1 than a classic English 4-4-2. In fact the Arsenal side of the late 90's (and early 2000's) were the most complete modern side in European football. They contained power, speed and skill as well as fluidity and understanding which helped the side find a perfect balance. Wenger and France pointed to a new way forward for football.

For decades English football had used the 4-4-2 formation. Ferguson had used it with Manchester United in the 1990's with Giggs and Beckham on the wings providing crosses for the two centre forwards. It was working brilliantly against English sides in the Premier League, yet in Europe United were not as powerful.

After their success in 1999 United possibly felt they were embarking on a new era in Europe, a time to dominate perhaps? Yet during the 1999/2000 campaign they were knocked out of Europe by del Bosque's Madrid side. Del Bosque's wing back system baffled United's coach and players, and they simply could not deal with the tactical difficulties posed.

After United were knocked out by Madrid, in 2000, Arrigo Sacchi said, *"Manchester are a very good side, their win last season was exceptional. Madrid, I believe, are more likely to win the Champions League on a regular basis. Their style of play, alone, means they are better equipped to dominate Europe."* Was Sacchi implying three at the back was the important aspect, or more that an overloaded midfield was the key for success? As we saw earlier, Alex Ferguson would follow this Champions League defeat with a revised approach in terms of style and formation – a revision to improve his side's performance in Europe.

During the following season Ferguson opted for a more controlled style of play and attempted to move to a 4-2-3-1 formation. Ferguson sought out Pep Guardiola to fill the holding midfielder role yet, when rebuffed by the Barca midfielder, instead spent £28m on the Argentinian Juan Sebastian Veron.

In turn, Ferguson's 'evolution' suffered some growing pains. As Rob Smyth wrote, in an article regarding Ferguson's tactical revolution, *"In the short term, the move was a disaster: by breaking up the midfield of Beckham-Keane-Scholes-Giggs, Ferguson killed a golden goose that was delivering a Premier League every season. Nor did it lead to an improvement in Europe."*

Although Veron didn't make the necessary impact, Ferguson continued to see the need to modernise his United side. With Carlos Queiroz as his assistant, United would continue to become more 'European' in their style yet it would take until 2006 for United's tactical revolution to take shape fully.

In the meantime, English football was welcoming two new tactical geniuses to its shores. These men were from the new generation of coaches who were developing new styles to succeed in the modern game.

In 2004 Liverpool hired Rafa Benitez and Chelsea brought in the Champion's League-winning coach Jose Mourinho. Both of these coaches had proved to have a great understanding of the European game. Before arriving in England both had won the UEFA Cup, and Mourinho the Champions League also. During their time in England Benitez used the 4-2-3-1 with Mourinho working between 4-3-3 and 4-2-3-1; both were of the view that their teams needed more balance and control to improve performance. Both men sought extra defensive support and found this with single forward formations.

Midfield overload

For many coaches the 4-4-2 was becoming too rigid, flat, and lacking in creativity. Overloading midfield areas enabled coaches to dominate possession and secure their defence more effectively. With the rise of the single holding player, used by many sides in a diamond 4-4-2, coaches had to find ways to get their creative players onto the ball as their No.10, their playmaker, was typically finding space in central areas difficult to find and exploit. This led to the 'roaming' *trequartista* who was forced to move away from central areas in order to find pockets of space.

Now, if the defensive midfielder's role was to stay with this player (the trequartista) he was often drawn away from his desired central position. This created an issue for a team's defensive balance because other players could and would exploit this space. Therefore it then became necessary to have *two* holding midfielders.

If coaches wished to have security with two defensive midfielders, yet also have a player to make the midfield a three, then a player needed to be sacrificed. Width was still important, yet two centre forwards, it appeared, were not. The single forward became the norm. In fact, this became the most important change to modern formations. Coaches simply could not allow two forwards to play up top anymore as they would lose the midfield dominance which they required.

The 4-2-3-1 'worked' because it offered new spatial options and problems for the opposition. According to Jonathan Wilson - Juanma Lillo, Pep Guardiola's mentor, said that 4–2–3–1 gave him the best distribution of players over the pitch; he felt that it offered the team the opportunity to play between units more and use angles more effectively.

When Rafa Benitez took over at Valencia, from Héctor Cúper in 2001, he changed the system which had helped the side reach two Champions League finals and introduced the 4-2-3-1. It was seen as a way to counter and combat the short passing game which sides in Spain were using. Benitez used two holding midfielders, Ruben Baraja and David Albelda, both players who were good passers of the ball and tactically disciplined, and used the Argentinian Pablo Aimar in the number 10, attacking midfield position.

Benitez would win the league in his first season and as Michael Cox said, regarding Valencia's La Liga success, *"The key was the fact that Valencia effectively played three central midfielders at a time when the rest of Spain was only fielding two."* It was simple really. Benitez overloaded the midfield and dominated the game.

The 4-2-3-1 would prove successful for Benitez and he won two La Liga titles and the UEFA Cup. Midfield dominance, allied with tactical discipline, was a blueprint for where the game was heading. It soon became a popular formation in Spanish football on the back of Benitez's success and one which he brought over to England while at Liverpool.

Rafa Benitez's 4-2-3-1 with Valencia 2001-2004

With the arrival of Benitez and Mourinho in English football, as well as Queiroz at Manchester United, English football became *very* European in its approach and the style of the Premier League changed markedly. The 4-2-3-1 became the formation of choice for most top coaches and importantly success in Europe was forthcoming because of it. By the mid 2000's the 'classic' English style of the 90's was no more. Midfield dominance was key, something 4-4-2 could not offer.

The value of the formation was that it helped sides keep possession as well as help protect the back four. It also gave licence to full backs to venture high up the pitch. Teams needed to overload midfield and attack with more potency while still staying defensively strong. It became necessary to have the right balance in the team between defence and attack. We have seen already how Real Madrid suffered from losing Makélélé . The use of two holding players to prevent counter attacks, break up play, and supply forwards was now a necessity.

The era of specialists

The move to 4-2-3-1 brought a key change in the evolution of players, notably the reduction in the influence and presence of the 'box-to-box' midfielder, a type of player who was very popular in the English game. Players like Bryan Robson and Roy Keane were the classic box-to-box players of the 80's and 90's and did very well in their careers. In the 2000's Liverpool's Steven Gerrard was the modern version. However, as the 4-2-3-1 became more prominent the need for the box-to-box player became minimised.

The game was becoming a place for the *specialist*, a player with a defined role, especially in midfield. It was a case of being either an attacking player or a defensive player. The rise of the specialist was seen in individuals like Didier Deschamps and Claude Makélélé. France had shown with their success in 1998 and 2000 how important the 'holding midfielder' was. Makélélé's value was only truly seen when he left Madrid for Chelsea; Jose Mourinho stated, after his side won the title in 2004/05, that the Frenchman was Chelsea's player of the season. Mourinho would, of course, see the need and value in this 'type' of player, Makélélé was everything a coach who sought to have defensive control and strength would want.

By the mid 2000's the two holding midfielders were seen as having specific roles; one would be the 'destroyer' and the other the 'creator'. This can be seen with Javier Mascherano and Xavi Alonso at Liverpool, or Michael Carrick and Owen Hargreaves at Manchester United. The 'destroyer' and the 'creator' highlighted what the 2000's were all about; it was a 'decade of specialists'.

Arrigo Sacchi was not happy about this evolution. The man who had envisioned the future game being one of *universality* was distraught at where the game had gone. For him the era of the specialists was damaging the quality of the game, as he said in an article in the Guardian in 2010, *"Today's football is about managing the characteristics of individuals. And that's why you see the proliferation of specialists. The individual has trumped the collective. But it's a sign of weakness. It's reactive, not pro-active."*

Was Sacchi - the great visionary - behind the times? Did he not see or at least appreciate what modern football required? The 4-2-3-1 helped sides find the perfect balance to achieve success; specialists were *key* for this to work.

Milan's diamond

There was, however, one side which would continue to use 4-4-2, and who were arguably the best side of the 2000's. Carlo Ancelotti would take over Milan in November 2001. Being a key player under Sacchi at Milan he was well versed in the 4-4-2 and blended the ideas of Sacchi with Capello's diamond - building his coaching philosophy from his two ex-coaches. He was initially criticised for his defensive approach at Milan but was keen, however, to ensure his midfield possessed creativity.

Ancelotti went about creating a side with a quality that perhaps no other side possessed. Players like Paolo Maldini, Alessandro Costacurta, Jaap Stam, Cafu, Alessandro Nesta, Andrea Pirlo, Clarence Seedorf, Gennaro Gattuso, Rui Costa, Kaka, Andriy Shevchenko, Filippo Inzaghi and Hernan Crespo were all part of his Milan side at some point, an *incredible* array of talent. It proved a success and he would take Milan to three Champions League finals in five seasons from 2003 to 2007. However, rather disappointingly, he would only win one league title during his eight years at the club.

In 2003 Ancelotti would face his old side Juve in the Champions League final. It was not a great spectacle and pretty disappointing considering the wealth of creative talent on show. A Milan midfield of Pirlo, Gattuso and Seedorf with Rui Costa playing in the playmaker role behind the talents of Andriy Shevchenko and the predator Filippo Inzaghi should have been creative yet normal play ended 0-0. It was a sign of Italian football's ability to 'cancel out' the opposition. Milan would end up winning on penalties.

That summer Ancelotti would add the Brazilian playmaker Kaká, a dynamic, creative and athletic playmaker. This was the new breed of playmaker, not like the Argentinian Juan Román Riquelme who - although a genius - lacked the physical attributes required for football's new era. The 'classic 10' was now becoming a thing of the past. Kaká was a new breed and Milan would thrive with him.

The midfield diamond of Pirlo, playing in the *regista* role - the deep lying playmaker - was supported by the defensive minded Gattuso with Clarence Seedorf supporting the attack. With Kaka at the point of the diamond it would make this the strongest midfield of the era, possessing athleticism, strength and an abundance of skill and inventiveness .

Going against the emerging trend Ancelotti would stick with two forwards, in a time when it was falling out of favour with many. In fact, of the top sides of the mid 2000's, it would only be Milan who would continue with the diamond formation.

However even Ancelotti would realise that his midfield (although brilliant in an attacking sense) could be left vulnerable defensively. This was proven by the second leg Champions League defeat to Deportivo La Coruna in 2004. Milan were 4-1 up from the first leg yet would lose 4-0 in Spain and get knocked out. A similar capitulation happened in the 2005 final versus Liverpool where a 3-0 half time lead was lost in the second half and Milan would lose on penalties. Was it a case of mentality or was the formation of two forwards (with a playmaker behind) exposing the side?

Carlo Ancelotti's Milan in the 2005 Champions League final. They played one of the most brilliant first halves witnessed, to go up 3-0, yet ended up conceding three in the second half and losing to Liverpool on penalties.

Ancelotti admitted that extra midfield cover was necessary and Massimo Ambrosini was brought in to offer more defensive solidity. After the 2005 final defeat to Liverpool Milan would become a one forward team with Kaka playing behind the lone forward. Even Ancelotti had realised the era of two forwards was now at an end and midfield overload and dominance was critical. In 2007 they would face Liverpool again in the Champions League final and this time, although not providing as splendid a performance, they would win 2-1. Was this a metaphor of the modern game? More pragmatism with less creativity?

Formation or style?

It is clear that the 4-2-3-1 formation has come a long way from its beginnings a decade ago. The extent of 4-2-3-1's rise would be seen at the 2010 World Cup where 18 of the 32 teams played some form of 4-2-3-1 at some stage. And by 2013 it appeared that nearly all of Europe's top sides were using it: Chelsea, Arsenal, Real Madrid, Bayern, Manchester United, Manchester City and AC Milan.

These sides were all building their tactics and strategy from the 4-2-3-1 framework. On paper this was proof of its popularity but looking deeper, past the simple line-ups, it appeared that it was becoming something different. Coaches were being innovative within the framework.

Across Europe the modern 4-2-3-1 has taken two key paths; for some coaches it has involved having four interchanging forwards who don't have fixed positions (Queiroz had almost mastered this at United between 2006 and 2008 with the four of Cristiano Ronaldo, Wayne Rooney, Carlos Tevez and Ryan Giggs).

This idea of interchanging forwards and fluid football was really only seen with Barcelona after United and this was in their strict positional (but fluid) 4-3-3 formation. The way Barca played it, with Messi in the '9' role became referred to as the 'false nine' formation, effectively playing *without* a centre forward.

Barca made this work best because they possessed the best players capable of executing the system, especially Messi who would drop deep to collect the ball. It was a tactic built on the strategy of overloading midfield areas with greater numbers and offering greater spatial problems for defences. But it wasn't a system without a forward, it was just one without a *fixed* one.

With a false nine system the key to success sees midfield runners and wingers exploit the open space behind the defence, with the need for overlapping and third man runs increased. When Messi moved out - a wide player or midfielder would exploit the space he left. Without a centre forward centre-backs were suddenly left without anyone to mark, it led to confusion between their unit and the midfield and this confusion helped players to find space to penetrate the opposition with incisive killer passes or quick dribbling runs. This varied movement allied with the importance of blistering pace has become of growing importance in the modern game.

This was Barca's masterful play and proof that rotation and *fluidity* was a formula for success. Why didn't others succeed when trying to replicate it, though? Well, perhaps fluidity of this type was too difficult to master without particular types of players?

The idea of a striker-less system was evident with Roma who, under coach Luciano Spalletti, experimented with a 4-6-0 first in 2007/2008 using Francesco Totti as the 'false nine'. Spain, following on from Guardiola's work developed it to near perfection in 2012 winning the European Championships again. They would defeat Italy 4-0 in the final, during which their positional movement was too much for Italy's defensive strategy. That performance was a clear indication that, of all the nations in world football, it is Spain who are the most progressive and adaptive.

Generally speaking, the most common style of football has seen the use of centre forwards playing as target men. Playing predominately with their back to goal the intention has been to hold up the ball and bring in, or release, midfield runners moving beyond them. This was seen to work for Jose Mourinho while at Chelsea and Inter Milan with Didier Drogba and Diego Militio respectively.

This type of forward is able to play in a single forward system because of their strength, ability to retain possession, and their ability to bring others into the game. Most often this has been seen in a 4-2-3-1 where the supporting three, either creative playmakers or forwards playing deeper, would seek to support the number nine by making deep penetrative runs which are harder for the opposition to track. It's a tactic to overcome the offside rule as much as to benefit from the growing importance of speed in the game.

The single forward system wasn't fluidity, as such, but it became the most popular form of the 4-2-3-1 from 2010 to 2013. Clubs like Bayern Munich, Borussia Dortmund, Real Madrid and Manchester City all utilised it and it helped them achieve success. The two German sides used it to great effect to reach the final of the Champions League in 2013, producing the so-called 'final of the 4-2-3-1's'. Forwards like Robert Lewandowski and Mario Mandžukić were integral for bringing in players like Marco Reus, Franck Ribéry and Arjen Robben. It was evident that, by the end of 2013, the formation for success was this *version* of the 4-2-3-1.

Across South America, with coaches such as Manuel Pellegrini, the formation was seen more as a 4-2-2-2, with the 10 playing higher up the pitch looking to drop into holes later on. Of course as the forward drops between units the formation is more akin to the 4-2-3-1 yet it is the use of width (and classic wingers) which offers different elements and challenges to the modern defence. Pellegrini's use of this with Manchester City (who had been used to a classic 4-2-3-1 under Roberto Mancini previously) brought title success and some of the best attacking football seen across Europe in 2013/14. However, they struggled to make a significant impact in Europe, pointing towards the problems of this set-up when seeking to dominate possession.

The return of the back three

We can see that the 4-2-3-1 (which many sides have profited from this past decade) has become somewhat predictable and, when this happens, it can lead to stalemates. Therefore a new style is often required to offer new problems for opposition sides. It may be that the back three system is a tactical move which coaches are seeking to employ. In fact a move to three at the back appears part of a natural cycle for modern football.

Earlier in this chapter it appeared that a back three was to become the preferred choice for coaches as we moved into the 21st century. And yet the opposite happened. The back three almost ceased to exist. Nevertheless, in recent years we have seen its resurgence. And at the most recent 2014 World Cup we saw the true return of the back three.

At the World Cup we saw many coaches utilizing a back three. Mexico, Chile and Costa Rica, for example, all employed a back three, yet the best example was from Holland under their coach Louis van Gaal. He decided to use it because of his side's defensive deficiencies yet it turned out to be a masterstroke. Holland would come third in the tournament, and would impress greatly with their compact and solid defence as well as their frightening transition play through Robin van Persie and Arjen Robben. Apparently van Gaal embraced the change as he had witnessed sides in Holland starting to use it after the recent success of Juventus in Italy.

Antonio Conte's Juventus have dominated Italian football with their 3-5-2 formation. Three Serie A titles in a row from 2012 to 2014 have not only proven that a back three 'works' but that a strategy based on hard work, team cohesion, and attacking variety can bring success. With the talent of Andrea Pirlo and Arturo Vidal in midfield, allied with the defensive strength of goalkeeper, Gigi Buffon, and a back three of Giorgio Chiellini, Andrea Barzagli and Leonardo Bonucci - Juve have been a formidable side in recent years. With the freedom a back three gives to the wing backs Juve have been solid defensively and ruthless in attack. The use of wing backs in Kwadwo Asamoah and Stephan Lichtsteiner offers Juve the defensive cover they desire as well as the energy, width, and quality that Conte wishes for in attack.

Perhaps it was not surprising to see Italian football seeking to resurrect the back three. For several years Napoli employed a three-at-the-back system, using a 3-4-3. This style was built on quick attacking play using the speed of Ezequiel Lavezzi out wide, Edinson Cavani through the centre, and Marek Hamšík playing as a playmaker in an inside right position. This formation and style provided some excellent football. Yet it has been Juve's 3-5-2 which has been most impressive in terms of success.

However it is not just Italy where the resurgence has been observed. In recent seasons both Barca and Bayern have moved to 'fluid systems' where they may start a match with a back four and then move to a back three. Ajax too, under Frank de

Boer, have sought to utilize this fluid system. It is no surprise that these coaches see a move to a back three, and more importantly a switch to a 3-4-3 as important for their ability to dominate and attack oppositions. The change is relatively simple; either the defensive midfielder drops in centrally (as we saw Sergio Busquets do under Tito Vilanova, a very common development in the modern game), which allows the two centre backs to split to cover the wide areas. Or a more recent development is to have holding midfielders cover the wide areas left vacant by the wing backs; the logic being that coaches would prefer to keep their central defensive pairing together, centrally, rather than split across the pitch.

The World Cup proved that the game has moved on once more and that a style and formation which was deemed dead has returned. It is conceivable that in the coming seasons we will see many more sides moving towards a back three system. This will open up new problems and new spatial opportunities which have been denied while 4-2-3-1 has been so prominent.

To counter or to pass

What is evident is that formations are no longer rigid but fluid and adaptable. And, ultimately, these formations must be allied with the *strategy* a coach wishes to play. Rather than saying what the future of formations will be, is it more important to address future style and strategy?

The past decade has certainly seen the rise of possession-based sides and coaches. Arsène Wenger, Marcelo Bielsa, Louis van Gaal, Luis Aragonés and of course Pep Guardiola would seek to dominate games with a possession-based style emanating from the Dutch Totalfootball philosophy. This 'tiki-taka' style of play, in which a team would seek to build up play through the thirds and play in the opposition's half is a tactic which asks a lot of the players in the team as it requires excellent technical ability and tactical understanding as well as the ability to play in tight areas.

Yet as Guardiola's Barca became more dominant sides sought the means to nullify their ability to penetrate. A clash of styles ensued as we saw with Bayern and Dortmund this past season: the battle of 'tiki-taka' and counter-pressing. A battle which we saw previously with Barca and Real Madrid under Guardiola and Mourinho.

When we look at the past three winners of the Champions League we see that counter-pressing looks to have superseded 'tiki-taka'. Chelsea in 2012 executed it well yet both 2013 and 2014 saw the finals of counter-pressing sides in Dortmund and Bayern and then Atlético Madrid and Real Madrid respectively. This transition-based tactic has helped sides expose teams while being defensively solid.

Universality

Have we seen the end of possession-based football's domination? Is this new counter attacking tactic the way forward? Have we seen the game evolve to a level where coaches effectively *allow* possession-based sides to have the ball?

It seems clear that the game has developed to levels where teams, both in and out of possession, have become extremely strict in terms of positioning, roles and movement. And it appears clear that defending and transition have never been more important. Which is why we will look into these factors, in greater detail, next.

Chapter 6: Pressing

"The opposition must be offered no way out. A possession game – Barcelona's game – requires you to win possession in the first place" The Guardian's Sid Lowe on Pep Guardiola's defensive pressing philosophy at Barcelona

Defensive neglect

It is heard at almost all levels (in all sports)… the cliché of *'attack wins games, defence wins championships'*, yet do people really understand the impact of this and the true importance that defending has on success?

Since the turn of the century football has progressed in many areas, and much attention has been given to what happens when a team is in possession. In fact, the rise of 'tiki-taka' with Barcelona and the obsession that the media and fans have with goalscorers and attackers points to a cultural emphasis on attacking. The purists will argue that attacking football is how football *should* be played, yet do we understand what this means?

Zdeněk Zeman, the Czech coach who has worked predominantly in Italian football with Lazio, Roma and Foggia is a proponent of 'all-out attack' football; he simply seeks to score more than the opposition. Although such an approach is entertaining the truth is that it is simply not conducive for success. English football saw Kevin Keegan, while coach at Newcastle United in the mid-90's, play a very attacking brand of football which was lauded as entertaining, yet he never managed to win anything. Both Zeman and Keegan sought to play a certain way yet neglected a key element to football: *defence*.

In fact when we look at the English Premier League over the last few years it has been home to a philosophy of attacking football. Many English sides, in recent history, have embraced this philosophy and it has resulted in some ludicrous scorelines between the top sides; scorelines which have pointed not so much to great attacking play but to a *neglect* of defending. This approach has coincided with a decline in the performances of English sides in the Champions League. Actually, it is no coincidence at all.

Simply put - defending as a team is essential for success, especially at the top levels of football. Quite frankly the top English sides forgot about this (we shall look at Chelsea's Champions League success, and why they were successful, shortly).

Perhaps some fans enjoyed the Keegan years but, remember, he never won anything with his style. English football lost its dominance in Europe because defensive organisation, seen under the tutelage of coaches like Mourinho, Benitez and Queiroz in their times at Chelsea, Liverpool and Manchester United respectively, was diminished. As we've also discussed, these coaches were world class European tacticians who understood the importance of defending and being organised. It was no surprise that during the 2000's their sides were dominating Europe. When all three left the Premier League, English football *changed*.

Roberto Di Matteo brought Chelsea European success in 2012 because he used the tactics which Jose Mourinho had previously instilled in his players. They defended resolutely to win the competition. Taking over from Andre Villas-Boas, a coach who sought a high pressing, possession-based style, Di Matteo changed Chelsea for the better in terms of their ability to win games. It was pragmatic and ultimately successful.

Compare this to Manchester City who, at the time, possessed some genuine world class players but who struggled in the Champions League. Why was this? Well it was because of their defensive approach. Their coach, Roberto Mancini, struggled for two seasons (2011-2013) in the group stages because of the way he set up his side to defend. His problem was that he failed to build an organised, tactically strong, cohesive side built for success in Europe.

What is needed at the top levels of the game, especially in Europe, is organisation and *having a strategy* when out of possession. In games against Real Madrid, Dortmund and Ajax the opposition all found holes and flaws in Manchester City's armour. Under Mancini, the team lacked cohesion, organisation, and discipline! Although he had top notch players in Vincent Kompany, Yaya Toure, David Silva and Sergio Aguero - Mancini's problem was that he put his trust into *individuals*, hoping or expecting them to produce moments of magic to win games. This may work in the Premier League but in Europe it requires a much stronger team performance, especially when you do not have the ball.

City struggled in Europe with Mancini because the defence manifested itself as 'disorganised individualism'. Setting up in a 4-2-3-1 (like other top sides across Europe) they didn't have a defensive strategy; when to drop, where to drop, and who to press. In order to succeed, and even win a game at the top level, these tactical elements have become essential.

Mancini had struggled before in Europe - when at Inter Milan – where his tactical naivety reflected his reliance on individuals. Inter struggled in the competition in a similar way to City yet when Mancini was replaced by Jose Mourinho, Inter would win the Champions League. Why? Because Mourinho understood the importance of being a strong and cohesive *team*. The lesson about success in Europe is clear; the whole overcomes the parts, no matter how good those individual players are.

In the 2013/14 season English football has seen the return of Mourinho to Chelsea and Manuel Pellegrini installed at Manchester City with both coaches bringing a wiser approach to their teams through their tactical understanding. These are coaches who appreciate the needs of the modern game. Even Arsène Wenger has seen the importance of being stronger defensively.

In his quest to replicate Barcelona, Wenger forgot (or neglected) the biggest factor as to why Barcelona are so great. *Barcelona (and Spain) are world class defensive sides.* Wenger's defensive inattention led to Arsenal being a shambles when out of possession; they didn't press quickly to stop counter attacks, they didn't press from the front, or drop off and deny space. The midfield looked disorganised and clueless when out of possession and they allowed too many 2v1 situations. They also failed to deal effectively with long balls and crosses. It was a defensive shambles.

Cesc Fàbregas summed it up when he spoke of the 'freedom' Wenger afforded him, something which the tactically astute and successful coach Guardiola was furious with. The Spanish are tactically as good as they are technically. Their ability on the ball is excellent, their movement and timing is mesmerising, yet their tactical *discipline* to keep their defensive shape, always focused on their tactical roles, is a reason why they have achieved as much as they have.

Wenger's failing was that he saw only passing, and ability on the ball. Without a defensive foundation, a side will not win anything.

It is clear that the rise of, and need for, a *collective approach* for sides, especially when defending, has become the main formula for success in the modern game. Barcelona proved that during their dominant years. Bayern embraced it and became Europe's best side. And Germany have reached the top of the world with their success, in Brazil, primarily through their collective spirit and togetherness. The future game will only increase this need for cohesion.

Spain's defensive might

At the 2012 European Championships there was an appreciation of a strong defence by some, and a general disregard of it by others. No surprise that those who prospered at the tournament did so on the back of their impressive defensive setups, notably the finalists: Italy and Spain. In turn, there were some quite awful displays of defending; Ireland in particular were abysmal, especially considering they came into the tournament on the back of such a resolute defence. Under Giovanni Trapattoni they were a shambles and deservedly eliminated in the group stages.

Another side which disappointed greatly was Holland. The Dutch were arguably the best side in the tournament when in possession; their speed of play, movement, and their skill on the ball was scintillating at times yet it was what they did defensively which led to their knockout in the group stages. In their game against Germany, their defending meant Germany took all three points.

Both sides played a 4-2-3-1 yet Holland seemingly neglected to focus on *team* defending. Holland's problems came from their chaotic defence and a lack of balance in midfield. A lack of midfield overload, the wrong type of players in various positions and, importantly, a lack of team defending cost the side qualification from the group. Compare this performance to their World Cup performance two years later and you see the difference in approach which van Gaal provided. They looked stronger, more resolute, and *worked as a team*.

When you consider the importance of collectivism then you can see why Spain have dominated international football since 2008. Their progression from a 4-3-3 under Luis Aragonés to a 'false nine' 4-2-4-0 under Vicente del Bosque, at the 2012 Euros, showed a growing maturity and controlled approach to games. With Sergio Busquets and Xavi Alonso playing as holding midfielders, Xavi and Iniesta centrally above them, Silva wider and Fàbregas as the 'false nine' - Spain simply dictated their games in the midfield.

Like Guardiola at Barcelona, del Bosque sought to fill his side with midfielders, at the expense of a 'true' forward. This tactic did not offer significant penetration throughout the tournament yet it allowed Spain to do what they wished for; control the midfield area and remain defensively strong (they did not concede a goal in any knockout game from 2008-2012; a quite astounding statistic). The tactic would also help prevent the onset of fatigue such that their command of possession and enhanced fitness would see Spain win the 2012 Euros tournament, annihilating an exhausted Italy 4-0 in the final.

And why did Spain fail so poorly at the 2014 World Cup? Well they lost their belief in their style of play. In Diego Costa they had a player who thrived playing a counter-pressing style. And the problem was that del Bosque could not just put such a player into the team and create a counter-pressing side. Spain played a confused style, not sure whether to dominate possession or use Costa's attributes. Spain looked like a side who didn't know who and what they were anymore. This is what cost them.

From 2008 to 2012 they knew who they were, they built their dominance and confidence from this. Yet in Brazil they looked scared, unsure and ultimately weak. Costa's introduction not only affected the balance and, perhaps, the harmony of the side but it rocked the fabric of the Spanish philosophy.

If del Bosque wanted to embrace a more counter-pressing strategy he would have been better suited playing players like Fàbregas, Pedro, and Koke (with Costa) as they are more vertical and direct in their play. He added a piece which was not going to work yet was not brave or willing to make the additional changes in style and personnel to make it work.

During their prevailing and successful years Spain and Barcelona would dominate midfield with their possession-based game. The tactic is not only a way to find space to penetrate the opposition it is also a defensive tactic in order to 'rest in possession'. Spanish football's emphasis on a high pressing approach is a tiring tactic for players thus resting when in possession is essential to keep a team's energy levels up.

During Barcelona's dominant period they became more and more fatigued (long term) as a unit which resulted in an overuse of their 'tiki-taka' football; it became common to see Barca have 70%+ possession in games. It was a near admission that they were conscious and fearful of losing the ball and having to work hard to win it back. As highlighted earlier, most of their players had not properly rested since the summer of 2007 due to international tournaments where they reached the finals each time, and pre-season tours to help market the club's brand.

At the 2014 World Cup Spain gave away possession too cheaply and were punished in transition, particularly by the Dutch in their 5-1 destruction of the Spaniards. The players were exhausted and unable to press to win the ball back, a tactic which had been their most essential weapon previously.

High pressing

For some in the game there is a misconception that the term 'defence' means 'defenders', this is *wrong* and those who stick to this idea are more likely to lose more games than they win. Defence is what the team does when not in possession of the ball. Effectively defence is a collective effort by the whole team. What Barca did better than any side before them was their ability to press as a team.

High defensive pressing is the style that Rinus Michels developed in Holland with Ajax in the late 60's, and is a method which Arrigo Sacchi's Milan mastered so well for great success, and which Barcelona and Spain recently perfected. This style means that, as a team, you press high up the pitch in order to win the ball back. Its value is that you prevent the opposition counter attacking and, if you win the ball back, you are closer to goal.

A high pressing game requires many factors to come together to be highly effective; notably it requires a collective approach and a deep understanding of the roles and positioning of all players. It also requires supreme fitness and a willingness to work hard and be selfless for the good of the team. It is a tactic that requires a real intelligence, an understanding of the triggers of when to go, where to show, and where to support.

Interestingly, English sides have often attempted a high pressing game; Graham Taylor's Watford in the 1980's were renowned for it, however what this side and many English sides lack, is the actual knowledge of *how* to press. A gung-ho approach was often how English coaches viewed 'pressing', which was easy to play around for most sides, as it lacked intelligence or strategy. Contrary to the English mentality - pressing does *not* mean running around like a lunatic hunting for the ball. It requires astuteness and understanding.

The truth is that not many sides can achieve success playing a high pressing game, yet if a good coach can impress this style on their team, the rewards are there. This is why Guardiola should be complimented for his ability to make it work so effectively when at Barca. Alex Ferguson remarked after the 2011 Champions League final that the way Barca pressured their opponents to win the ball back was *"breath-taking"*.

Of course the downfall to this defensive style is the vulnerability behind the defence as the defensive line is very high. Thus it is important to have quick and intelligent defenders, who are adept at playing 1v1s. It is vital they can read and win the ball if the opposition play a longer clearance out. On top of this is the need to have a goalkeeper who acts like a sweeper, being able to read and clear up in the (massive) space allowed behind the defensive press. Yet Guardiola wanted his forwards to work hard to stop this happening. Here's how.

Firstly, the initial press. Importantly Barcelona started pressing the *instant* they lost possession. Of course that is the perfect time to press because the opposing player who has just won the ball has exerted energy in winning possession and does not have a clear idea of what decision he will make now he has the ball. Barcelona therefore attempted to dispossess (or at least rush) the player before he could give the ball to a better-placed teammate and start an attack.

The key is that Barca pressed in packs which was made easier thanks to their possession-based style. Because they passed over short distances of 10-15 yards there were always several players around the ball, so if they lost possession, there would be a number of players able to press quickly to win it back. If only one or two players press, it's too easy for the opponent to pass around them. Team defending, working as one, this is the key.

Now if Barca hadn't won the ball back within five seconds of losing it, they would retreat and build a compact ten-man wall behind the ball in order to prevent the opposition playing through them. It was methodical and well drilled. The players nearest to the ball pressed to stop an attack yet those further away took up their defensive positions to close the space and compress the team. In a similar mentality to Sacchi at Milan the distance between the front man in the wall and the last defender was meant to be only 25 to 30 metres.

This defensive setup has become the hallmark of the gegenpressing strategy which we will come to next. Yet Barca were the team most adept at playing a high press and a mid-press effectively. In fact in the final in 2009 against Manchester United, after Barca had taken the lead, they opted to defend with this deeper 'wall', nullifying the space for United to play through and behind. It was eleven *precisely* positioned opponents and it prevented United creating many chances.

When Barca were set up in this defensive block they simply waited for a chance to press once more. The tactic is all about waiting for the *right* moment to press again. The moment is not chosen on instinct, there are very precise prompts that tell them when to press; a trigger such as a poor touch, or a player's head going down can be the time to go and press again. Or it could be that the team seek to shepherd the ball to a player or area of the pitch where they can press once more. It is very intelligent and very effective. And it is these principles which have helped counter-pressing become such a formidable tactic in recent years.

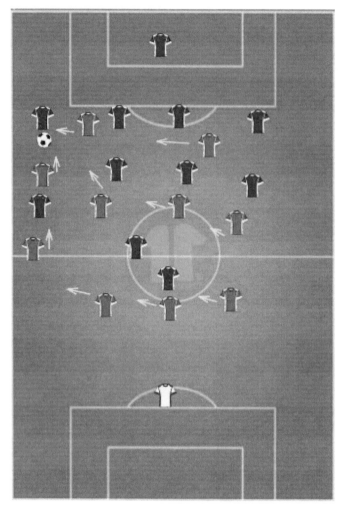

An example of Barca's high pressing game in transition. The full back has won the ball back yet is confronted by four players around the ball immediately. Look, also, at how the defence is set up - as a back three - with the holding midfielder supporting in front and the goalkeeper's position higher up to play as the keeper sweeper if necessary. This should allow the team to stop the opposing team playing forward and attacking as well as seeking to win possession back by forcing an error.

Gegenpressing

Now although there are different ways to defend, the central element which is often lost on many coaches, fans and even managers, is that defending and attacking are not mutually exclusive. The most important moment in football comes in *transition*.

Jose Mourinho argues that transitions are the most essential part of the game: *"When you lose the ball, you are most vulnerable, when you win it, you have your best chance to score."*

Watch Spain and Barcelona at their best when they win or lose the ball and how quickly they transition, watch a Mourinho side when they win the ball in their own half… in a matter of seconds they are down the other end. This is how important, how crucial, transition is to football. Manchester United from 2006 to 2008 had perfected counter-attacking football with the speed of players like Ronaldo and Rooney. Put simply, the best side's transition quickly and effectively. And this is where the success of gegenpressing has come from.

While Barcelona and Spain were showing the value in a high pressing game, coaches were looking for ways to counter their style and tactic. Jose Mourinho would use a deep defensive block with Inter Milan in the Champions League semi-final in 2010 to overcome Barcelona in the semi-final and Bayern in the final. His objective was to cede possession and territory higher up the pitch yet restrict space behind his compact block. It was seen as a masterpiece of defensive organization. He would continue this tactic with Real Madrid from 2010 to 2013, especially in the games against Barca. He was showing the value of counter-attacking football, of transition; it was not simply 'defend-at-all-costs' as others played against Barca.

At the same time, a new strategy was being developed which was focused on pressure and transition. We have spoken of gegenpressing previously, and will look more at how this style has become popular and successful in recent years.

It was Jürgen Klopp at Dortmund who developed and executed the 'counter-pressing' tactic to great effect. In the makeup of the 4-2-3-1 Klopp would work on the defensive organization of his side to nullify space behind the defence as well as making it difficult to play between them. Dropping his forwards off to a point 10 yards ahead of the halfway line, he would allow the opposition to have the ball in their defensive third, the aim being to draw the opposition into the mid-third and then to pounce with frightening speed and intensity in order to win the ball back and counter.

This compact mid-block meant there was a lack of space for the opposition to penetrate through and behind. Setting out in a 4-4-1-1 formation the team would make a strong defensive block which was tough for sides to break down and penetrate through. Of course the aim was to draw the opposition in, win the ball back and transition with frightening speed. Dortmund's counter attacks were truly incredible to watch.

Now an important part of this tactic is the effectiveness of the centre forward. Their ability and dynamism to press when out of possession is central to the success of the tactic. It was not about winning the ball but being able to force the play, contain the opposition, and force errors. To be successful the forward must be a hard worker and sharp in his approach.

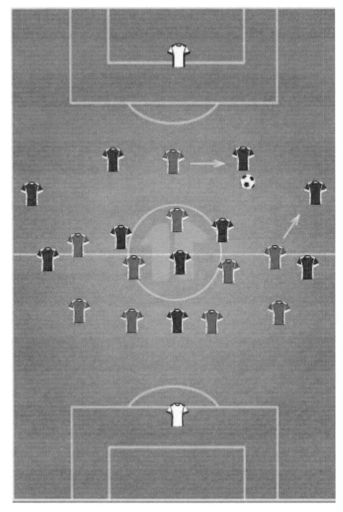

An example of how gegenpressing works. The centre forward seeks to force the central defender to play to the left, where the wide midfielder seeks to press and win the ball back. See the compactness of the team, preventing space in-between. The lack of space behind means any runs and passes over the block can be dealt with by the defence or goalkeeper.

We have seen already how Jupp Heynckes replicated Dortmund's gegenpressing method in the 2012/13 season with Bayern and executed it to perfection. In the semi-final against Barcelona, and as mentioned in Chapter 4, Heynckes said Bayern were *"tactically brilliant"*. He was right. They were excellent too against Arsenal and Juventus earlier in the competition. He was talking about their execution when out of possession.

Using the gegenpressing strategy Bayern nullified sides who sought to play a possession-based game and punished them ruthlessly on the counter attack. Against

Barca they would win 7-0 on aggregate. It was ruthless and suffocating pressure and proof that counter-pressing, when done right, could nullify 'tiki-taka'.

Jupp Heynckes coached his side to know when to press and when to delay. The players understood how to force and contain the opposition, how to restrict space and how to nullify the opposition's options. As mentioned in Chapter 4, Philipp Lahm called their approach (quite appropriately) *"aggressive pressure"* and this idea has become a focus of the modern game.

Of course, it is not too different to how Sacchi's Milan and Guardiola's Barca played; the ideas of collectivism, of a whole unit working together to apply pressure on the opposition, knowing the triggers of when and where to press.

And in the 2013/14 season we witnessed the rise of a new counter-pressing force in Atlético Madrid. Under the tutelage of Diego Simeone the club has propelled itself to the top levels of the European game. In 2012 Simeone took the side to Europa League success and then defeated Champions League winners Chelsea in the European Super Cup (4-1) in August 2012. The signs were there that Atleti were becoming a force, built on defensive organisation and using a deep defensive block, as well as utilising ruthless counter attacks.

In 2013/14 they would win La Liga (the first time a team other than Barca or Real Madrid had won it since Rafa Benitez's Valencia in 2004) and reach the Champions League final. They were a minute from winning a historic double only to concede a set piece in the dying moments and lose in extra time. However Atleti and their coach had proved their credentials, in a similar fashion to Dortmund the season before; they had shown their ability to compete with the top sides. And their strength? An extremely organised defensive block with sublime transitional play.

Tiki-taka vs counter-pressing

Chelsea's Champions League run in 2012 proved the value in approaching games with a level of *pragmatism*. How they setup against Barcelona, Bayern, and even Benfica was an admission that they could not compete with these sides by dominating the game with possession and long build-ups. They simply did not have the personnel to implement an open brand of football.

Roberto Di Matteo admitted their vulnerabilities and used their strengths to counter them. He went back to the method which had suited Chelsea so well for many seasons, with a mentality which was schooled by Jose Mourinho during his time at the club. Defend deep and compact, and counter attack with quick wingers and the power of a strong number nine.

Chelsea's tactical decision to defend in numbers and to stifle any space and time for players like Lionel Messi was the correct decision in hindsight. However, this defensive approach has been criticised by the 'purists' of the game. Many fans and pundits accused Chelsea of not *deserving* the trophy. It appeared that the purists believed that the manner and style in which the trophy was won placed a shadow over the winners. Johan Cruyff stated, after Chelsea lifted the trophy, *"A football team can forget everything and still win. I'd choose to take the steps we take at Ajax, towards the football that we all want to see."*

This is quite ludicrous. If Chelsea won the competition, then they deserved to… surely?!? Is Cruyff serious when he believes that it is better not to win if you play defensive football? Surely a good coach will change their formation or strategy to suit the game and opposition in an effort to improve their side's performance and chances.

Cruyff, though, had learnt, as a coach, that stubbornness in one's philosophy can prove costly. His 'Dream Team' lost 4-0 to AC Milan in 1994 when his reluctance to change things cost Barca the game. Capello's tactics stifled Barca and Milan were ruthless on the counter attack. This stubbornness effectively ended Cruyff's reign and prevented that side from going on to achieve more.

Di Matteo was pragmatic and he operated how he saw best… in very much the way of the man whose shadow lingered over Stamford Bridge: Jose Mourinho. Di Matteo adopted tactics which reflected the team's strengths as much as the weaknesses of the side.

Yet based on what Barcelona have achieved, especially their consistent challenging for top honours, it appears that it is beneficial to value a possession-based game: to have the ball and dictate the game, rather than to trust the opposition not to score. If sides are serious about being one of the best and most consistent sides in Europe then do they need to develop a style which utilises a more possession-based style of football, and attack with fluency?

There will be those that say that possession-based football has been shown to be more effective because having over 60% possession in a game correlates to an increased rate of success (based on a large sample size of games). In the past decade, in particular, possession statistics have become obsessed over, with coaches like Arsène Wenger seeking to have over 60% in each game. Guardiola would take possession to another level at Barca and then at Bayern with consistent 70%+ possession in games. It seemed this is the model. Is it really? No, it appears not.

Recently we have started to see that sides are *willing* to allow the opposition to have possession of the ball. This means we are starting to see games where possession statistics mean little. The context of the game cannot be explained in 'who had more of the ball' because both sides are not seeking to have possession. What has become more important, especially in the higher echelons of the game, is creating and converting chances.

Ultimately possession doesn't count for much unless you finish your chances. Of course if you have more possession this, statistically, increases your chances of scoring as you have more opportunities; however, we are really talking about the *quality* of chances created here.

Barca, during their highly successful period, made their possession count for something by producing a high number of *high quality* scoring opportunities. They showed patience, intelligence and great decision-making to convert possession into goals. Yet as they became more stifled by ever-improving oppositions those quality chances were reduced. And those who were able to counter more effectively started creating more chances. Possession started to become a problem, not a solution.

This strategy was shown to work, particularly for Inter and Chelsea in 2010 and 2012. In the semi-final against Barcelona in 2010 Inter held the ball for just 21.5% of the two matches, yet still managed to win 3-2 on aggregate. Even in the final (against Louis van Gaal's Bayern Munich) Inter Milan had the ball for only 30% of the game, yet still won 2-0. It appeared to show that a defensive counter attacking strategy could succeed over an Ajax *Totalfootball* philosophy.

What is clear is that possession-based football may not be the answer to everything in the modern and future game. Teams have evolved into appreciating the value of allowing the opposition to have possession; being more defensively secure and denying the opposition good goal scoring opportunities appears more important. This approach may seem higher risk as you are giving your opponents the opportunity to have the ball (which may in turn create more chances) yet with improvements in team defending sides are showing more focus and discipline in their defending and greater intelligence and efficiency in transition.

Using possession stats to judge a team is wrong. You judge teams by their ability to convert their chances. You judge them by the final score. That is what matters. And this is where the rise of counter-pressing originated from. It is about denying the opposition chances and creating great chances to score in transition: it is quality over quantity. It is about controlling the game without possession.

Counter-pressing has become a model for success at the top levels of the game; with Chelsea, Bayern and Real Madrid winning the Champions League from 2012 to 2014. And with Dortmund and Atlético Madrid reaching finals too, it does seem that counter-pressing has overtaken tiki-taka football in the modern game. German football is now regarded as the pinnacle of world football and their World Cup success certainly pointed towards their ability to press and counter attack with ruthless precision and efficiency. However, Joachim Löw has seen the necessity of possession, and in controlling games with possession. He has sought to learn from Guardiola at Bayern and embrace both tiki-taka *and* counter-pressing in his side's play. Germany showed versatility and variety in their tactical approach at the World Cup, a key reason why they won the tournament.

So while some have said that we are witnessing the death of tiki-taka through the exits of Spain and Bayern in the World Cup and Champions League last season, it is a slight exaggeration. Perhaps tiki-taka simply needs modernising? The game is developing at rapid speed and new styles and systems are being cultivated in order to counter opposition sides. The level of in-depth analysis and the rise of technology has catalysed the game's evolution. The game of the future will require sides to be flexible, fluid and versatile. One style alone will not be good enough for success.

This look at modern defending points to one clear thing, one which differentiates between the good and great sides… their coaches. Their attention to *detail* in preparing their teams to defend and attack as a team has become paramount to success. There is the idea that setting up a side to be defensively organised is easy. This is not true. To get a team to defend as one, whether pressing high or dropping off, takes time, great coaching and importantly great persuasive skills. Success appears to rest on the quality of the coach. This is why coaches like Guardiola, Heynckes, Mourinho, Ancelotti, Klopp and Diego Simeone have become so successful. They have convinced their players to 'buy in' to their philosophy, to sacrifice the self for the team. Great coaching and great persuasion. And this is where we will look next.

Chapter 7: Team-building

"We have a team spirit and an ability to work together that I've never experienced." Jupp
Heynckes, at Bayern Munich

Collectivism

We have seen the evolution of tactics and formations over the past decade, the
importance of team defending, and of course we have witnessed the ever-improving
quality of players across the whole team. Yet the modern game has also taught us
something else which is central to success: the importance of teamwork.

As we saw in the previous chapter, the growing focus and need for pressing has seen
team defending become essential. Just like Sacchi's Milan side (which was drilled to
near-perfection in what they did off the ball) modern teams have embraced the
importance of defending as a *whole*.

Barcelona's success was often viewed as great attacking football with Messi's skill
and finishing allied to Xavi and Iniesta's talent on the ball. Yet their true route to
success was how they pressed and won the ball back as a team. At their peak, in
2011, it was complete harmony and *togetherness*. Meanwhile, the rise of Germany's
top sides and their national side came about ultimately because of their ability to
blend quality with teamwork and togetherness.

Atlético and Real Madrid's successes in 2013/14 came from their coaches' abilities
to bring in cohesion and a willingness to sacrifice for the squad. It appears simple
really, to achieve success you need to be a team and to be a team you need a coach
who can bring a group together.

Sacrifice the me for we

It can be said to convince a group of individuals to give up their *self* for the team is
the hardest task of a modern coach. To have the persuasive skills and man-
management ability to convince highly paid and often highly egotistical players to
work and sacrifice themselves for the team, especially when out of possession, is the
most important task of a coach.

Our look at football's development has flagged up coaches like Mourinho,
Ferguson, Guardiola, Ancelotti, Simeone, and Klopp, who have all shown an ability
to bring a group of players together and create a united team, and not just that - but

make them believe they are the best in the world. *Team building* and motivation is therefore the most important facet of a modern coach.

When Pep Guardiola took over as first team coach at Barcelona, in 2008, he knew he had inherited a talented group of individuals but was aware they were not a 'team'. There was a lack of commitment and too many cliques and divisions. Standards had dropped since the Champions League success of 2006. He knew that his job was to create the right environment and conditions for his players to fulfil their potential; he sought to make them into a unified team, and it is this that made Barcelona such a great team from 2008 to 2011.

Guardiola made training sessions secluded, away from the fans and media; he sought to create an environment of oneness and togetherness. He insisted that the players mix together when they ate and forced them all to speak Catalan. He was aware that small groups and cliques were toxic when looking to produce a successful team. He understood that total unity is what makes the difference between converting a good group of players into an excellent team. He convinced his players of the need to be unified and cohesive.

His influences were based on Cruyff's teaching - based on the Ajax Totalfootball philosophy. Rinus Michels fittingly titled his book *"Teambuilding"*, pointing to the fact that perhaps it was the most fundamental thing for being successful in football. The lessons of that Ajax side and philosophy were for players to sacrifice themselves for the team, yet still to shine individually and ultimately win games. When writing about that great Ajax side, Guardiola wrote: *"All the players, of different quality without exception were aware of their mission on the field of play. They demonstrated a tactical discipline and enormous capacity to apply all that at just the right time."*

During the summer of 2010 to the end of 2011 Barcelona were simply at *one* with each other, showing such brilliant cohesion, understanding and balance that the acclaim of being the 'best ever' side was not far from being true.

The whole is greater than its parts

The idea of having a 'go to guy' is not uncommon. In fact, to be a world-class winning side you often need genuine world class ability. Yet when that player becomes *too* important, when the focus and balance of the team becomes unhealthy, that is when success can lead to failure. A successful winning side cannot be just about one player. A reliance on one player often makes a team one dimensional, predictable, and easier to play against.

Although there can only (often) be one 'star' in a team, it is important, almost essential, to have supporting players in the side who can offer the team more dynamism and variability. Bill Cartwright, a basketball player who played for the

Chicago Bulls under Phil Jackson and with Michael Jordan, a player who won three NBA championships, wrote in Jackson's book *Sacred Hoops*, *"Most teams have guys who want to win but aren't willing to do what it takes. What it takes is to give yourself over to the team and play your part. That may not always make you happy, but you've got to do it. Because when you do, that's when you win."*

During Barcelona's dominant period what was important was how the team's success came from the supporting cast. It was not always about Lionel Messi. Messi can be said to be the Michael Jordan of football; for three years he was the near perfect team mate who provided those key moments of individual brilliance. A player, like Jordan, who could come up with something special when it mattered most.

Yet like Jordan, the players around Messi became over-reliant on him. His talents were so brilliant that it appeared that his team mates were placing too much hope on him and reducing their own effectiveness. As Messi soared to great individual heights it was clear that this was having a negative effect on the quality of Barcelona as a team.

Recall how in the 2012/13 season no player, apart from Messi, scored over 20 goals. Fàbregas, Xavi, Alexis and Pedro all reached the mid-teens, David Villa reached 9 due to his injury in December. Yet Messi scored 73 goals! The impressiveness of Messi's achievements were startling and one cannot take that away. However, as the team became more and more 'Messi-centred', the balance and therefore effectiveness of the team was lost. Messi *was* Barcelona. His evolution had taken him to becoming the focal point of *everything*. One man, however, cannot win things by himself, it takes a team to do it.

Now compare that to Bayern Munich. By all accounts it was van Gaal's inability to control a dressing room packed full of big players and bigger personalities that proved his downfall and was the reason why he left in 2011. And it was here, crucially, where Jupp Heynckes succeeded; bringing together this squad of talented players and bonding them together.

Bayern Munich reached the Champions League final in 2010 and 2012. They possessed some great players but were overcome by a stronger Inter 'team' in 2010 and a more together and focused Chelsea side in 2012. It was almost like their individual brilliance in players like Robben, Ribéry and Gomez was not enough. To go from second to first they needed to be a better team, they needed to sacrifice themselves for the team. In the 2012/13 season they looked unified; they had achieved 'togetherness'.

After the 4-0 defeat of Barcelona in the Champions League semi-final, in 2013, Jupp Heynckes stated that Bayern's teamwork was key to their success. *"The team were outstanding in executing the tactical plan. That was top-class in terms of physical effort and fighting spirit. It's fantastic teamwork."* Heynckes achieved an unprecedented treble that season.

It is clear that the top modern coaches realise that, in order to succeed, they need to take individuals and create a team. This was Sacchi's achievement at Milan and Guardiola's at Barca; playing a system and style where, as Sacchi explained, *"Players are connected to one another, which moves together as if was a single player."*

In 2011, talking to *The Guardian* Sacchi explained, *"Today few teams know how to do this. Few teams work as a unit. They are all made up of little groups. There is no great connection, nor a good distribution of players around the pitch."* It would appear that Sacchi's words have been listened to as the value of teamwork has risen in recent years. Yet there was a coach who was ahead of time in this respect. That man is Jose Mourinho.

The group one

Jose Mourinho has dominated the past decade of football. He regards himself as the "Special One", a statement which is hard not to argue with. Yet what is it which makes him so 'special'? Yes he is tactically excellent and has been fortunate to work with top sides who possess top players. But the truth is that Mourinho, like Alex Ferguson, Louis van Gaal, Pep Guardiola and Arrigo Sacchi has the ability to produce great *teams*. Mourinho has the ability to motivate and persuade his players to sacrifice their own egos for the good of the side. He has convinced his players at Porto, Chelsea, Inter, and even at Real Madrid of the need to be a *united* group. And he has been successful because of it.

The lesson of Samuel Eto'o is a great example of how Mourinho can convince those to sacrifice the 'me for the we'. Eto'o is known for his strong ego and individual approach yet at Inter Milan in 2009/2010 Mourinho played him as a left winger; he was instructed to work hard defensively, to track back, and help the side when out of possession. This was not something Eto'o was used to, and thus it was remarkable to see a player with a reputation for being selfish playing so… selflessly. Mourinho had convinced Eto'o to play for the team, not himself. Inter would win the treble that season. Coincidence?

Inter's success was proof of Mourinho's ability as a motivator and persuader, as well as being a great tactician. Mourinho's biggest asset was, and still is, bringing together a group of players and making them one unit, united together. This has shown to make them difficult to break down both on the pitch and mentally as a team. It is this which made Porto victorious in 2003/2004, a collective spirit of togetherness - belief and trust in each other. It's what helped Chelsea achieve back-to-back Premier League titles in 2005 and 2006, and what brought treble success to Inter Milan in 2010.

Mourinho almost achieved the same level of success at Madrid yet in 2012/13 the side fell apart when players like Iker Casillas and Sergio Ramos started to lose their belief in the team and philosophy of Mourinho. The 'harmony' had been lost, egos prevailed, and failure ensued.

When Carlo Ancelotti arrived at the Bernabeu to replace Mourinho in the summer of 2013 he brought a harmony and togetherness to Madrid which had been lost. His trust in players and man-management skills helped Madrid to win their 10th European crown in their 4-1 defeat of rivals Atlético Madrid.

Former Real Madrid coach Leo Beenhakker has seen what Ancelotti achieved at Madrid, stating that, *"[Ancelotti] is showing he is a master with the way he manages well all these figures. He seems to have them all really plugged in. They are all committed, not just 11, not 14, but more. All of them. He knows how to manage very complicated matters."*

Carlo Ancelotti's beautifully 'balanced' and together 2014 Champions League winning Real Madrid side. This was the 4-3-3 which destroyed Guardiola's Bayern in the semi-final second leg 4-0, with Madrid winning the tie 5-0. The side's transition-based approach was ruthless yet the key was how the team played as a cohesive group. This was the pinnacle performance of Madrid's season.

This is what Heynckes mastered at Bayern in 2012/13. In turn, when Dortmund defied the odds to reach the Champions League final in 2013, their success was not built on money but the value of being a team; their coach knowing the importance of being a whole unit. We have just seen how important the defensive strategy of gegenpressing has been for German football - perfected by Dortmund and Bayern in recent years – but above all it is a tactic which requires high work rate, anticipation, cohesion, and trust. Teamwork at its best.

This story of team cohesion epitomises how Klopp values, and how he generated, team spirit and togetherness while at Mainz. After he'd led the club to promotion in 2004 he settled on an unlikely pre-season trip. As he explained, *"We took the team to a lake in Sweden where there was no electricity. We went for five days without food. They had to do this [he whistles and, using an imaginary fishing rod, casts off]. The other coaches said: 'Don't you think it's better to train playing football?' No. I wanted the team to feel that they can survive everything. My assistant coach thinks I'm an idiot. He asks if we can train there. No. Can we run there? No. But we can swim and fish! We were like Bravehearts. You can stick a knife in me here – no problem. We went to the Bundesliga and people could not believe how strong we were."*

Devil in the detail

Arrigo Sacchi was a coach who was meticulous in his preparation of a team, obsessed with the positioning and space between units. For him it was important that all the players were as one, and focused on their objectives, especially when out of possession. Guardiola was the same at Barca.

At Barcelona, Guardiola revolutionised a club under his image and ideals. He persuaded the team to buy into his methods, tactics and approach, and by doing so they became a great success. Arsène Wenger admits that this side was the best he had seen: *"Until now, in my life, it's the best team I've played against. The first time we played them at the Emirates, the first half an hour was the best I've seen."*

Guardiola would organise and prepare his team for each game with *meticulous* planning. Perhaps only Mourinho can be compared to Guardiola, in terms of in-depth tactical preparation and the precision of a player's movement, positioning and strategy. Compare this to Arsène Wenger who has a different approach. Wenger does not believe in micro-managing his side. When asked about the rivalry between him and Guardiola, about the 'talent' of Guardiola as a coach, Wenger replied, *"Football is not a chess game. It belongs to the players. We prepare the team to do well but don't forget that the main heroes are on the pitch, not on the bench."* Is Wenger wrong?

Wenger's philosophy is about the *players*, about giving them ownership, responsibility and the freedom to choose and make decisions. Guardiola, however, is about managing the group to minute perfection. Each detail is covered, every step planned. Sacchi too knew the importance of this method, so too does Louis van Gaal.

The lesson appears to be that at the top levels of the game the coach is *not* a facilitator of the players but their leader and general. Sacchi is right, the game has not changed much from his time. Wenger, however, appears unwilling to accept this. His belief in management is admirable but it has been his undoing as a coach. It is why he has taken his team 'close' to European success yet never all the way. Success has always been about the influence of the coach on his players. Talented players coached superbly will achieve success.

Wenger may believe in *Totalfootball*, may strive to emulate the quality and style of Sacchi's Milan and Guardiola's Barca, but he has neglected a vital ingredient of greatness. The recent successes of coaches like Mourinho, Guardiola, Simeone and Klopp is no fluke. The reason for their success appears to be about their level of *detail*.

We have seen already that a focus on what sides do when out of possession is integral to success, with the top coaches knowing how important team defending is, working as one whole organism to achieve the goal of denying the opposition chances and goals. There is also no doubt that zonal defending and marking has taken precedent over man-marking too.

And we cannot ignore the importance of set-pieces in modern and future football. This is an area which seems to get overlooked when we think of the game and its development. Set-pieces in tightly contested games are often the difference. Coaches like Mourinho and Simeone are excellent at planning and implementing creative and structured set-pieces. It is these moments when the detail and focus becomes apparent.

These coaches are the model of the future game. Through strong leadership and principles, through the nurturing and development of players and, importantly, the ability to build a united and committed team, coaches can seek to be successful. Allied with a great tactical and technical knowledge the modern coach is a fundamental requisite for success. Formations may be important, but it is teamwork, collectivism and selflessness which are central to success in the future game.

Arrigo Sacchi has always been a believer that the team is more important than the individual and the modern game has become testament to this belief. He also believes that as the team becomes more unified, it can move towards one of *universality*.

In the past decade this philosophy has struggled to make an impact… until now. It appears that Sacchi's philosophy has the potential to become real. And as we will see with the evolution of each position, players and teams are becoming more fluid and 'complete'. Football, it seems clear, is heading towards a future of universality.

Chapter 8: Keeper Sweeper

Over the next few chapters, we shall look at the roles of various positions and it makes sense to start with the goalkeeper, the player who wears the number 1. When we talk about a specialist position and how the role of the 'specialist' is changing, we must regard the goalkeeper as the only *true* specialist in the side - which makes him or her extremely important. And, as we will see, this is perhaps the most evolved role of all in terms of its development path over the past twenty years.

To possess a top quality goalkeeper is arguably one of the most important requirements for success. We have seen already that defending has been enhanced, and that more has been asked of forwards to press and defend higher up the pitch. A goalkeeper, however, holds the most crucial and demanding role - he has the most to lose should he make a mistake. A forward may miss nine chances and score one goal and be regarded as the hero, whereas a keeper may save nine and concede one and be regarded as the villain. It is a tough job where there is little room for mistakes. Therefore a modern keeper must be consistent, attentive, and a great decision maker. Yet he must also be a player. Something which hasn't always been the case.

Ruud Gullit once said that, *"A goalie is a goalie because he can't play soccer"*, and at one point in the history of football this statement was not far off the mark. There was very little similarity between the keeper and his ten other teammates. He was simply not regarded as a 'footballer'. However, this all changed in 1992.

The back pass rule

In the past, a keeper's role would have been to make saves, take crosses, and punt the ball down the field. However, the introduction of the 'back pass rule' in 1992 changed all that. It was introduced in order to discourage time-wasting and ultra-defensive play. It came on the back of the 1990 World Cup in Italy where games were described as 'exceedingly dull' due to constant back passes and keepers simply holding on to the ball. They would even drop the ball on the floor and, when pressed by the opposition, simply pick it back up again. One example, familiar to many, was that of the example of the Republic of Ireland's Pat Bonner. He kept the ball for over six minutes against Egypt by dribbling it around his box and picking it up again.

The rules needed to change in order to make the game more entertaining. And so it came to pass. The back pass rule means that if a teammate passes the ball to his keeper with his feet the keeper is not allowed to pick the ball up, he must use his feet like an outfield player. He can only pick it up, in his area, courtesy of a pass from a teammate's head or chest. The rule also affected throw-ins; the keeper could not use his hands if receiving a throw from his team.

A rule was also introduced that stipulated if a keeper dropped the ball, he could not pick it back up. And finally to prevent time wasting and to keep the game flowing, the 'six second' rule was introduced which meant that a keeper could only have the ball in his hands for six seconds after which he must release the ball into play by either kicking, throwing, or dropping the ball. These changes drastically changed the needs and role of the goalkeeper.

Distribution

There is a well-known phrase in football that states: "The goalie is the first line of attack". It implies that the starting point for most attacks comes from the keeper. Whether he has collected a cross, or he has a goal kick, the keeper has a number of moments in the game when he has possession of the ball and can initiate or influence play.

The introduction of the back-pass rule completely changed goalkeeping. No longer were keepers simply able to pick up the ball, they were now *forced* to focus more on their footwork; they were now a *footballer*. Initially there was a difficult period of adjustment for many keepers whose whole world had been turned upside down. Those keepers, who had played in the 1980's, had not been developed to use their feet and were used to a certain way and style.

To be told they had to change was a massive culture shock. What resulted was a lot of rushed and hurried clearances which most often went out of play or to the opposition. There was certainly a sense of fear with the new rule; keepers' trusty weapons – their hands – could not be relied on as they had been.

There were, however, some great goalkeepers during the 1990's who adapted and prospered under the new rule. For others, the change in the rules did not necessarily affect their quality as a keeper at all. In particular, Danish keeper Peter Schmeichel and Germany's Oliver Kahn can be identified.

Both Schmeichel and Kahn were giants in terms of their size, dominance, and keeping abilities. The signing of Schmeichel was a major coup for Alex Ferguson when he joined Manchester United in 1991 and he further proved his quality when helping Denmark win the 1992 European Championship. Without question his influence helped United become the force they became in the Premier League.

Kahn, meanwhile, moved to Bayern Munich in 1994 and spent 14 years at the club, becoming one of the greatest keepers in the history of the game. His shot stopping talent as well as his aerial dominance made him the perfect keeper for that era.

Yet being a top keeper in the present game is no longer about solely being a good shot stopper. While searching for a goalkeeper, a manager will now look for someone who is *comfortable* with the ball at his feet. Brendan Rodgers, while manger of Swansea, bought the Dutch keeper Michel Vorm in 2011, and made some important comments in relation to what he, as a possession-based and progressive coach, seeks in his keeper.

"For us it was then the case of looking to get in the right type of goalkeeper. There were many good goalkeepers who could have been available but we needed one that was going to suit our style and Michel was one that was on our list. After looking at his style and his game I think his attributes suit us perfectly. He makes saves, which is important for a keeper. But for how we play, we like to build the game from behind, it is vital that the goalkeeper is comfortable with his feet. You will find nearly all Dutch goalkeepers understand and manage the game very well and he is a player that not only does that but he controls the game well from behind and will help us construct the game from the back."

This quote encapsulates what the modern keeper requires to succeed. Great distribution skills and ball control as well as intelligent game management. Game management incorporates the tactical understanding needed to control the tempo of the game, to make good decisions, and to provide great positioning to receive a pass.

Louis van Gaal, the visionary and progressive coach at Ajax in the early 1990's, saw a young Edwin van der Sar as the perfect keeper suited to the new rules and the style of play he sought at Ajax. The young keeper was put into the Ajax squad and would experience UEFA Cup and Champions League success in 1992 and 1995 respectively. He would be voted Europe's best goalkeeper in 1995. Van der Sar was a very accomplished goalkeeper yet it was his ability with the ball at his feet which distinguished him as the best. His excellent distribution skills and composure were sought out by Alex Ferguson at Manchester United in 1999 to replace Peter Schmeichel yet van der Sar, at this time, would move to Juventus and United would end up signing the French World Cup winner Fabien Barthez.

Barthez was a player who often enjoyed playing with the ball at his feet (often putting fear into the fans at Old Trafford for his flamboyant skill). He was not something English football had witnessed much of, previously. In England keepers were still traditional in their approach – a no frills service which often involved kicking it high and long to avoid letting the ball near the goal. Barthez however looked like an outfield player and sought to play like one. He was, however, caught out several times trying to play out from the back or seeking to sweep up attacking play.

In a Champions League game against Deportivo La Coruna, in October 2001, Barthez was guilty of coming out and completely missing the ball, gifting two goals in a 3-2 defeat. A month later he was again guilty of errors, this time gifting Manchester United's rivals Arsenal two goals. His first error was a poor pass out straight to Thierry Henry who put away the goal with ease. The second goal saw

Barthez coming out to sweep a through ball - completely missing it, and gifting Henry another goal. Barthez was a good keeper yet too error prone for a top side like United. United needed better and would find great success when they finally landed van der Sar in 2005. We saw already how this signing was important for their progress towards becoming the best side in Europe thanks to the strength they now had in goal.

The modern keeper

The new century would see a rise in the quality and quantity of the modern keeper. In 2001 Juventus replaced van der Sar, who struggled with the demands of Italian football, with Parma's Gianluigi Buffon, paying £32m for the keeper (and making him the most expensive keeper in history). It was money well spent though - as the Italian has proven to be one of the best in his time at Juve and for Italy. His contribution towards Italy's success at the 2006 World Cup earned him second place in the Ballon d'Or world player of the year award, which Fabio Cannavaro, his defensive teammate won. Buffon's strength, authority , and shot stopping ability are some of the best around. However he, perhaps, comes second to a Spaniard as the best of the 21st century.

In 1999 Real Madrid turned to a young Iker Casillas as their keeper. A player who would become one of the greatest keepers of all time. Although he didn't have the size and intimidator's prowess of a Schmeichel, Khan, or even van der Sar, Casillas was an excellent keeper who showed great reflexes and agility. He was entirely suited to the way Madrid played at that time, with a focus on *playing* out from the back and through the thirds.

Ron Atkinson, a previous Manchester United manager, once called him a *"lucky goalkeeper who is always in the right position"*. Perhaps a typical English viewpoint but the truth is that Casillas was an excellent keeper who had superb anticipation skills and agility. In his first few seasons he would win the Champions League and La Liga twice. A decade later and he is the most successful keeper ever: three Champions Leagues, five La Ligas, a World Cup, and two European Championships with Spain. He is Spain's most capped player with over 150 caps and the keeper with the most appearances in the Champions League. It is fair to say that Casillas is the greatest keeper of the 21st century.

But is not just Casillas who shows what a modern goalkeeper needs to have. It is Spanish football overall. Spanish football has been ahead of the rest when developing modern keepers. Casillas, Pepe Reina, Victor Valdes and David de Gea all *look* like outfield players in terms of their size and appearance as well as their ability with the ball. Perhaps unsurprisingly Reina and Valdes both developed at Barcelona's academy which makes sense when you consider the philosophy which the club promotes in terms of technical excellence and possession. For a side like Barcelona the keeper is a key 'player' on the team and therefore must be adept at playing with his feet.

According to *Opta* statistics, in 2011/12 Pepe Reina of Liverpool created more goalscoring chances for his teammates than any other goalkeeper in the English Premier League. Rafa Benitez had bought him for Liverpool because of his distribution skills and in that 2011/12 year - he created five opportunities.

As for Victor Valdes, he was a key part in Barcelona's rise to dominance between 2003 and 2013 winning three Champions Leagues and six La Ligas. Yet he has been regarded poorly by many in the media and by fans across Europe - not valued for what he offers the team.

What Valdes offered Barca more than anything was his ability with the ball. He is arguably the best distributor of the ball in Europe and it is little surprise that Barca have been able to play their possession-based game because of him.

The stats would prove it. *Opta* found that Valdes had the most number of successful passes by a goalkeeper in Spain in 2009/2010 (823) and 2010/11 (617). With many goalkeepers expected to play the ball 'safe', regardless of success, Valdes averaged more than 80% pass completion during his time under Guardiola. The percentage is impressive but the key was the distance of the passes. Guardiola's style was not to play long balls but to play a shorter possession-based game, to which Valdes was central.

In turn, Valdes completed the primary role of the keeper - to keep the ball out the goal – with great success. He has only averaged more than one goal per game (across a season) once in his career and that was in his debut season. He has broken numerous records at domestic level, including a record number of consecutive clean sheets at home. In 2011/12 he broke Barca's record for the most minutes without conceding a goal when he went 896 minutes without a goal being scored.

It has probably taken Valdes longer than it should to receive acknowledgement for his abilities. It was the arrival of Pep Guardiola that led to his reputation being enhanced as he became an integral part of the way Barcelona played - as 'sweeper keeper'; a role taken from the Dutch philosophy.

Keeper sweeper

The 'keeper sweeper' has emerged in the past decade because of the changing role of the keeper and teams' broader defensive developments. In order to master the keeper sweeper role a goalie is involved in the game from the first minute until the last - 'reading' the game at all times, and communicating with, and directing, his teammates. He must be willing to engage in active play when required.

While at Ajax, van der Sar played the sweeper role because van Gaal insisted that his side pressed high up the pitch. This meant there was a lot of space behind the defensive line which could be exploited. The keeper was therefore a key part of making sure any balls over the top were dealt with. Guardiola sought the same at Barcelona; while playing a high pressing game he needed a high defensive line which required Valdes to patrol the areas behind the defence.

As coaches saw the value in using a high defensive line the modern goalkeeper started to spend more time outside the goal area than inside. This was to eliminate goalscoring opportunities early in the move before shots could be attempted.

Manuel Neuer, arguably the best goalkeeper of the current era, has emerged as one of the most dynamic sweepers in the game. Under the tutelage of Guardiola at Bayern, playing a much higher defensive line than Heynckes had done previously, Neuer has further enhanced his sweeping skills. His speed, anticipation, and confidence with the ball at his feet as well his heading ability has allowed his defence to play and press yet further up the pitch.

Although this sweeper role looked dangerous in the second leg against Real Madrid in the Champions League semi-final, where there were several poorly timed clearances Neuer proved the value of his role in arguably his best performance for his country at the 2014 World Cup against Algeria. Erik Kirschbaum wrote for Reuters that, *"Neuer stopped seven Algeria shots and defused a number of dangerous counter-attacks playing like a sweeper with an astonishing 19 touches of the ball outside the penalty area and 59 in total."*

Against Algeria, with a high defensive line and wet pitch, sweeping was essential yet dangerous. As Neuer said to reporters post-game, *"I had to risk my neck at times. Sure there was a risk but I had to take the chance."* His coach Joachim Löw was pleased with his keeper and his duties, stressing that Germany weren't troubled by shots because of Neuer's sweeping role: *"He didn't have a lot to do on the goal line but he showed how strong he is away from the goal."*

Neuer would win the Golden Glove award for his performances at the World Cup and was a major reason for Germany's success. His presence, positioning, handling, and shot-stopping - as well as distribution and sweeping skills - make him the best keeper in the modern game.

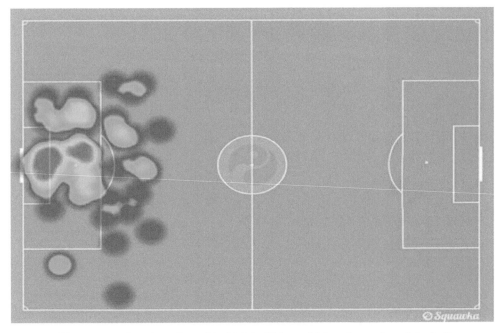

Heat map taken from June 30, 2014 of Manuel Neuer's touches of the ball versus Algeria in the 2014 World Cup

In twenty years the role of the keeper has dramatically changed. The keeper must now be a complete player: he must be a great shot stopper, his handling skills to catch and punch from crosses and set pieces must be superb, and he needs to be a great passer of the ball. As well as this are the psychological attributes required to achieve success in the modern game. Concentration, anticipation, bravery and a 'demand and command' of the area. To succeed in the modern game a keeper needs all these skills.

It is evident that the modern keeper is the 11th player on the team; he must be adept at being part of the 'team' and no longer just a bystander to the game. Modern teams utilise all 11 players when in possession of the ball, and the goalkeeper needs the ball-playing attributes of an outfielder.

Currently, we are witnessing the emergence of young and talented goalkeepers like Manchester United's David De Gea, Chelsea's Thibaut Courtois, and Barcelona's new keeper Marc-André ter Stegen. These players have all the attributes needed for elite level sides. One change, though, for the modern keeper is that while a top keeper in previous years would begin to peak and mature in their late 20's, these young keepers are expected to be mature and focused by the time they reach 20 years of age.

Chapter 9: Modern Libero

We have seen so far how changes in tactics and formations, as well as the evolution of defending, has opened new spatial dimensions and options. The game itself has required a higher quality of player to deal with the speed and technical needs of the sport, as evidenced with the modern goalkeeper. In turn, as we enter a new era in football, it is evident that football's cyclical evolution has contributed to the rise and return of the 'libero'.

A need to exploit space

Due to the obsession with midfield overloads and dominating possession, coaches have sought new ways to overload areas and find space and time on the pitch. Teams have often cancelled each other out in these midfield areas meaning that, at times, the game has become a stalemate. Coaches have attempted to use 'false nines' to overload the midfield, or use a narrow form of the 4-2-3-1, leaving one forward isolated against two defenders and five midfielders who seek to control the middle. Teams have sought to dominate midfields and games with possession and numbers. None more so than Pep Guardiola with both Barcelona and Bayern.

With this need to overload central areas we have seen full backs given increased licence to attack the flanks. Coaches have sought to nullify this attacking threat by having these players marked and tracked, thus restricting their space. Effectively we have seen a game in which each player is marked, except one. As the 'one forward' formation becomes more popular due to coaches using 4-2-3-1 there is one player who is always free (discounting the keeper) and we have seen the central defender's position changing to help their side retain possession.

Against one forward formations the central defender has been given more space and freedom, and he has become a key part of building attacks. We are now witnessing the return of the libero, the playmaking centre back.

The classic libero

In the past we had world-class liberos such as Franz Beckenbauer, Franco Baresi and Matthias Sammer, as well as Lothar Matthäus and also Glenn Hoddle. In fact, these two final players were midfielders who moved back deeper into defence in the latter years of their careers. These legends of the game were the playmakers of the team, excellent passers of the ball who could also carry the ball and break the opposition's defensive lines. They controlled games, swept up opposition threats, and started their own team's attacks.

Across Europe during the 1980's and 1990's this type of player was thriving in back three systems, most notably in Italian and German club football (international success was there too). Brazil and Holland, playing four at the back systems, also looked to produce ball playing defenders because their styles required it. Unfortunately, the subsequent move away from back three formations reduced the need for a libero sweeper type player; four at the back typically meant zonal marking and the playmaker moved forwards up the pitch.

English football never particularly valued the libero, the formational philosophy of the nation was 4-4-2 and this was used to promote a direct style of football. Whilst this stopped many sides from embracing a ball playing centre back, Liverpool and Nottingham Forest - during the 1980s - did see the value in ball playing defenders and built their success on these types of individuals. Yet the FA of England, and the coaches who attended their courses, did not take heed or seek to develop this type of 'key' player. For them, a defender's job was to defend, to head the ball, tackle, and stop the ball from going in the goal, *nothing* more.

Thus English teams (exceptions noted) have rarely trusted the defender who can 'play'. It was evidenced by the defensive, negative mindset of English football, one which promoted a 'safety first' philosophy over attempting to play. It was no surprise that England fell behind other nations, those who valued a possession-based approach; nations who sought to build out from the back, and therefore who needed players who could deal with these needs.

Technical excellence

As we enter the 21st century we can see it has become essential to have a team where *all* players can play with confidence and technical ability. Top coaches have sought central defenders who wish to play out and develop play through the thirds. Playing 'out from the back' has become a popular phrase used by many top coaches and teams.

The modern game, in fact, has become dominated by ball playing defenders; players like Thiago Silva, David Luiz, Sergio Ramos, Vincent Kompany, Mats Hummels, Giorgio Chiellini and Gerard Pique - players who are arguably the best defenders in the modern game. There is a trend to this list, something they all have in common. As well as their ability to defend; to tackle, spoil play and intercept, they are also known for their ability *with* the ball. Notably, their ability to *carry* the ball. The modern defender is not just a great passer of the ball, he is adept and confident at *running* with it.

World class defenders in the modern game are confident and willing to take the ball out and drive with it into forward areas, as modern systems promote it. This is why Pique was so important for Guardiola's Barca side, and why Guardiola wanted to move Javier Mascherano deeper into defence. He required players with a midfield intelligence, with an ability to pass with quality, and with an ability to drive into midfield to help overload those key areas. And now, at Bayern Guardiola, Guardiola wants Javi Martinez to play in this deeper role also. He wants Martinez to be his libero.

If players are free to bring the ball out they must be adept at doing so, they must have the technical excellence and tactical intelligence to be effective in this role. Mats Hummels, one of Europe's best defenders over the past few years, is an excellent reader of the game, a great defender. Yet he also plays the libero role superbly. For Dortmund and Germany he can be seen driving the ball out of his defensive area into midfield, breaking the opposition's defensive lines.

However no-one better epitomises the modern libero than David Luiz, Paris Saint-Germain's Brazilian central defender. Yes he is a player who most certainly mixes opinion. For some he is an extremely talented player, for others he is a liability because of his perceived lack of discipline and control as a central defender. Many point to his poor positioning and desire to chase the ball. However, when watching Luiz you see a player who characterises what the modern game requires: he is positive, progressive, and always seeking to attack. Along with his Brazilian and club teammate Thiago Silva, arguably the world's best defender, the two of them can effectively play a type of 'double pivot' from defence, both having the ability to move forward into areas which their midfielders' movements have created for them to exploit.

The 2014 World Cup in Brazil showed us the libero in action. As the 4-2-3-1 became more predictable coaches sought to alter their styles in order to get their players into possession. The use of three at the back systems was seen with Chile, Holland and Mexico, with Argentina and Italy also seeking to use it at some point. Players like Chiellini of Italy and Rafa Marquez of Mexico were excellent examples of the modern libero being brought back to the modern game. And as sides seek to embrace three at the back formations, it will only help this type of player in terms of their freedom and ability to drive out with the ball.

Chiellini has become accustomed to a three at the back system in his time under Antonio Conte at Juventus. Conte plays a 3-5-2 which has brought three Serie A titles in a row from 2011 to 2014. This formation allows his side to offer new problems to the opposition. His three man defence of Chiellini, Barzagli, and Leonardo Bonucci all have the ability and freedom to carry the ball into forward areas. The team is, effectively, capable of playing the structured three at the back system as well as having *three* capable liberos to drive out with the ball. Tactically it is fascinating as it poses serious questions of the opposition.

As sides move away from the 4-2-3-1, coaches like Guardiola and Frank De Boer at Ajax have sought to bring in fluid formations which move from a four to a three when in possession. This has seen players like Sergio Busquets move from being a holding midfielder into something deeper during the game. The great tactician Marcelo Bielsa, at Marseille, will switch between a three or four man defence based on the number of centre forwards the opposition have - always seeking to have an overload and thus the freedom for one player to drive out with the ball. During his time as coach at Athletic Bilbao Bielsa used Javi Martinez as his libero, giving him the licence to be his playmaker and take the ball into midfield.

Coaches are seeking to adapt and anticipate where the game is heading and attempting to offer new problems to the opposition. Modern coaches like Guardiola, Bielsa and Conte are offering new problems for the opposition. It is absorbing to witness these tactical developments and, of course, the associated technical components required for these styles to 'work'.

Seeing this evolution and the return of the modern libero is an enthralling development in the world of modern football. What this emergence shows is that players are becoming more adept technically in *all* positions. A defender is no longer someone who just heads and tackles, he is now a key part of the team when in possession; he is the team's deep lying playmaker.

Chapter 10: The Wing Back

It has been said that 'full back' is the easiest position to play in football; it is where a coach might seek to 'hide' his weaker players. Historically, full back was seen as a functional and safe role on the pitch. That view, however, is becoming questioned in the modern game as more is asked of the full-back. In this chapter we will assess the changing role of the full back and discuss the importance and future of this position. While other positions are changing and evolving, the modern full back may become the most significant change on the pitch.

The classic winger

The role of the winger has changed markedly since the 1990's. In the era of David Beckham and Ryan Giggs it was about beating your man on the outside and delivering the ball. It was about creating a yard of space to deliver a precise cross. The winger's role was marked very precisely; they were to occupy the 'channel' and supply balls to their strikers.

As the 2000's dawned - the winger became a different type of player. As we saw earlier, football started to see a growing number of inverted wingers coming into the game. Portugal's Luis Figo and the Czech Pavel Nedved would show where the game was going with their dazzling dribbling and scoring ability. Thierry Henry developed from a winger while at Monaco and Juventus to an inside/centre forward in his time at Arsenal.

Ronaldinho mesmerised Barca's Camp Nou with his skill and speed, coming off from wide and running at the heart of the opposition. And Arjen Robben excelled when playing on the right and seeking to cut inside and go for goal while at Chelsea, Real Madrid, and Bayern. The best we have seen this century are Cristiano Ronaldo and Lionel Messi. All were given the freedom to drive inside with the ball.

The game changed markedly in the mid-2000's; the classic 'winger' became the goalscorer, no longer merely the assistant. In an attacking sense this change led to sides having a lack of 'width'. The inverted winger's movement, and their changing role, led to space in wide areas being created. The landscape of the game changed, the evolution of the winger would impact how teams functioned, and ultimately how they defended.

Those players who drove inside, more than outside, were now defended against differently. Previously, defenders would want to force wingers inside as it was more congested and they were forcing them onto their 'unfavoured' foot. This even led to some coaches playing inverted full backs to counter these threats; both Rafa Benitez and Jose Mourinho played the Spanish full back Álvaro Arbeloa at left back when playing Barcelona to counter the threat of Lionel Messi who would come in off the right wing onto his favoured left side, for both Liverpool and Real Madrid respectively.

Attacking licence

The previous 'full back' - players like Paolo Maldini, Stuart Pearce, Lilian Thuram and Javier Zanetti - have all been regarded as great players, or more importantly, great *defenders*. However, the modern game is asking more of the full back in terms of attacking. Because of the inverted winger, the modern full back must be an attacking outlet for his side. And so the game is showing...

If you were asked to name the best full backs in the game now you would list: Philipp Lahm, Dani Alves, David Alaba, Lukasz Piszczek, Jordi Alba, Ashley Cole, Bacary Sagna, Pablo Zabaleta and Marcelo. When you think of these players you think of their attacking threat more than their defending strengths. In fact many of the modern full backs are not *hugely* talented defenders at all, their strength comes from their attacking capabilities.

The attacking full back, or should we say 'wing back', is not a new phenomenon necessarily. We have seen attacking full backs for decades in the game. The most classic examples are those of Roberto Carlos and Cafu for Brazil, however what we are seeing is a rise in the quantity of this type of player, so much so that the full back is no longer seen as a defender.

Because the winger has become such a dangerous player they are marked more closely and often denied the 1v1 situations they crave. To help them create these opportunities full backs are important to help take a defender away by making overlapping runs past the winger (the intention being to distract a defender and thus create more space and opportunity for the winger). The best example of this (and working to near perfection) is Bayern with Robben and Lahm over the last few seasons. Lahm's intelligent deep runs create space for Robben to drive inside, yet he often seeks to play the overlapping run to enable Lahm to create crosses for goals.

Bayern achieved much success with this approach under Jupp Heynckes between 2011 and 2013 and Lahm became the 'classic' winger of the team, as did David Alaba on the left. The role wasn't about defending per se, it was more about supporting the attack to help Bayern dominate the game and provide greater goal scoring chances. What is clear is that in the modern (and future) game, how we view the full back role needs to change; they are no longer defenders but modern wingers.

Diagonal runs

The modern full back has become essential to a side's success. No longer are they there to be 'functional', they are now key elements to a side's attacking play. And because of this they need to have the attributes required to excel in their role. They need to be excellent at: running with the ball, crossing, and *must* be superb in 1v1 duels.

Many of the players we have mentioned previously display the attributes of being attacking players because many of them were once wide players who were moved back. Ashley Cole is a good example of this; at U14 he was deemed a 'maybe' as a left midfielder, yet as left back he exceled. In a similar way to the modern central defender, forward-minded players have been moved deeper to play in defence.

And full backs are now showing a *further* step in their evolution. These players are starting to move in *diagonal* lines. What does this mean? Well let's look at Bayern and Guardiola. In players like Lahm, Rafinha and Alaba, Guardiola has them not only playing and moving wide and high in vertical lines but now moving into midfield areas to exploit space centrally. They are moving diagonally. As midfielders move away from their central positions - either deeper, or more forward - attacking full backs are exploiting this space. Such movements can be very difficult to mark or track meaning such movements can be very damaging to the opposition.

An example of how Guardiola's system opens space for Rafinha. The positional rotation of Schweinsteiger and Robben creates space to be exploited centrally. This spatial freedom and movement means the full back is no longer instructed to work in straight lines but is free to move diagonally also.

This idea of movement and positional rotation is becoming necessary for top sides to exploit smarter defences. Vertical lines, or even horizontal ones are too *rigid*, the game is becoming diagonal, and Guardiola is leading the way in showing how effective that can be.

And in Philipp Lahm Bayern and Germany have the absolute prototype of the modern wing back (or even perhaps modern player – yet we'll come to this later). Lahm is a world class wing back, able to play wide as well as centrally. He is excellent in attack; his passing and crossing is sublime yet compared to other 'world class' wing backs Lahm is also excellent when defending too. Put simply, Lahm is *the* prototype for the future wing back.

Defensive balance

As a position begins to progress we see the implications across the team. As more coaches seek to use their full backs as modern wingers, the defensive balance of the side needs to be reviewed. Of course not every coach believes in the attacking freedom afforded to these players. Jose Mourinho prefers a 'safe' full back option who will defend more than attack, a la Álvaro Arbeloa at Madrid and Branislav Ivanovic at Chelsea. As we've seen, Mourinho is a defensive-minded coach who prefers to have six players behind the ball at all times in order to make his side hard to break down and be countered.

Pep Guardiola, often seen as the antithesis of Mourinho, shared a similar approach in his time at Barcelona, though. He used a lopsided full back/wing back pairing of Eric Abidal and Dani Alves. Abidal was his 'safe' defensive choice and Alves was his attacking winger. Abidal covered round to create Guardiola's ideal 3+1 defensive cover. Although on paper Guardiola's Barca played a 4-3-3 you have to question if he really ever played with four at the back.

There was always a question as to whether Alves should even be regarded as a full back. His role was to play a mid-to-high wide role to provide width in order to exploit space, or to pull defenders across to create space centrally. His role was key for Barca's success yet it was never truly considered a *defensive* one. In fact Alves was actually more of a liability - defensively - for the team. It didn't matter though, it was what he offered in possession that mattered; he was everything a coach would want (in an attacking sense) from the modern wing back.

His attacking licence was not an issue as he was covered sufficiently. In their prime (2009 to 2011) Barca had a balanced back three of Puyol, Pique and Abidal who provided the cover for Alves to attack. In the classic sense of the 'four becoming a three' the full back would be allowed to attack one side while the other would drop back to make a three and Barca did this (but in the aforementioned more lopsided way). Yet, in the past few years, we have seen a resurgence of two attacking full backs. The Cafu and Carlos approach has returned! This has had significant implications for the classic full back, as well as the back four itself.

The return of a back three

In recent seasons we have seen coaches giving their full backs much more freedom to attack and get forward, *on both sides*, at the same time. Guardiola's successor at Barcelona, Tito Vilanova used Jordi Alba on the left, as much as a winger than a full back. It meant Alba and Alves were both *allowed* to join the attack which meant a greater expectancy on Sergio Busquets to drop in to make a back three. Offering both players the freedom to push forward meant Barca lost their defensive balance, yet it does not mean it was a flawed idea. We saw earlier, for example, how Antonio Conte embraced the use of wing backs in Kwadwo Asamoah and Stephan Lichtsteiner playing in his 3-5-2 system. Both players offered Juve the defensive cover they desire as well as the energy, width, and quality that Conte seeks in attack.

Four at the back suited sides who wanted to defend zonally and cover the width of the pitch more effectively while providing defensive overloads in central and wide areas. Think of players like Stuart Pearce, Lee Dixon and even Paolo Maldini, who played as, and knew they were, defenders. However, as the game progresses the back four has become restrictive. With full backs needed more in attacking areas, and required to provide and exploit attacking overloads - moving to a back three is not an issue for sides defensively.

Effectively coaches cannot rely on a back four when the full backs have little or no interest in defending. Brazil found this out in the hardest way possible at The 2014 World Cup in the semi-final against Germany when their 'full backs' Maicon and Marcelo abandoned any defensive responsibility leaving their two centre halves seriously exposed. Germany exploited this tactical failing and won the game 7-1, the heaviest defeat for Brazilian football ever. It was a lesson that wing backs need to be covered by three central defenders!

Ultimately the game has changed and the role of the modern full back is one of the most significant of these changes. The way we view the full back must adjust, and modern progressive coaches are showing ways to make this possible. We are seeing already that the classic full back is becoming obsolete and that it is the *wing back* which will be necessary for sides to succeed in the coming years.

Chapter 11: The 'Water Carrier'

As we take our journey across football's evolution we can see that, so far, each position has been transformed to suit the needs of the modern game. As we move into midfield we will look at the developing role of the 'holding midfielder', a position which has grown hugely in importance this past decade.

An undervalued asset

Eric Cantona once remarked that his French teammate Didier Deschamps was merely the *"the water carrier"*, meaning his job was simply to supply the ball to the better players. What Cantona failed to recognize was that there was nothing *wrong* with a player having this role; what was wrong was to think that such a player was not as important a part of the side as the so called 'flair' players. Cantona's view was naïve and arrogant because Deschamps' role and influence was, in fact, *essential*. Without a player like Deschamps how would the 'talented players' get the ball, and who would do the work for the team on the defensive side?

Cantona's disrespect and disregard for Deschamps had a twist though. Cantona wouldn't be part of the French squads which won the 1998 World Cup and 2000 Euros, however Deschamps would be fundamental to the team; he was the captain, the coach on the pitch. The truth was that possessing a world class 'water carrier' was not a waste, it was a recipe for triumph.

As we saw earlier, clubs and coaches in the 1990's started to see the value of the 'holding midfielder': a player who would offer defensive security to the side and cover the gaps between the units of defence and midfield, an area where the opposition's number 10, the *trequartista*, liked to operate. The defensive midfielder became important as a way to nullify the threat of the playmaker.

English football was late to utilise this *type* of player - the trequartista - and it took the arrival of players like Gianfranco Zola and Dennis Bergkamp as well as coaches like Wenger, Mourinho and Benitez to evolve the English style. Both of these foreign imports excelled due to the freedom and space they found playing between the orthodox 4-4-2 formations of English sides which was prevalent in the late 90's.

Eventually English football caught up and coaches started to see the need and value in having a purely defensive midfielder in place. Away from the typical 'box-to-box' midfielder of that era, this type of midfielder was willing to stay disciplined and allow the players in front of him to attack, while he stayed positioned in the middle of the pitch, in front of his defence.

Many fans see this type of player as safe, boring, and ultimately a waste yet, like Cantona, yet they are naïve to the importance that the 'water carrier' has. And there has been none better at proving the importance of this than Claude Makélélé.

The Makélélé role

If you asked many fans, after Chelsea won their first Premier League title in 2005, who their player of the season was you would probably hear names like Frank Lampard or Didier Drogba. Instead, their manager, Jose Mourinho, declared Claude Makélélé as Chelsea's 'player of the year'. The importance that Makélélé had on Chelsea's success would not be seen or understood by many fans, or even many pundits, yet for their coach he was crucial.

Before he moved to Chelsea he was at Real Madrid, where he won the Champions League in 2002 and La Liga in 2001 and 2003. However in the summer of 2003 the club believed that he was surplus to requirements and accepted a bid of £16m from the *nouveau riche* Chelsea. It was to be a grave mistake on the part of Madrid; although they possessed attacking talents - the 'Galacticos' - in Zidane, Ronaldo, Figo, and Raúl, they (Florentino Perez) were ignorant to think that they did not require a defensive midfielder who could help provide the team with the *balance* which Makélélé provided.

The issue had been that Makélélé had demanded to be rewarded with the same wage as the top earners at the club, yet Madrid's president Florentino Perez flatly refused. When David Beckham arrived it was clear what their intentions were: they sought to add another Galactico and profit from shirt sales, forgetting that success comes from the balance between attack and defence, with a defensive midfielder central to needs.

Makélélé was only truly appreciated for what he did after he left. It seems that the strengths of many 'under-valued' players are only seen in their absence! Without the Frenchman the void in Madrid's midfield was evident. Zidane saw the issue of replacing Makélélé with Beckham, and sagely observed: *"Why put another layer of gold paint on the Bentley when you are losing the entire engine."*

Fernando Hierro, one of Real Madrid's greatest players and captains, criticized Perez for allowing Makélélé to leave; *"I think Claude has this kind of gift – he's been the best player in the team for years yet people just don't notice him, don't notice what he does. But you ask anyone at Real Madrid during the years we were talking about and they will tell you he was the best player at Real."*

The players could see it, but their president did not. And Madrid's loss would be Chelsea's gain. The Frenchman enhanced Chelsea between 2003 and 2006 helping them to win two league titles under Jose Mourinho. He was so accomplished in his role that this specific position has become known as 'the Makélélé role'.

After Claude came a need for 'a Makélélé' in many top sides and this saw the emergence of players like Michael Essien, who stepped into the role at Chelsea to support (and ultimately replace) Makélélé. Marcos Senna helped Spain find 'balance' and offered the defensive support the team needed to win the 2008 Euros. Esteban Cambiasso would be key for Inter Milan's treble success under Mourinho in 2010 and both Javier Mascherano and Genero Gattuso for Liverpool and AC Milan respectively helped their sides with their aggressive defensive approaches. In the 21st century the defensive midfielder was no longer merely a 'water carrier' but was now officially an essential component for a team's success.

The Little Witch

As we saw from the evolution of the 4-2-3-1 formation, as the decade went on the key to the midfield was to possess a 'destroyer' and a 'creator'. One would break up the attacks, and the other would create and provide for his side. This partnership became a fundamental element for a side's balance and, ultimately, their success. The 'creator', referred to as a 'deep lying playmaker', or *regista*, became a prominent player in the late 90's and early 2000's.

The role of the deep lying playmaker was perfected by two of the most graceful and technically gifted players to have played the game in the past twenty years: Juan Sebastian Veron and Andrea Pirlo. The regista emerged, in this position on the pitch, is because of the way coaches attempted to stifle the trequartista - they needed to find a place to get the best from their creative players. Some refer to the role as the 'quarterback' position, a reference to American Football and the player who leads the offence and provides passes to the players in attack.

We have spoken of Veron already and how his time in English football was seen as something of a 'failure'.

Veron's range of passing, his touch, vision and elegance on the pitch was a delight to watch. His elegance was often mistaken for laziness yet he was so athletic, so sure of his talents that he never felt the need to run around like a lunatic. He was a perfect Argentinian playmaker: technically excellent, individualistic, and someone who played at his own pace.

Veron originally moved from Boca Juniors to Serie A with Sampdoria under the management of Sven Goran Eriksson, and would break into the Argentinian World Cup squad in 1998, supported by the more rugged and hardworking Diego Simeone. It was the classic destroyer and playmaker duo and Veron would dictate the game, showing his varied passing ability and excellent vision.

Veron would follow Eriksson to Parma and would win the SuperCoppa Italia in 1999. He was the key provider for his fellow Argentinian Hernan Crespo. And both would be moving together, once more following Eriksson. This time it was to Lazio; Veron moved for £18m and Crespo would go too for £35m. The partnership would go on to win the Serie A title, the SuperCoppa, and the Super Cup in 2000. At this time Veron was considered one of the greatest midfielders in world football.

His move to Manchester could have been great yet it ended up being seen as a flop . The fact that his time at Manchester United did not work was, in part, due to the difficulties United's midfield had in *adapting* to a new style. For so long they were used to a four man flat midfield. Veron couldn't fit in and they could not adapt to him.

Veron was expected to play in the centre with Roy Keane, but the two proved incompatible. Keane was not like Simeone, he was a box-to-box midfielder who importantly led and organised the side. He would not acquiesce to Veron's wish to be his worker, allowing Veron to control games. For his previous clubs and country Veron was used to controlling games and was often afforded a free role where he would roam and dictate the play. Keane would not permit him this role and Veron could not adapt to what was expected of him.

Many will argue that the pace and intensity of the Premier League was an issue yet it was more about his ability to govern games and set the tempo. Under Marcelo Bielsa, for Argentina, Veron excelled because he was given the freedom to control the team. Under Bielsa's high tempo attacking style Veron would be the playmaker that exposed sides with his long range and creative passing.

Veron had all the ability and intelligence to be regarded as one of the best deep lying playmakers in the game however his move to Manchester United was undermined by bad timing. Andrea Pirlo, on the other hand, was more fortunate with his timing. It would be Pirlo who would take the crown as the 21st century's best *regista*.

The Architect

Pirlo is perhaps the most successful example, in the modern European game, of the deep lying playmaker. Whereas the 'destroyer' was becoming the favoured choice of many, Milan's coach, Carlo Ancelotti, wished to have a playmaker play in the holding midfielder position in his 4-4-2 diamond formation. It was Pirlo's range of passing, his vision, and his intelligence which helped Milan to two Champions League successes in the 2000's, in 2003 and 2007. Like Veron, Pirlo is a tempo dictator, a player who controls game with possession and the timing and precision of the killer pass.

Pirlo was originally a trequartista, a classic number 10, who played behind the forward. However, he was moved deeper by his coach at Brescia, Carlo Mazzone, who saw great potential in the deeper playmaking role. It was an inspired decision. Pirlo moved to Inter Milan yet it was his move to their rivals, AC Milan, which brought out the best in him. He was bought by Milan's coach Fatih Terim in 2001 for €18m (although Terim would be sacked at the beginning of the 2001 season and replaced by Carlo Ancelotti).

Ancelotti had a midfield of creative genius - Pirlo, Seedorf, Rui Costa and later Kaka - which was a joy to watch. Pirlo controlled the games and provided the key passes to the forwards. When Ancelotti added more 'physicality' in the midfield with Gennaro Gattuso and then Massimo Ambrosini Pirlo was given less defensive responsibility and greater liberty to create and command games. At Milan Pirlo would reach three Champions League finals in 2003, 2005 and 2007 winning two of them, as well as winning the World Cup with Italy in 2006. Pirlo's influence on both club and country highlighted his world class talent and his importance to his team's success.

In 2011 Milan decided that Pirlo was no longer in their plans and allowed him to leave. Juventus signed him on a free transfer, a move which would inspire the player and the club. Three Serie A titles in a row would be forthcoming with Pirlo the key player in the side. He proved that, even in his 30's, he still had the class and vision to lead his side to success. Without doubt, Pirlo is one of the greatest players of the 21st century; and without question *the best* regista. And his role and success brought a new generation of deep lying playmakers through.

English adaptation

Although Veron didn't work out at United it was clear that they required a player of his type in their team. When Keane departed in 2005 Ferguson sought out Michael Carrick from Spurs, filling the void of playmaker which Ferguson and Queiroz desired. Without the burden and pressure from Keane, Carrick excelled and it was no coincidence that United would go on to have the most successful period in the club's history after he arrived. Perhaps Veron would have blossomed without Keane in the side in the same way?

Carrick is now 33 years of age and has been underrated by many fans for too long in England. His international career should have far exceeded 31 caps as his quality has been proven at United. His ability to play the short pass and retain possession, as well as his ability to provide the longer killer pass from deep, has made him a valuable part of United's style.

Carrick's critics come from those same people who don't see the value in the regista, who view these players as simple or even boring passers of the ball, who believe they are playing 'safe'; this is delusional and naïve. Carrick would have been perfect for England over the past 10 years, playing the deeper role he has done so well for United since 2005. Yet he has been overlooked because of the ignorance of certain coaches, media, and fans.

For the past decade coaches have been guilty of playing the 'stars' of Gerrard and Lampard in the rigid 4-4-2 which has meant there has been no place for Carrick in the side. Imagine if England's midfield had been Scholes and Carrick, like it had been for United for many years. One imagines that England would have done much better.

At Liverpool Rafa Benitez saw the need for a deep lying playmaker and brought in Xavi Alonso from Real Sociedad in 2004 for £11m. That season Liverpool would win the Champions League, with Alonso scoring in the final. Alonso's partnership with Dietmar Hamann, and then Javier Mascherano, brought out the best in his abilities, with his freedom to provide deep penetrative passes for Liverpool's forwards. His value and reputation was enhanced later in his time at Liverpool, with the English media particularly starting to appreciate, and see the value in, this type of midfielder.

Alonso would move to Real Madrid for £30m in 2009 and would become a key part of Mourinho's Madrid side as well as a pivotal player in Vicente del Bosque's Spain squad, winning the World Cup and Euros in 2010 and 2012. He would be key to Real Madrid's Champions League success in 2014 under Carlo Ancelotti, although he missed the final due to suspension. Alonso, although perhaps not as great as Pirlo, has proved to be an integral part of his club and international sides' successes.

What is evident is that the deep lying midfielder has been shown to be a key part of success over the last decade. In turn, the water carrier has evolved into something much more, and perhaps it is Sergio Busquets who demonstrates this more than any other.

A world class pivot

In 2008, when Pep Guardiola arrived at Camp Nou, he inherited a talented side which had lost focus and discipline. He sought to improve this with the removal of certain players and the arrival of others. He possessed players like Samuel Eto'o, Thierry Henry and the young precocious star Lionel Messi, along with Carlos Puyol, Xavi, and Andrés Iniesta. It was a side with the potential to be great. Yet the key role for the new coach, the one which Guardiola knew only so well, was the *anchor* of the side, the holding midfielder.

As a player for Barcelona in the 1990's this is where Guardiola played under Cruyff, who spoke of Guardiola as his 'pivot' - a key player in the side, keeping possession and setting the tempo. In that first treble-winning season, Guardiola had the option to use Yaya Toure, the strong Ivorian bought from Monaco the season before. However, he favoured a young academy player who he had worked with for Barca B instead. His name was Sergio Busquets.

Many were unsure about Guardiola's decision; this young, tall, somewhat gangly player, was surely not good enough to play for Barcelona? Toure offered the size and physicality which many holding players possessed across Europe. Yet Busquets had already shown his worth to the coach and the players.

Since his arrival into the Barca first team there is no escaping the fact that Busquets has become a world-class player and is arguably the best player in his position. Guardiola saw himself in Busquets, and simply replicated his role when he played at Barca. Busquets is, in many ways, the modern Guardiola.

You can see just how vital Busquets is to the Barcelona style as well as to Spain. His ability to dictate the tempo is incredible and he has the great talent for knowing where his team mates are before his receives the ball. His vision and awareness allow him to keep possession and play passes quickly, nullifying any pressure from defenders.

The praise Busquets receives from his coaches and peers highlights his importance to the side. As Javier Mascherano, who would have seen Busquets as his competition when he initially moved to Camp Nou, explained, *"Xavi and Iniesta are the most creative midfielders in the world, but, above all, there is Busquets. He has the talent to play for any team anywhere in the world, but he's made to play for this team. Literally, he's the perfect guy. He robs the ball, he has superb technical skills and brings tactical order. I watch him and try to learn from him."* High praise indeed.

Xavi regards Busquets as the best one-touch passer of the ball in the world; a huge compliment, and an indication of his necessity to the side. As Xavi said, *"I've never seen a player with so many tactical options during the game, who's got so much quality as well as physical presence – it's incredible."* He added, *"Busi sees you quickly, he always takes the simple option. He reads the game well and moves the ball with precision, in as few touches a possible."*

Busquets' role as the 'pivot' or 'anchor' enables Barcelona to play the expansive football they wish because he offers such solidity and confidence on the ball. He is the modern midfielder; strong, agile, disciplined and excellent both defensively and in possession. His discipline (both positional and tactical), his understanding and anticipation to read the game, as well as his selflessness, have made Busquets a key asset to the side.

As Busquets says, *"The coach knows that I am an obedient player who likes to help out and if I have to run to the wing to cover someone's position, great. I genuinely enjoy watching the full-back run up the pitch and going across to fill in."*

Although Deschamps and Makélélé type players were integral to their sides' successes, the role of the holding midfielder has changed markedly since their day.

The role has progressed to suit the needs of the modern game and we are now seeing a new breed of holding midfielder where the role now is evidently more than just being a 'water carrier'.

The deep lying playmakers in Veron, Pirlo, Carrick and Xavi Alonso have shown the importance again of exploiting space offered by the opposition and having players with technical skills who can punish sides. These players however required a 'destroyer' next to them who could do their defensive work; Gattuso and Mascherano, for example, allowed their playmakers more time and space.

However Guardiola saw, in Busquets, the *future* of the holding midfielder; the ability to start attacks *and* dictate play. The defensive midfielder, therefore, is now required to do two jobs: break up attacks and start them. He is no longer *just* a destroyer or a creator, he must now be *both*.

Since Guardiola moved to Bayern we have seen the emergence of Philipp Lahm (yes, the player in the previous chapter who was regarded as the world's best wing back!) who has now proven his capabilities playing the pivot role under Guardiola. Many questioned the logic of this at first, however Lahm silenced his doubters, showing a confidence in his play which has had people marvelling at his ability.

Lahm's defensive excellence allied with his technical quality when in possession has made him a key and influential player for Bayern and Germany. What is significant is that - in Lahm - we see a world class player who is capable of playing in multiple positions. He is one of the new breed of players who can be regarded as 'complete', a superb multi-functional player who is showing us where the game is moving… towards *universality*.

Chapter 12: The Complete Midfielder

In most games midfield is where the game is won and lost. This is why Pep Guardiola, in particular, obsesses over the midfield areas, and dominating the game in these areas. And as the game has become more fluid, as formations have changed in order to help teams dominate and exploit space, we have seen the development of the modern central midfielder. Or rather, we have seen the *re-emergence* of the so-called 'extinct' box-to-box midfielder.

The box-to-box midfielder

Often regarded as the most dynamic and complete player in a team, the central midfielder, or the 'box-to-box' midfielder is the engine, the creator, the leader. A player capable of defending at one end of the field as well as playing a key role in his team's attacking moves at the other. This player is the one who can 'do it all'. Until the 'specialist' emerged he was the type of player that dominated football over a decade ago.

When Arrigo Sacchi was at Milan in 1989 he possessed two of the best players in world football in Ruud Gullit and Marco van Basten, both were key figures who led the side's attacking play. Yet it would be their Dutch compatriot Frank Rijkaard who would be the *ultimate* key player for the team. The reason? He was the most complete player of his generation.

Arriving at Milan after Holland's Euro 1988 success Rijkaard was the extra piece the team needed, propelling Milan to the top of European football. Initially seen as a central defender Sacchi saw in him an ability to play higher up in the midfield. He suited the ideas of universality perfectly. As Sacchi said in an interview, *"Rijkaard was a phenomenal midfielder, a truly formidable player."* And as his ex-teammate, and one of the greatest defenders to play the game, Franco Baresi added, *"He had everything, he knew how to defend, knew how to attack, score goals. Rijkaard's arrival completed a great squad."*

When Rijkaard moved back to Ajax in 1993 to play for Louis van Gaal he was one of the most complete players in European football and enabled van Gaal to play his fluid 4-3-3 system. Rijkaard played the libero role, moving between a sweeper behind the defence, or playing ahead of them in the holding midfielder role. His influence and quality turned Ajax into the best side in Europe.

We would see this 'type' of complete midfielder become synonymous with Ajax's youth system with the emergence of both Clarence Seedorf and Edgar Davids in the early 1990's. Along with Rijkaard and Gullit these players would share their cultural history with the Surinamese, one of Holland's former African colonies. With the migration of the Surinamese into Holland Ajax would benefit hugely with this influx of talent. The strength and power which these players provided offered a different dynamic for Ajax and Holland, similar to what France achieved in the late 1990's through their African colonial links. However Holland would struggle to achieve the same success as Ajax and France due to the conflict in the national side between the Surinamese players and the 'white' Dutch players.

Ajax, however, would achieve great success with Seedorf and Davids. Both would be central to Ajax's rise to the top of Europe and the club's Champions League success in 1995, excelling under the management and philosophy of Louis van Gaal. Seedorf was a more attacking player but he could play anywhere, thanks in part to Ajax's developmental philosophy towards producing 'all-round' players. His career after Ajax would take him to Italy and Spain, winning the Champions League for Real Madrid in 1998 and twice for AC Milan in 2003 and 2007. Seedorf would become one of the most complete and dominant midfielders of the 1990's and 2000's, a true example of what a modern midfielder should be.

Edgar Davids, known as 'The Pitbull', was a much more defensively-minded player but he had the skill and poise which Ajax expected in its players. Yet it was his engine, his energy, and determination, which would define his influence and make him one of the most important players for both Ajax and later Juventus. He would also play a primary role in helping Frank Rijkaard in 2003 at Barcelona (we will come to this later).

In Rijkaard, Seedorf, and Davids we see the prototype of the complete midfielder. It is little surprise that it would be Ajax and Louis van Gaal who would lead the way with the development of this type of player.

In English football the best example of this type of player is Roy Keane. Alex Ferguson sought to replace his midfield general Bryan Robson and in 1993 found his successor playing for Brian Clough's Nottingham Forest side. Forest had just been relegated from the Premier League and Ferguson could not resist luring the Irishman to Old Trafford, stealing him from the grips of Blackburn Rovers manager Kenny Dalglish. Keane was like Robson; aggressive, driven, committed and *very* effective. He was a leader on the pitch in the way he conducted himself and led the side to great success.

Keane would become United's captain in 1997 and one of his most notable performances, and greatest shows of influence, came in the second leg tie of the Champions League semi-final against Juventus in 1999. Keane would get booked in that game which meant he would be banned for the final. His reaction epitomized who he was; he got on with his job. That night's performance is regarded as one of the finest individual displays in football history.

United were 2-0 down in Turin after just 10 minutes, and their hopes of reaching the final hung by a thread. And then... a corner from Beckham was headed in by Keane. 2-1. 10 minutes later and he was booked for a foul on Zidane. Knowing he would be out of the final he put a performance in that showed who he was, as a player, as much as the position he played. Keane would make sure the team would battle through, showing such drive and intensity that Juve just couldn't cope. United would win 3-2 and qualify for the final.

As Alex Ferguson said in his recent autobiography, *"It was the most emphatic display of selflessness I have seen on a football field. Pounding over every blade of grass, competing as if he would rather die of exhaustion than lose, he inspired all around him. I felt it was an honour to be associated with such a player."*

United would go on to win the treble that season, with Keane's influence and leadership a central force for the club's success.

Keane, along with players like Patrick Vieira and Steven Gerrard, was the classic midfielder of the late 1990's. However, as the 2000's arrived, it was evident that this type of midfielder was fading away. The 'specialists' were starting to dominate.

Rotating double pivots

By the time that Chelsea won the Premier League in 2004 it was clear that the box-to-box midfielder was no longer seen as essential for many top teams and coaches. In fact this player was now a hindrance for coaches who sought 'control' and 'balance' in their side. A player running all over the pitch would leave gaps for the opposition to exploit.

This was the situation with Gerrard at Liverpool under Benitez, where Gerrard's energy and enthusiasm for doing everything was not what Benitez's tactical approach in midfield consisted of. This is why Gerrard was put at right midfield and later played as a support striker. He was not, for Benitez at least, disciplined enough to play in the 'middle'.

Speaking in 2006, after being criticized for playing Gerrard on the right, Benitez defended his decision: *"We have more balance with Momo Sissoko and Xabi Alonso there, and with Stevie wider. That works for our team. He goes inside and scores 23 goals. That surely is a good role for him."* The problem for Gerrard was that, according to Benitez, he 'ran too much'.

Gerrard's desire to influence games meant that he had been running all over the place and for a coach like Benitez this meant his side lacked tactical and positional control. Simply put, Gerrard lacked the discipline which the Spanish coach required from his central midfield players. It was this lack of discipline that meant, from very early on, that Benitez was looking for a more suitable position for Liverpool's talented player.

Liverpool's line-up for the 2006 FA Cup final versus West Ham.
The formation moved between a 4-2-3-1 and 4-4-2, with Gerrard playing predominately on the
right. He would score twice in the game and Liverpool would win on penalties.

As we've seen, during the 2000's, modern coaches required specific players for specific roles and, as mentioned, two holding players became popular with many sides utilizing the 'classic' midfield partnership of the 'destroyer' and the 'playmaker' in the 4-2-3-1. By the 2012 Euros most sides were using this midfield double pivot; France, England, Spain, Germany and Holland all used it. However, there is a major difference in having a formation and putting the right players into their respective roles.

The Dutch played Nigel de Jong and Mark van Bommel as their two defensive midfielders, both of whom were specialist 'destroyers'. On paper they may have allowed the Dutch to attack more freely as they offered more defensive cover to the side, yet what actually happened was that the gap between attack and defence was too open as neither player wanted to push forward. This left a big gap in the side which the opposition could exploit and counter against. Holland's coach, Bert van Marwijk, showed a lack of appreciation for what the modern game required. Holland were exposed on the counter, numerous times. Playing two spoilers, and no deep lying playmaker, meant that there was no tempo controller in there; no-one to help support the attack.

The winners - Spain - used both Busquets and Alonso who (as we saw in the past chapter) were both excellent at supporting the attack with their passing and creativity. With Xavi and Iniesta centrally above them, and Fàbregas and Silva wider (looking to get in behind) Spain dominated their games with this midfield overload. The level of technical quality in that midfield meant Spain could control possession and games with ease. It was no surprise they won the tournament.

Spain's 2012 final line-up vs Italy. Note the use of the 'false nine' in Fàbregas which allowed Spain to dominate midfield with six midfielders in their side. This was the hallmark of Spain and Barcelona's success and why they were able to control games so well.

Yet it would be Germany who would show the most progressive and modern approach to the double pivot. Bastian Schweinsteiger and Sami Khedira's partnership showed the discipline and knowledge of when to go forward and support the attack, and when to hold and support the defence. This 'rotating double pivot' enabled both players to fulfil attack-supporting roles. If Schweinsteiger was marked then Khedira rotated with him. Both players showed their dual ability to rotate and play either role.

With two players rotating life becomes very challenging for the opposition. It was a combination which worked well for Germany, yet which was perfected by Bayern Munich the following season.

This evolution in how the German midfield double pivot worked was a key reason why Bayern were so eager to capture Javi Martinez in the summer of 2012. They saw in Luis Gustavo a talented destroyer but not a midfielder who could offer them rotation and ability on both sides of the ball. The logic was that Schweinsteiger would be easier to track if he was the only one making runs.

The chemistry, almost symmetry, which Schweinsteiger and Martinez had in the 2012/13 season meant that Bayern's build up play through midfield, their movement to create and exploit space, and their ability to both move forward to support the attack became a central reason why Bayern dominated games and competitions that year. And, of course, both these players' complete talent in terms of technical skill, tactical intelligence, and physicality meant that, when out of possession, they had a wonderful ability to read the game, screen passes, and press.

In the Champions League semi-final of 2013, Bayern proved to have mastered the midfield, overpowering and dominating Barca's midfield with strength, skill and intelligence. The effectiveness of Schweinsteiger and Martinez in the rotating double pivot provided a perfect balance for the side and it is no wonder they won an unprecedented treble that season. Martinez was central to their success, in particular, as he offered them the 'complete' role which they missed in previous seasons using 'destroyers' in Mark van Bommel, Tymoshchuk, and Luis Gustavo.

In Bastian Schweinsteiger we see a great example of the modern 'complete' midfielder. Impressively he has adapted his game moving from being a right sided midfielder to a holding midfielder and now into a complete midfielder. He moves up the pitch and finds pockets of space which are created thanks to the attacking four ahead of him and the runs of his overlapping full backs. They force the defence back and ultimately allow more space for his late runs.

Bayern's rotating double pivot. The line-up versus Barcelona in the first leg of the Champions League semi-final where they won 4-0. Note the movement of Schweinsteiger who pushes forward to support the attack, with Martinez staying in the holding role to provide defensive cover for his side. Through the game this movement would be switched, based on the space ahead. Also, these two players would move forward to create space for the other to exploit in the middle of the pitch. This rotating double pivot was unpredictable and the movement hard to track.

The previous destroyer/playmaker combination was becoming predictable and in need of a change. No longer was a 'destroyer' required at the top level, now it was necessary to have a complete midfielder. In turn, having two of this 'type' of player allowed a coach to rotate the roles of 'holding' and 'supporting' the attack. Thus the rotating double pivot meant that the 'specialists' of years before were now more versatile and able to rotate roles. Sides became less predictable and were able to exploit the opposition more effectively. The 'rotating' double pivot would underpin the rise and success of German football.

The rise of the complete midfielder

By the time the 2014 World Cup came around it was clear that German football led the evolution of midfield play. Both their national team and their two biggest clubs - Bayern and Dortmund - have proven to be ahead of the rest in this new midfield setup. They have shown an understanding of the need for balance and have got it almost perfect.

What was becoming evident with the 4-2-3-1 was that the '10', often seen as the playmaker, was preventing sides from dominating midfield. Although the formation allowed for a three man midfield, a classic playmaker did not have the defensive components required to help his side when out of possession.

Signs of this were being seen in the 2011/12 Champions League. In the semi-final between Real Madrid and Bayern - Madrid were abject, particularly in midfield. They were overrun, a problem which had occurred against Barca for the majority of games between Mourinho and Guardiola. The problem was Mesut Özil. As great a playmaker as Özil was, he did not give the side the defensive balance or support when out of possession and against better sides (especially those who played with a three man midfield) Madrid were swamped.

It was no surprise therefore that Luka Modric arrived as a replacement for Özil. Modric is what can be termed a complete midfielder; a very talented footballer who possesses the technical skills to keep possession, create goals, and - importantly - offer defensive reliability. Mourinho knew that a three man midfield involving Modric would be more adept and able to provide the success Madrid required.

Ironically it would be Mourinho's successor Carlo Ancelotti who would find this midfield balance, a move which brought the Champions League success Mourinho could not achieve. Modric excelled in his role ahead of Xabi Alonso yet it was Ángel Di María (a player we will touch on more later) who proved his versatility and talent in the centre of the pitch. This midfield had dynamism, cohesion, and was effective both in attack and defence. It was why Madrid won the Champions League in 2014.

At the German national team level, Joachim Löw learnt his lesson regarding Özil and played him wide left for Germany during the World Cup... a smart decision. His replacement was Toni Kroos, a great midfielder who is able to control games, create, and score goals for club and country. Kroos is another midfielder who has come through Bayern Munich's academy (evidence of a development model which is developing *modern* players), a player who has all the attributes required to succeed in this complete midfield role. It is not surprising that since Kroos has broken into the Bayern and German XIs that success has been forthcoming.

At the World Cup Germany not only dominated the midfield battle in all their games, but they offered attacking rotation and threat as all three of their midfield could play in different positions. What Germany showed was that the midfield had evolved once more; this time Löw utilized more of a single pivot with a double pivot ahead, yet importantly in each position was a player who can be regarded as a complete midfielder.

Whether it was Schweinsteiger, Khedira, Lahm or Kroos, Löw knew that they could rotate and thus provide the opposition with many problems to solve. The best case of Germany's midfield strength came in the semi-final defeat of Brazil (a side playing a 'classic' 4-2-3-1) where Brazil's double pivot of Fernandinho and Luis Gustavo were simply overrun by Germany's dynamic, strong, and ruthless midfield.

A new breed of midfielder

Over the past few years, we have seen the decline of the specialist and the rise of the all-rounder. The box-to-box midfielder has returned! But this is the 2.0 version. You can see this new type of midfielder emerging across Europe.

Juventus and Chile midfielder Arturo Vidal is regarded as one of the best and most complete midfielders in the game. It is no surprise that Bayern had sought to bring Vidal to Munich before they attained Javi Martinez. They saw in him the attributes their system and philosophy required. Bayern's loss has been Juve's gain, mind you; Vidal has provided the forward impetus and support, as well as defensive cover, to aid Andrea Pirlo and has been a strong reason for Juve's domestic dominance in recent years.

A similar player to Vidal is Dortmund's Ilkay Gündogan, who looks to have all the quality and attributes required to be one of Europe's best midfielders. Another German to add to their ever-rising list of complete midfielders.

In England, Yaya Toure is perhaps the most complete midfielder since Patrick Vieira and Michael Essien in terms of his physical, technical, and tactical ability. He has proven that he is one of the best modern 'box-to-box' midfielders and in the 2013/14 season, with the introduction of Fernandinho, Manchester City possessed the most dominant midfield in the league. That is one of the main reasons why they won the league.

At Chelsea Nemanja Matic looks to have the potential to be one of the most complete midfielders in the game and at Arsenal, Arsène Wenger is seeking to change the Gunners' approach to fit in with a more German model. He has moved away from the Spanish 4-3-3 and implemented a 4-2-3-1 which has suited the attributes of both Alex Oxlade-Chamberlain and Aaron Ramsay who, when played in these central roles, have excelled because of their 'complete' abilities.

Just as the 'all-rounder' was becoming extinct, replaced by a world of specialists, it now appears that the position-specific specialist is experiencing the same fate. More evidence that football really does move in cycles.

With this evolution the contemporary 'box-to-box' midfielder now possesses *all* the attributes to play in the modern game. This player can 'do it all' when in possession and out of possession. He can drop in to make a back three, screen and press in midfield, and move forward to support the attack. He is the complete player… intelligent and creative in his approach, defensive minded, strong, and skilful. A *complete* player.

But is this skillset now a requirement for *every* player? Are we seeing a move towards a team full of this type of player? Are Germany and Bayern showing us that football is moving to *universality*? That the modern player is required to do and be *everything*?

Chapter 13: The Trequartista

"His type is an endangered species. Something special will be lost from football if they die out altogether." The BBC's Tim Vickery on Juan Roman Riquelme

The classic '10'

At the turn of the century the number 10, the *trequartista*, was dominant in football. It was a golden era for this type of player. The creative brilliance of trequartistas like Francesco Totti, Rivaldo, Jari Litmanen, Alessandro Del Piero, Zinedine Zidane, Rui Costa, Dennis Bergkamp, Gianfranco Zola and Juan Roman Riquelme were lighting up the game. These players were the 'classic' 10, playing between the forward line and midfield, controlling games and dictating play. They all possessed skill, creativity, and vision. They were the geniuses of their sides.

Players like Bergkamp, Zidane, and Kaka would continue to prosper into the mid-2000's, but the role of the playmaker had changed and certain players got left behind; notably the Argentinian Juan Roman Riquelme.

In many countries - such as Argentina, Holland and Italy - the number 10 is a cult figure. He is iconic. The player in this position is seen romantically as an artist, a man who can produce moments of brilliance. The No.10 shirt carries a sense of expectation and responsibility, especially true in Argentina where Diego Maradona became a god-like figure to the nation. At the turn of the century Riquelme personified what the '10' was about for Argentinians and purists of the game; technically brilliant, creative, self-regulating, languid and… *rigid*.

Riquelme, for all his talent, wasn't the most athletic or hardworking of playmakers, yet in possession he was magnificent. His game was built on playing between the lines and, when he was afforded the time and space to exploit matters, he was superlative. During the 1990's the 10 would take up a position between the opposition's defence and midfield and seek to run the game in this area. For many years this worked and these players became masters on the pitch… however the 4-2-3-1 effectively closed off this space.

As the century progressed, and tactics changed, the 10 position required a player with more dynamism and Riquelme's lack of mobility and zip prevented him shifting his game to meet more contemporary needs.

A need to evolve

In the past decade the role of the 10 has seen dramatic changes. As coaches sought to stifle the space which the 10 liked to operate in - with the introduction of the defensive midfielder - the 10 had to change how they played. No longer could the 10 simply stay 'in the hole' between the defence and midfield, because many sides were now plugging that space with defensive midfielders. The introduction of *two* holding midfielders was introduced to near guarantee that the space for the '10' was shut off entirely. The spaces which the trequartista loved to exploit had been taken away.

Coaches therefore needed to adapt their playmaker's role. Instead of playing 'in the hole' they now sought to make their 10's more lateral in their movement, to play wider in order to create space for both themselves and others. The reasoning was that this creative player could find more space and time to create for the team, or that if the defensive midfielder was instructed to stay close to the playmaker, then their movement *away* from central areas would open space centrally for others to exploit.

During the mid-2000's, as the game became more physical and athletic, it was evident that the 10 had evolved to become more of a strong midfielder who would possess not just skill but athleticism too. Players like Kaka at Milan, Steven Gerrard at Liverpool, and Frank Lampard at Chelsea were not the classic type of 10 yet they excelled in this position for their clubs. It was little surprise that these three clubs were challenging for the Champions League between the years of 2004 and 2007. They were also managed by the most tactically brilliant coaches of that time in Ancelotti, Mourinho, and Benitez.

And then came Manchester United who would take the 10 further. For over a decade United had played a functional yet effective 4-4-2 with classic wingers and box-to-box midfielders behind two centre forwards. Paul Scholes in particular had shone in this role, being a key provider and scorer of goals in the late 90's / early 2000's. Yet United's new vision meant a change was to occur.

Under their assistant, Carlos Queiroz, United had been building a squad of young players who possessed the skill and intelligence to play a *modern* type of football. Using a 4-2-3-1 and with players like Cristiano Ronaldo, Wayne Rooney, Carlos Tevez and Ryan Giggs playing in a fluid attacking four – in which any player could take up a position as a central forward, winger, or playmaker - United would become Europe's best side between 2007-2009. There was no 'fixed' 10 in this system, the key was 'attacking fluidity'.

Behind this fluid four was now Paul Scholes, who was finally getting the recognition his career deserved. Scholes was proving to be the best playmaking midfielder of his generation, yet instead of playing between the lines - like he did before - he was now playing deeper providing the forward line with more opportunity and space to punish defences. Queiroz's work would enable United to reach back-to-back Champions League finals in 2008 and 2009.

Manchester United's 4-2-3-1 in 2007/2008.
The forwards' ability to interchange and rotate showed a new step in football's evolution.

Dynamic technicians

In the 2009 Champions League final United would face off against a Barcelona side that were enjoying one of their greatest-ever seasons. Led by Pep Guardiola they had the chance to make history and win an unprecedented treble. It was not easy though, as their elimination of Chelsea in the semi-final had proved.

Universality

Chelsea's dominance and physicality appeared too much for Barca's skilful technicians yet it was a moment of brilliance from Andrés Iniesta in the final moments of the second leg which could be argued to be the *most* significant goal of the modern era. Call it fate but *that goal* changed the trajectory of the modern game *significantly*.

In stoppage time of the second leg at Stamford Bridge with the score 1-0 to Chelsea, Barcelona looked to be going out. It had not been a good game for Guardiola's side, in fact they hadn't achieved a shot on target. And then Lionel Messi picked up the ball in Chelsea's penalty area, he looked up and saw Andrés Iniesta waiting on the edge of the area. As the ball was passed across - Iniesta set himself for a one-touch finish where he put the ball into the top corner of the goal. A goal which would put Barcelona into the final and on course to make history.

Had Chelsea progressed it would have been an all-English final for the second year running and have affirmed the dominance of English football. It may have even proven the need for 'physicality' to succeed in this era of the game. It would have shown that Barca's style under Pep Guardiola was 'lacking' in strength and size. Had they lost, it is conceivable that Barca could well have 're-evaluated' their approach. Instead *that* goal put them in the final and revolutionised the game.

In the final, there were many who believed Manchester United were favourites. As Alex Ferguson said in Guillem Balague's biography of Pep Guardiola: *"We really should have won that game, we were a better team at the time."* And for the first ten minutes it appeared United would be too much for Guardiola's side. That was before Andrés Iniesta rushed past two of United's midfielders and fed Samuel Eto'o the ball. Eto'o powered into the area and dispatched a goal past van der Sar, Barca were 1-0 up early on, and never looked back.

During that game Barca grew in authority and in those 90 minutes took away United's crown as Europe's best. A second half goal by Messi would make it 2-0 and secure the trophy. United were good, yet Barca were better. And with that performance a new type of playmaker had cemented their place on centre stage.

Barcelona's 2009 Champions League starting XI.
The midfield trio of Busquets, Xavi and Iniesta would become one of the greatest to grace the game.
Xavi would control games with Iniesta the key playmaker of the side.

The rise of the little man

As discussed, the turn of the century was the 'era of the trequartista', and the following few years were most certainly the era of the 'fluid 10' with players who roamed into wide areas in order to create the time and space to expose the opposition. But, just as the athletically powerful '10' was prospering, a new type was coming through, one which was set to dominate football and change the course of the future game more than any other.

Universality

When Barcelona lifted the Champions League in 2006 it was a sign of things to come. Although Ronaldinho and Samuel Eto'o would steal the spotlight the success that night pointed to where the game was going; players like Xavi and Deco highlighted the new type of playmaking midfielder.

Deco had previously conquered Europe with Porto under Jose Mourinho in 2004, showing his brilliance in the '10' role. He was a sign of things to come. The 2006 success pointed towards something special growing in Cataluña and with the burgeoning talent of Andrés Iniesta and the young, but brilliant, Lionel Messi it appeared that Barcelona were on the cusp of greatness. Yet it would take Guardiola's arrival in 2008 to turn that potential into true greatness.

It was a model and philosophy which had been developing for two decades at Barcelona, and, two years after their 2006 Champions League success (i.e. the 2008/2009 season) it seemed that all that work and planning through the youth system, the philosophy which had been laid down by Johan Cruyff twenty years previously, was truly bearing fruit. The core of Xavi, Iniesta and Messi became synonymous with Barca's style as well and these players were seen as the modern playmakers. They possessed skill, poise, craft, vision, intelligence *and* they were all 'small'.

In this golden age for Spanish football, football was now facing a revolution in terms of style and type of player. At the 2008 Euros, Spain faced Germany in the final. Their 1-0 success proved that height, physicality and strength were no longer essential for success. The signs were showing that in the modern game dynamic technicians were needed.

Spain's coach in 2008, Luis Aragonés, saw that possession-based football was what Spain was built for and they would prosper from embracing it. He put his faith in Xavi Hernandez at the 2008 Euros - seeing in the midfielder the ability to lead and control games. Xavi's growing influence and impact for Spain and Barcelona turned him into the best midfielder of his generation. His ability to control games was unprecedented. Aragonés and Guardiola had embraced his talent and brought out the best in him.

Xavi's midfield partner would be Andrés Iniesta, arguably the greatest playmaker of the 21st century. Barcelona and Spain would dominate games with his skill, poise, and control. As Alex Ferguson said, prior to the 2009 Champions League final, *"I'm not obsessed with Messi, Iniesta is the danger. He's fantastic. He makes the team work. The way he finds passes, his movement and his ability to create space is incredible. He's so important for Barcelona."* Xavi and Iniesta, a perfect combination, technicians ideally suited to the contemporary game and its needs.

In the modern world of football, with restricted space and time, the importance of players finding and exploiting space and possessing excellent technical ability, poise, and vision would become essential when attempting to unlock defences. What Spain had proven was that they had *produced* players who could deal with these demands.

As success often leads to replication, the Spanish/Barcelona model became the ideal of many clubs and managers around Europe. You can call the 'type' of player mentioned above as the 'little man' and the little men have certainly seen their stock rise across Europe. Many top sides have decided that, to achieve success, they need to possess this type of technician.

The advantages that the 'little man' has over the bigger one is clear when you look at the effectiveness of the top players in world football. The ability to dribble, run at speed, turn and create goals are all important characteristics common to these players. In fact, speed and agility have become the key for these players. Watch Messi or Iniesta pick up the ball and glide past players with ease, cutting in and out to get through. It is their centre of gravity which makes them so effective. As they are smaller they have better balance and torque when turning and running at pace.

Because of the dominance of Barcelona the world of football became awash with these small playmakers. The small technician became critical for success from 2008 to 2011. Players such as David Silva, Cesc Fàbregas, Sami Nasri, Mario Götze, Isco, Eden Hazard, Shinji Kagawa and Juan Mata were all excelling for their clubs. This list can be categorized as containing 'dynamic technicians', yet there were two players in particular who would prove that the 'classic 10' could still have a place in the modern game, under the right coach. Their story is significant as we unfurl the development of the modern 10.

Mourinho's 10's

While Barcelona were displaying the playmaker's evolution, Jose Mourinho, ever the antithesis to Pep Guardiola, was seeking to prove that the classic trequartista could still 'work' in the modern game.

In 2009, Jose Mourinho was at Inter Milan. He sought a playmaker who could excel in his formation. He found him in Wesley Sneijder, the Dutch playmaker who had endured a difficult time at Real Madrid. He was brought to Inter Milan to be a key man in Mourinho's new project and Mourinho moulded the side around Sneijder, making players like Samuel Eto'o, Goran Pandev and Diego Milito do the defensive work from the front, allowing Sneijder to play a free role behind the striker.

The 2009/2010 season would be a great success for both player and club. A record treble-winning season and a World Cup final marked a great 12 months for Sneijder. Nicknamed "the Sniper" for his playmaking ability to assist and his pinpoint set piece deliveries, Sneijder grew into his role as Inter's trequartista. His performances were rewarded by UEFA and he was named as the best midfielder of the 2009/2010 season, and shortlisted for the 2010 Ballon D'Or. Lionel Messi took the accolade yet there is a strong case that Sneijder *should* have won it that year.

Another playmaking 10 that Mourinho worked with was Mesut Özil, perhaps the most talented playmaker of his generation. After impressing for Germany's U21 side at the 2009 U21 European Championships Özil then showcased his talent on the biggest stage - at the 2010 World Cup - taking Germany to a semi-final with some mesmerising displays. A move to a big club was imminent and it was Real Madrid who would come for him.

The German playmaker excelled at Real Madrid under Mourinho and then moved to Arsenal in 2013. Özil would benefit from the tutelage of Jose Mourinho and with the attacking talents of Cristiano Ronaldo and Karim Benzema he would provide the highest number of assists in European football during his time at Madrid and prove to be one of the best playmakers in world football.

However, there is a question mark over Sneijder and Özil. Yes they are fantastic players... but are they suitable to the modern game and what it requires of its players? Despite their track records there have been arguments that suggest Sneijder's *inflexibility* in a modern world of fluid positions has made his role redundant. There is an argument that he lacks the flexibility of movement which the current game requires.

If Sneijder had been playing during the late 90's and early 2000's it is conceivable that he could have been one of the greats. During the 90's Sneijder would have been blessed with time and space which he could have exploited and prospered in, yet this space and time has disappeared or at least become minimised.

It is important to note that whereas many regard Sneijder as an 'attacking midfielder' he is in fact more of a 'second striker', and this is where the problems of his suitability arise. Under Mourinho he was not instructed to track back and help his midfield when defending. His role was to wait for a counter attack and be in space to receive the ball. Other managers, since, have asked him to play deeper and support his midfield, to make a 'three' which we discussed earlier. Like Özil, defending is not something he wishes to do.

As great as these playmakers are when in possession, they do not give their side defensive balance or support when out of possession and against better sides, especially those who play with a three man midfield they fail to provide the team with the cover and support which is required. There is very little room in that midfield three for a luxury player. As we saw in the previous chapter, success requires 'complete' midfielders.

In the summer of 2012 it appeared that Mourinho had learnt his lesson regarding the '10'. Perhaps it was a lesson from the previous season's failure in the Champions League semi-final against Bayern. Although the tie went to penalties, Madrid were abject in midfield. A midfield two of Sami Khedira and Xavi Alonso can outplay many sides, yet against a side possessing Schweinsteiger, Gustavo, and Toni Kroos, they were overloaded. Simply put Özil did not provide the defensive support required and Madrid were over-run.

This semi-final exit appeared to be the reason that Luka Modric was signed. Modric is a very talented footballer and, as we saw in the previous chapter, a more complete player than Özil. His reliability in possession offers more support defensively. In 2013/2014 Modric - alongside Ángel Di María and Xabi Alonso - offered Madrid the ability to play a three man midfield and dominate games - one reason why they won the Champions League. What is evident is that the 'complete' midfielder has replaced the classic playmaker in the central areas. So is there a place for the playmaker in the modern game?

The Özil situation was reflected in the case of Juan Mata in England. Ever since Juan Mata arrived in English football he has been a revelation. Chelsea's player of the season for two years running highlighted how important he was for the club and the team. He helped them win the Champions League and Europa League too in that time. He became Chelsea's 'key' man. Mata is a classic trequartista, a player who excels as the archetypal '10'. He drifts wide (often to the right) but enjoys the space between the opposition's defence and midfield.

However, with the return of Jose Mourinho at Chelsea Mata was not seen as a key part of the side. Instead, the Brazilian Oscar was the player given the '10' role. Mourinho prefers Oscar because of what he offers defensively. Mourinho had determined what the modern game requires, and appears to no longer trust or see value in players who often neglect their defensive duties and fail to drop back to make a three man midfield. There are many similarities with Oscar and Modric and it is clear that Mourinho has gravitated towards a three man midfield rather than rely on a classic 10 in the 'hole'.

We have seen the lack of suitability with Spain's Isco, too; a very talented playmaker who moved to Real Madrid from Malaga in 2013. The problem was that he didn't fit into Ancelotti's system and thus was often sitting on the bench rather than playing. The central midfield area has become a place for midfielders, not playmakers.

Fluid playmakers

In the summer of 2012 Dortmund would lose Shinji Kagawa to Manchester United, meaning their academy product Mario Götze would step into the central playmaker role. Dortmund looked to be more of a complete side with Götze in that role and would reach the Champions League final and face Bayern. Götze pointed towards a new type of playmaking midfielder.

Unlike a classic trequartista like Mata, Özil, or Kagawa, Götze was much more *dynamic*. He roamed into wide areas, playing like a winger, or even a forward when required. He could drop deeper, overload the midfield and seek to link play. And he could be a playmaker in central areas when required. In an attacking sense he could do it all.

And importantly - defensively - he could press, track, and support the team. As we saw earlier, the importance of the whole team participating in the defensive phase is fundamental and Götze offered Dortmund this more than Kagawa did.

It was a huge loss for Dortmund to lose Götze, especially losing him to their rivals Bayern. The Munich club were able to take a world class player from their rivals as well as add a complete playmaker to play alongside another new modern playmaker in Thiago Alcantara. Guardiola was building a midfield filled with the new generation of complete, playmaking midfielders. A clear move to universality?

In the summer of 2014 the World Cup pointed to the importance of this 'type' of playmaker. The standout player was James Rodriquez, the Colombian Number 10. Shining during his time at Porto, Rodriquez moved to Monaco in 2013 for €45 million. After his sensational performance in the World Cup where he scored six goals for his country, he became eagerly sought after, and it would be Real Madrid who would pay €75 million for him.

Rodriquez is a modern forward; similar to Götze (who would score the winner in the World Cup final for Germany playing as a false nine). He is capable of playing in a multitude of positions across the forward line. Central, wide, and up front is not an issue for him, an asset which makes him extremely valuable in a game where versatility and movement is becoming more important. In Rodriquez and Götze we have the modern playmakers: fluid players. The classic trequartista has been left behind by football's evolution, fixed and rigid has been replaced by fluidity. It is another step towards universality.

However, while Götze and Rodriquez are sublime players the greatest version of this player is still Lionel Messi. Messi is the most complete player to grace the game, perhaps ever. And while we touch on him more in the coming chapters, it is important to state that when we are talking about the modern playmaker, Messi, like Lahm earlier, is the perfect prototype for this role.

As we can see, in the space of 15 years the '10' has evolved significantly. The modern playmaker must be more than a creative attacking talent, he must be flexible and importantly willing to do his work when out of possession. Just as the fixed trequartista was replaced by the dynamic and athletic midfielder in the early 2000's, so it appears the same trend has happened once more. The speed of this evolution highlights how quickly the game is changing. Evidence once more that football is forever in flux.

It is becoming plain in today's game is that *every* player should have the components and 'key skills' which the modern game requires. This is why we are seeing the development and growth of universality; the idea that *every* player on the pitch should possess the key attributes of a footballer.

Chapter 14: The Inside Forward

In the late 1990's players like Ryan Giggs, Pavel Nedved, and Luis Figo were thriving in a game where 'verticality' of movement was the norm. These players were extremely effective at what they did and provided and scored many goals for their teams. Yet the 'winger' at this time was still expected to be a crosser of the ball, a supplier to the centre forwards. However, as the 2000's arrived, the evolution of the winger became clearer. A new breed was emerging.

We have seen already how the modern full back had evolved to become the modern winger because of changes to the winger's role. The modern winger was a player who sought to exploit the *central* areas and, as the game became more 'fluid' and interchangeable, coaches saw that these dynamic players were able to do more than just cross and assist. They found that their dribbling skills could be invaluable for scoring goals too.

A new way of playing

When Arsène Wenger arrived at Arsenal in 1996 he encountered a league which was rigid and fixed in terms of positions and tactics. He knew he could bring a new approach, new ideas to the game. And so it proved. We have seen already how he embraced the foreign transfer market and built a strong and powerful side, yet it was what he did with his wingers which was truly impressive.

Wenger bought Marc Overmars from Ajax and unleashed one of the most dynamic, quick, and skilful players in world football on the English league. Developed by Louis van Gaal Overmars possessed more flexibility in his play and his movement into central areas was not commonplace for most wingers; even Ryan Giggs at Manchester United didn't come as centrally as perhaps his talent warranted (perhaps because he was never played on the right, thus enabling him to come 'inside' on his left foot). A winger at this time, in England, attacked the 'channel' and looked to cross the ball. Yet Overmars was different. And Wenger would be one of the first to truly embrace this type of approach.

Added to Overmars came the arrival of others like Freddie Ljungberg and Robert Pires; players who helped Arsenal achieve success with their fluid and dynamic style of play. Yet it was the signing of Thierry Henry who would become Arsenal's greatest 'inverted winger'.

When Thierry Henry came into the Premier League, few could have really known the impact he would have on English football. With Henry, Dennis Bergkamp, and many of the French national team, Arsenal's style would transform the English Premier League. Technical excellence mixed with strength and speed would typify

Arsenal and, as the club rose to become a major force in England, Henry's development would epitomise this rise.

Henry arrived after a torrid time in Italy with Juventus where he was used as a classic left winger. Wenger knew him from their time together at Monaco and knew he could do more and, consequently, sought to develop Henry into a forward. Seeing Henry rise from a timid player who lacked confidence, into one of the greatest players to play in England was captivating.

With his positional development Henry would drop from his central role into wide and deep positions where he would receive the ball with more time and space, allowing him to drive at defenders with his frightening speed. This type of movement was revolutionary in a very rigid and fixed league. He found space and, with his pace and dribbling ability, he terrorised defences and helped raise Arsenal to the top of English football.

Wenger would seek to add more of this type of player to his team in the following years. The signings of Jose Antonio Reyes, Robin van Persie, Aleksandr Hleb, Theo Walcott and Andrei Arshavin were all made to play as inside forwards, coming from the wing into central areas. None, however, could achieve what Henry had achieved for the club.

Ferguson's evolution

There was no doubt that Alex Ferguson had seen what Wenger had done with Thierry Henry. He had seen where his Manchester United side was lacking and sought to address it. Manchester United is a great example of a side which moved from being a classic wide-play team into something more akin to where European football was heading.

We have seen already that, at the turn of the century, they would embark on a change of philosophy, as Ferguson sought to develop the team. As already touched upon, the case of David Beckham would highlight the evolution of United and football.

At the turn of the century David Beckham was regarded as one of the world's best players. In 2001 he would be voted second (once again) in the FIFA player of the year awards, this time coming behind Luis Figo. Manchester United had won the Premier League for the third time in a row, confirming their status as one of Europe's best sides. But, even though they won the Champions League in 1999, they were still struggling in Europe.

By the summer of 2003, however, United were looking to make a significant change. Ferguson sought out two players to replace Beckham: Ronaldinho and Arjen Robben. These were two very quick dribblers with sublime skill, who could score as well as create goals. As we've seen, United missed out on both yet in missing out they brought in Cristiano Ronaldo instead. Beckham moved to Madrid and United had the new 'type' of player to replace him. The difference between Beckham and Ronaldo was evident; the modern winger was not a crosser but a *forward*, he was now the goalscorer.

It was not an easy transition. United's centre forward Ruud van Nistelrooy did not like it. He missed Beckham's deliveries, the timing and precision of the calculated balls Beckham offered. Ronaldo was not in tune with the Dutch forward, he retained the ball for too long and looked to enjoy 1v1 skills more than provide assists. However, Ferguson saw in Ronaldo the future of football. Ronaldo was kept and the Dutchman moved on.

Both Beckham and van Nistelrooy were replaced by the modern 21st century player. Classic wide play, the English style of crossing, and finishing, was becoming a dying style. The dynamic inside forward was the future.

The inside forward

After 2003 the game was now in a clear state of flux. The role of the winger was changing drastically and the rise of the inside forward came about because coaches started to *invert* their wingers. Many of these players started playing on the opposite side to the classic set up, which would have seen a left footer playing on the left. Inversion allowed players to drive inside onto their favoured side. This promoted movement into central, goal scoring areas. In turn, there was also the freedom afforded to these players to roam and find space.

Under Mourinho in the 2004/05 season Chelsea excelled with the skill, speed, and dynamism of Arjen Robben and Damien Duff, playing as inside forwards in a 4-3-3. Elsewhere, Barcelona were thriving under the skills of Ronaldinho, and United were clearly evolving their style with Cristiano Ronaldo.

Ronaldinho showed how effective the new type of winger could be when he was allowed to cut inside, and he was christened World Player of the Year in 2004 and 2005. It was the transformation of the modern forward; dynamic, with the freedom to move between units and possessing skill and finishing abilities which mesmerised defences and fans alike.

As the 2000's gave birth to the inside forward, more of this 'type' of player emerged and there is no doubt as to the most complete and prolific of these individuals. Both Cristiano Ronaldo and Lionel Messi were 'wingers', yet both were regarded as 'inside forwards' who would come inside from wide positions onto their favoured foot.

In 2014 the game has become awash with inverted wingers and inside forwards. Players like Gareth Bale, Marco Reus, Neymar, Alexis Sanchez, Ángel Di María and Franck Ribéry have triumphed in the freedom which the modern game provides for such a type of player. These players in the 90's would have been seen as 'wingers', yet today they are able to do and show much more.

And in Franck Ribéry we see possibly the world's best wide player. His own progress as a player coincides with how the modern game has changed and points to a sign of the future.

The universal forward

Ribéry joined Bayern Munich in 2007 from Marseille for a then club record fee of €25m. This was after Zinedine Zidane had labelled Ribéry the *"Jewel of French football."* Bright things were expected of the Frenchman but it was not easy for Ribéry who experienced injury issues early on. However, when Jupp Heynckes arrived in 2011 his performance levels increased and he became a vital and important part of Bayern's success. In fact many put Bayern's rise to the top of Europe down to Ribéry, a player who many believe is 'irreplaceable' in the side.

Franck Ribéry is a complete player in terms of his technical, tactical, physical and mental capabilities. He works for the team, tracks back, and is dominant in his 1v1 battles. There are not many better wingers than him in the game at this time. His off-the-ball movement, which shows creativity and intelligence, pulls defenders all over the place.

In defence, there is perhaps no better 'forward' who defends as well as Ribéry. And it is this willingness and desire to do defensive duties which makes him the world's best at this time. His energy and stamina - working up and down the pitch constantly - makes him a truly wonderful player to watch.

He is selfless in his willingness to work for the team and yet has that bit of 'magic' to make things happen. Tactically he offers variety to his game yet also maintains his discipline, showing good decision-making throughout matches on where and when to move.

In July 2013 Joachim Löw, Germany's head coach put forward the suggestion that Ribéry was the best player in German football, stating that his 'defensive play' and his ability to 'amaze' were fundamental to his accomplishments. *"He is characterised by outstanding technical skills and an incredible feel for the rhythm of the game. But what was particularly noteworthy was his defensive play, which he celebrated as passionately as his inimitable dribbles."*

Universality

It is hard to disagree with Löw's statement regarding the Frenchman. Ribéry has become the world's best left-sided player because of his ability to do *everything* in that role; in possession he can drive inside and outside and look to cross or shoot. He can cross from deep or run to the by-line and be the provider or the playmaker as well as the scorer of goals. He is not 'glitz and glamour' like Cristiano Ronaldo yet is extremely effective and possesses such doggedness and drive that he must frighten those he plays against. And this is when he is attacking.

What Franck Ribéry personifies is the modern player and what is required in today's game. There is no place for hiding in attack or defence anymore. The role of the modern winger needs to be focused defensively as well as offensively. In combination with Robben (who at Bayern has become more consistent, effective, and even more dynamic), Bayern's success is, in large part, down to the work of these two players - in *and* out of possession.

We are now seeing players like Eden Hazard at Chelsea coming through to fulfil contemporary needs, too. Schalke's Julian Draxler looks to be the quintessential modern inside forward (another product of the German youth development system). Real Madrid's Jese Rodriguez also appears to be a player who has the complete game required for the modern way. And perhaps the most versatile inside forward, right now, is Ángel Di María, who has become one of the most complete and *universal* players in Europe.

It's clear that the need to be a universal player is becoming more common and necessary. As the game embraces increased fluidity, the inside forward, the modern winger, has become a crucial player in the side and their movement is central to their role. No longer does this player stay in the 'channels', they now exploit space all over the pitch, making the job of marking them so much harder and making their effectiveness and impact so much greater.

Chapter 15: The Dying Breed

For all the various styles and tactics employed in the game of football, the intention is the same for everyone - to win! And in order to win you need to score more goals than the other side. Which means the scoring of goals is, obviously, very much an essential act in football. It is therefore surprising and puzzling that the man who is supposed to be the scorer of goals, the 'striker', appears to be a dying breed in the modern game.

During the 1990's the game was dominated by forwards like the Brazilian pair of Ronaldo and Romario, Christian Vieri, Gabriel Batistuta, Jürgen Klinsmann and the English pair of Alan Shearer and Teddy Sheringham. As the 2000's arrived, however, players like Thierry Henry, Raúl, David Trezeguet and Patrick Kluivert became the prevailing 'type' of centre forward of their era.

As the 4-2-3-1 became the formation of choice for most top coaches the game changed markedly. The role of the forward in particular changed, notably the use of a single forward. Coaches could not allow two forwards to play 'up top' as doing so would undermine the midfield dominance that coaches craved.

And so solo forward formations became the trend, giving rise to players like Ruud van Nistelrooy, Andrei Shevchenko, Zlatan Ibrahimović, Didier Drogba and Samuel Eto'o.

The complete forward

Now if there is one thing which has become clearer as this book has gone on - it is that the modern game requires both functionality and versatility from its players. The modern forward is not just a classic number 9 who waits for the chance opportunity to poach his goal: the Filippo Inzaghi style of centre forward. The 'poacher' who waits in the box for a chance to score. No, this player became a dying breed and the game could not 'carry' such individuals.

A single forward tactic needed a player with the ability to be flexible and varied in their approach to the game. During the 2000's the Inzaghi type striker started to go into decline, en-route to becoming *extinct*. The modern game required more.

So what does a world class forward need to possess nowadays? Technically they require an excellent touch, the ability to finish with both feet with limited touches in tight areas, the ability to use their head, and an ability to combine and create goals for others. They must also be able to run with the ball and dribble to beat players.

Tactically they require excellent positioning, movement, and the ability to find and exploit space both behind, and in front of, defences. The modern forward is also required to play and move wide; they cannot be restricted centrally. And they must also offer the team a lot out of possession, being a major figure in a side's defensive strategy.

Physically they require explosive speed, agility, and balance - especially when under pressure. Mentally they need to be intelligent, able to read and anticipate the game, able to play in the future. Finally they need to be confident, positive, and determined. The modern game requires 'complete' elements in its forward players. David Villa is all of these things.

One can argue that David Villa has been one of the best, and perhaps the most undervalued, forward in world football over the past decade. His international performances, the goals and the success they have brought, all point to his world class calibre. His quality, versatility, and goal scoring prowess have given rise to this 'complete' forward.

Villa changed the way forward play is regarded. Although players like Samuel Eto'o were already thriving in the Spanish league (Eto'o had dynamism, speed and finishing ability) Villa was showing that forwards could roam away from central areas.

By the end of 2006, Villa had become an integral part of Luis Aragonés' Spanish national team after Raúl's departure. The decision to move on from Spain's 'Prince' was justified. In fact, it can be argued that removing such a dominant and overbearing presence was paramount for the resultant success of the national side. It was a symbolic move of football's evolution; Spain had moved into the 21st century.

Although Spain would only reach the knockout stage of the 2006 World Cup, losing 3-1 to France, the signs were clear that Spain were improving on the international stage under Aragonés and his new look forward line up of Villa and Fernando Torres - Villa would play more as a right winger in a 4-3-3 formation - would see Villa score three goals at the 2006 tournament.

At the 2008 Euros Spain and Villa would finally banish the 'underachievers' tag and would mark the start of some splendid years for Spanish football. With Villa and Torres up front, Spain appeared blessed with true world class quality in their side.

Villa would continue his international scoring form at the World Cup in 2010 where he would finish joint top scorer with five goals. His goals would be a major part of Spain's progression to the final and their overall success.

In 2012 Villa became Spain's all-time top goal scorer overtaking Raúl's tally of 44 goals. In turn, his record in tournaments proves how important he is when the pressure is on. His goals are not just tallied against the *lesser* sides but against some of the world's best *and* at key moments.

Some believe that Villa did not get the recognition he deserved because of his loyalty to Valencia. When he moved to Barcelona in the summer of 2010 it was significant for him and the club. He was perfect for Barca's style and his influence and movement would be provide Barca with the depth, width, and goals they required.

As Cruyff said of Villa's influence, *"Villa is not only there to finish plays. Villa is synonymous with depth. It means always being ready to open passing lanes, to draw defenders and thus freeing space for others."* It was little surprise that with Villa in the side Barca would play some of the best football ever seen.

A need to be universal

By 2011 the world of football was in the midst of a revolution. Barcelona's success pointed towards a new way forward and many were wondering if the 'classic' centre forward was to become a thing of the past. Attention focused more on players like Messi, Ronaldo, and Villa. Tactics shifted towards 'false nines' and a move towards striker-less formations. Universal type formations for universal type players.

The move away from the classic striker towards a more 'complete' forward has meant more football played on the floor at high speed. Forwards like Wayne Rooney, Robin van Persie, Luis Suárez and Radamel Falcao have emerged as players who have mastered the '9.5 role', where they move between the 9 and 10 positions, moving deep to provide and hold up the ball, and pushing into centre forward positions to score goals.

Never has universality been so important to football; and the '9.5' is an example of this, a player who can be both creator and scorer. They are playmakers and goal scorers in one (even showing an impressive aerial ability). The most complete, universal forwards in the present game are Lionel Messi and Cristiano Ronaldo.

At Barcelona, Guardiola was seeking to bring the best out of his star player - Messi - and decided that sacrificing a centre forward to offer Messi more space was worthwhile. His tactical brain and willingness to experiment helped football progress and gave other coaches and players ideas of how to exploit oppositions. Messi started out wide right yet moved centrally and became a revelation. Playing between a 9 and 10, a tactical move which gave rise to the terms 'false nine' and the '9.5' Messi propelled himself to levels not seen since Maradona, Pelé, or Cruyff.

Size and power

With only one choice of forward, coaches had a decision to make. Whereas the earlier trend was a big man/little man combination, they now had to choose between the two. It was interesting to see this decision influence the game.

Universality

In the previous decades of football, particularly in England, the 'big' centre forward was commonplace in most sides. He offered height for headers, and strength for physical battles. During a period of football when the ball was often spent in the air rather than on the floor this player prospered. However, across Europe the centre forward was valued more highly in terms of talent and the 'big man' needed more than just heading ability.

In the early 2000's the English league was ruled by the strength, power and skill of forwards like Alan Shearer, Teddy Sheringham and Thierry Henry. Different types of players yet ruthless goalscorers. In 2004 when Jose Mourinho arrived at Chelsea he brought in another dominant forward in the Ivorian - Didier Drogba. Drogba's ability to hold up play, create, and score goals propelled Chelsea to the top of English football. Drogba became the perfect prototype of the lone forward.

The need for movement had become a central factor at the top levels of the game at this time. The game had become more about *space* and therefore required smart players, coaches and teams who looked to find ways to locate and exploit this. The top players were required to be masters of creating and exploiting; being able to drag defenders away, move deep, wide and beyond, to receive or to create space for others.

Didier Drogba was one of the best at this and, under the guidance of Mourinho, he evolved his game from a classic number 9 target man, to a much more dynamic forward. His movement into wide areas created space for players like Frank Lampard to exploit, which produced many goals for the Englishman.

Mourinho has built his success on this type of forward. At Porto he used Benni McCarthy to secure Champions League success. He created one of the most dominant forwards in English football in Drogba at Chelsea. He made Ibrahimovic Serie A's top goal scorer, and brought in Diego Milito to be the target man for his treble winning Inter side in 2009/2010.

As the game embraced dominant forwards, more sides were seeking players similar to Drogba, players who offer more than just goals. Previous poachers like Michael Owen, Ruud van Nistelrooy, Andy Cole, Filippo Inzaghi and even Fernando Torres – players who had brought success to their sides - were no longer seen as essential by top coaches.

Accordingly, we saw the rise of players like Robert Lewandowski, Zlatan Ibrahimovic, Mario Madzukic, Edinson Cavani, Diego Costa and Mario Balotelli. Powerful players with the ability to hold up the ball, bring others into the game, and score goals with their heads and feet.

Exploiting modern defenders

It is interesting here to point to the evolution of defenders as to why this type of forward was more imposing. The modern game was requiring ball playing defenders who could build out from the back, and although these players were better technically in possession, they appeared to be becoming *less* capable defensively.

The game became one which valued defenders who could *play* more than they could actually defend, leading to a reduction in defensive quality. It seemed that modern defenders were lacking in the skills necessary to deal with 'big' forwards. Coaches saw this as something to take advantage of. As defenders became more inclined to defend on the floor, the aerial threat of players like Ibrahimovic, Fernando Llorente and Diego Costa became more pronounced.

As detailed, overall, the game had become about midfielders and had embraced small slight technical players – therefore a more physical approach and style could be seen to overpower such players and teams. Strong forwards overpowered defenders whose abilities lay not so much in 'defending'.

It was Bayern who really took this approach to heart and made 'dominating' opponents an art form. In the 2012/13 season Bayern put pressure on opposition defences from wide areas and through the middle with Robben, Ribéry and Thomas Müller behind a centre forward in Mario Mandžukić. It was extremely effective (as the 7-0 aggregate defeat of Barca proved!). Size and power allied with skill appeared the way forward.

Mandžukić was as complete a forward as Bayern would want, possessing the ability to 'move' into areas that allowed teammates to move in behind and exploit the space he vacated. This movement becomes hard to defend against. His defensive ability to press tirelessly to contain and rush opposition defences (he even pressed the defensive midfielder, effectively working three players single-handedly) made him, like Lewandowski at Dortmund, a key asset to Bayern's defensive setup. Mario Gomez, by comparison, was a more rigid classic target man, and had proven incapable or unwilling to do what Mandžukić did.

And when Guardiola arrived the side was enhanced further. The talents of Mandžukić were furthered and the overall attacking approach became more dynamic, varied, and fluid. Guardiola developed Bayern to be a side who played the ball on the floor and importantly on the floor in the area. The Croatian had scored 19 goals for Bayern under Heynckes in 2012/13, yet under Guardiola he scored 28. And it wasn't just Mandžukić who excelled. Arjen Robben and Franck Ribéry scored more than before, and Mario Götze reached 15 goals, yet the key difference was the contribution of Thomas Müller, who scored 24 goals, 13 goals more than the season before.

The German forward is a player of the past and future in one. He looks unorthodox and gangly and comparisons with Gerd Müller, the great German forward of the 1960-70's is not far off. Müller scores goals - unconventional, ugly goals at times and he is not a player you associate with the 'pretty' modern game. But Thomas Müller is one of the most intelligent, versatile players in the modern game. He is a goalscorer, a creator, and 'understands' space more than most players in the game. He, like Mario Götze, Sergio Aguero, Luis Suárez and, of course, Lionel Messi is the perfect example of the universal forward.

Strike partnerships

Yet while Bayern were moving towards fluid attacking football, as close to *Totalfootball* in the modern game as we have got, other coaches were looking at introducing a strategy which had seemingly been lost. With the change in the striker's role and the evolution of modern defenders, coaches were alerted to the vulnerabilities of modern defences and pointed towards the idea that perhaps *another* centre forward could cause even more damage.

For a decade, defences had learnt to deal with a single forward, yet what would happen when another was introduced? By 2013 coaches started to answer this question on the pitch. And, as we know, answers most often lie in the past.

The classic strike partnership was one of the most consistent facets of football for decades. The 80's and 90's was a golden era for the strike partnership, it was the time when the 4-4-2 was very much the formation of choice for many (notably English sides). Two forwards was a necessity.

Across Europe at that time, the twin striker setup utilised the *trequartista* who played behind a poacher. During the 90's this is where Del Piero, Zidane and Baggio excelled. It was a partnership yet not in the English way of viewing it.

Arsène Wenger is credited with being a key vehicle for change in England yet he did not deviate from the 4-4-2 in terms of set-up - he worked the system to suit the needs of his players. Bergkamp and Henry played the 9 and 10 roles and the team stood out. In fact it was one of the greatest 'partnerships' English football had witnessed.

The arrival of continental coaches would see the need to move away from the 4-4-2 of England to a more balanced and midfield-dominated formation. The classic front two appeared a thing of the past. Was it simply a case of the modern game not requiring a front two? Was a compact and overloaded midfield more important than goal scorers? Or was it that wide players driving in from outside were the *new* type of forward, able to exploit more space in wide areas? It appeared teams could deploy a single forward, or have a three pronged forward attack with wide forwards, but a classic central two was not possible.

Renaissance of a dying breed

In the 2013/14 season a two man strike partnership started to emerge across Europe. Manchester City's new coach - Manuel Pellegrini - utilised a 4-2-2-2 that recognised the need and value in two forwards. The move back towards a big man/little man combination in Álvaro Negredo and Sergio Aguero proved clinical and brought many goals. Liverpool also sought to develop a strike partnership with Luis Suárez and Daniel Sturridge delivering an abundance of goals and attacking entertainment. The two man strike force had returned.

Perhaps the most dominant partnership across Europe was that of Zlatan and Cavani at Paris Saint-Germain. Both players have been used as single targets for many years yet have shown an understanding and ability to move and create for others. The way they played was fascinating, in many ways they were used as single forwards, yet interchanged and moved for *each other* to create space. With their attributes and intelligence it has become one of the most dangerous partnerships seen.

We also saw Juventus sign a strike partnership of Carlos Tevez and Fernando Llorente (winning Serie A), with Fiorentina also seeking to embrace a partnership in Mario Gomez and Giuseppe Rossi. And then there is Atlético Madrid, who defied the odds by winning La Liga and being a minute away from lifting the Champions League.

Atlético played some of the best football in Europe and, yes, they used a strike partnership. David Villa and Diego Costa were clinical and ruthless in their approach and Atlético became one of Europe's best sides that season. Both players are intelligent, and move to create space deep and wide.

In some ways the teams listed above (and their coaches) are going against the accepted norm by using two forwards. Somehow they are made out, by certain pundits, as being 'old fashioned' in their approach. But the return of a forward two is not old fashioned; it's a modern take that offers success. Why should coaches feel restricted to using just one forward when they have two great ones to choose from? Could we start to see more clubs using this approach?

We saw at the World Cup that Louis van Gaal used a two man forward line of van Persie and Robben to great effect. Bayern look set to have a partnership of Lewandowski and Müller for the 2014/15 season. Barcelona may even play with two forwards in Neymar and Luis Suárez with Lionel Messi behind. The resurgence of strike partnerships appear to be something we will see more of.

Universality

Now of course some will say it is a move back to 4-4-2, but is it really? At times it looks like it, yet it is hard to identify a definitive formation, especially in possession. Whilst it is clear that there are teams using two forwards, these modern versions are *very* different to the classic ones.

Contemporary forwards in this fluid 4-4-2 rotate, roam deep and wide, and seek to move defenders. The old classic forward two would stay between the 18 yard box and goal, and would play a predictable (albeit often effective) game. Modern strategies and tactics are more intelligent and fluid. And with that you require players who are both intelligent and capable of adapting to different roles and positions. This is universality, and this is what we are starting to see more of.

Ultimately it is evident that the modern forward has needed to become more dynamic, more flexible and more mobile to suit the needs of the modern game. The forward has had to evolve as much as any other player in order to stay relevant. One, two, and three forward systems are reliant on movement and fluidity. It is why when we talk of universal players and systems the forward has had to evolve the most. He must be a goalscorer, a playmaker, a target man and the first line of defence. *Complete* is the word.

Part III | The Future Game

Chapter 16: Visionaries

"Football is not about eleven individuals, but about the dynamic system made up of those individuals." Valeriy Lobanovskyi

The past two decades have given us some exceptional managers, men such as Fabio Capello, Marcello Lippi, Vicente del Bosque, Carlo Ancelotti, Alex Ferguson and Jose Mourinho. These men have achieved stellar success and have become regarded as some of the greatest managers in the game. Yet, have they sought to take the game to new levels, sought to change football? Not really.

Although all have been successful, none of these men have managed the game in a way which can be said to go against the norm (although, perhaps, Ancelotti's Milan side could be said to be 'different' to what others were doing at that time). Although the record books would regard these men as greats, although their players and fans would say they are the best, it is difficult to suggest any of these men were true *visionaries*.

Football has evolved because there have been key men who have shaped and advanced the game. Men who have taken the game to new levels with ideas beyond the accepted norm. This chapter will look at the influence of the game's true visionaries: those who have influenced, inspired, and changed the game and who have given the game the possibility of universality.

Totalfootball's constant influence

Rinus Michels was a Dutch coach who achieved great things with Ajax and Holland in the late sixties and early seventies. He is the man credited with the creation of the football philosophy *Totalfootball*. Based on what has happened to football since his time, Michels can be argued to be the most influential coach in football history.

Totalfootball was seen by Michels to be the interchanging of positions across the pitch. Players would move into spaces freely, rotate, and cover for each other while always being on the move. The idea of space was key and, for him, success came from how you controlled it.

A high pressing game enabled the whole team to stay compact and close, creating pressure on the opposition to limit their time on the ball. And when in attack - it was as though a whole team was attacking you. Totalfootball was near poetry when executed correctly. Each player understood the tactical setup and how one another's movement impacted on their position. Complete harmony, unison, and understanding.

Of course many tried to counteract the style and at times succeeded. But it was Ajax, playing under Stefan Kovacs (and led by the genius of Johan Cruyff the player) that defeated Inter Milan in the 1972 European final to put (as Jonathan Wilson wrote) *"another nail into the coffin of the old-school catenaccio… Ajax proved that creative attack is the real lifeblood of the game."*

The fact that Totalfootball has continued to thrive across the decades and different generations of players and coaches shows how it has captured the imagination. People want to play a style of football which entertains as well as succeeds!

There was another coach at the time of Michels who was also a believer in the ideas of Totalfootball, and who had a major influence on the development of *universality*. Valeriy Lobanovskyi's time at Dynamo Kiev would see him develop and prove his theories on the game of football - where was a believer in the *wholeness* of the game. It was *"less about individuals than about coalitions and the connections between them."*

Lobanovskyi's philosophy was, *"To create the ensemble, a collective of believers who subordinate themselves to the common playing idea."* He saw football as a *"dynamic system, in which the aim was to produce the optimal level of energy in the optimal pattern."*

Lobanovskyi was very much ahead of his time in the 1970's, and was obsessed with preparation, in terms of physical training, diet, and rehabilitation. And it would be Lobanovskyi who would coin the phrase *universality*.

His training methods covered 'set moves' in which players would work on patterns of play which were to be rehearsed and executed to perfection pre-game. It was key that his players developed a greater understanding of their roles in the system and what they should be doing. Lobanovskyi sought to educate his players as a team in 'intelligent' football.

Critics of Lobanovskyi would say he 'stifled individuality' yet in truth what he did was make players aware that they were *not* individuals, but part of a unit. And that their skills would only be needed in the 'context of the system'. As he said, *"The tactics are not chosen to suit the best players, they must fit our play. Everybody must fulfil the coach's demands first, and only then perform his individual mastery."*

Think of modern coaches like Jose Mourinho, Louis van Gaal, Diego Simeone and Pep Guardiola, for a moment. They have become the modern versions of Lobanovskyi in terms of their approach, demands, and team-focused philosophies. Yet before we reach the modern visionaries, we must continue to discuss those coaches who brought the game into the 21st century.

An Italian revolution

Arrigo Sacchi was an admirer of the philosophy of Michels and sought to achieve a similar style of football while coach at AC Milan. His back-to-back European Cup successes in 1989 and 1990 have still not been matched since. What set his side's success apart was the level of performance, and their quality and movement… which was captivating.

The fact that three of Holland's finest players – Marco van Basten, Ruud Gullit and Frank Rijkaard – were part of the team highlighted Sacchi's admiration and appreciation for Dutch players, and the Dutch philosophy, and helped make Milan Europe's best.

When Sacchi arrived at Milan he was an outlier in terms of his approach to the game. While the rest of Italy was playing a defensive, negative game, Sacchi sought attacking football. And like those visionaries before him he did not wish to focus so much on the individual, but build a cohesive attacking 'team'.

Sacchi appreciated the Dutch Totalfootball approach and embraced it in his style, but he also sought to leave a legacy, to leave a mark on the game. As he said, *"If you want to go down in history you don't just need to win, you have to entertain."* He added, *"My greatest objective was to make people enjoy themselves."*

And as we have seen, those who make a long-term lasting impression have been the 'entertainers'. As Jorge Valdano, the ex-Argentina player who is a fan of creative, attacking football, said, *"We remember Arrigo Sacchi's AC Milan side more than we remember Fabio Capello's AC Milan side, even though Capello's Milan were more successful."* It is this idea which appeals to the visionaries; success yes, but one must leave a lasting impression.

Whilst managing, Sacchi was keen to stress the importance of pressing for his side, and the tactical genius of Italian football. It was not as aggressive pressure as Ajax did, it was more calculated, more akin to *gegenpressing* now. As he commented, *"Our pressing was psychological as much as physical."* It was team defending, working as a unit, knowing the triggers, the timings and being as one; in synergy together.

The arrival of the three Dutch players underpinned the success of Sacchi's Milan. It allowed the 'new football' to come into Italian football. It was entertaining, attacking football. The Dutch players brought the quality and attacking impetus which Milan required. Schooled in the Dutch football philosophy and culture they suited Sacchi's approach perfectly.

The success of Milan was allied with the success of the Dutch national team which, in 1988, lifted the European Championships with goals from Milan's attacking partnership of Gullit and van Basten. Led by Rinus Michels it was almost perfect that Michels and Sacchi, both of whom embraced the concept of Totalfootball, would prove the strength of this philosophy across the game at that time.

The Dream Team

Johan Cruyff, Michels protégé, became Barca coach in 1988 and would take Barca to European Cup success in 1992. Building on his beliefs of the game in line with Michels' Totalfootball approach - he would produce one of the greatest sides in football history.

For Cruyff Totalfootball was a simple concept, in an interview with *Champions Matchday* Magazine in July 2014 Cruyff explained his concept of Totalfootball: *"Football is throwing the opposition into chaos. If you get past your man, you throw the opposition into chaos. Creating a one-man advantage using positional play has the same effect. If you don't get past your man, or create that extra man advantage, then the opposition stays organised, and nothing happens. The one man advantage is total football."*

The idea of teamwork is stressed once more from the Dutchman: *"Everyone who has played at a high level knows, I never played alone, we always did it together. It's about the team, you do that well, you do that well, so I do my job and you do yours. That mentality is transmitted to all the players and anyone who doesn't do that, he's on his way to being one of the dropouts."*

Cruyff would see in a young Pep Guardiola a player who possessed the intelligence and supreme passing ability Cruyff sought from his midfield pivot. Guardiola was to be the fulcrum for Barca's 'Dream Team' providing cover and support for players like Ronald Koeman, Michael Laudrup, Hristo Stoichkov and Romário.

The quality of player allied with the coaching methods and philosophy of Cruyff should have seen Barca achieve even more. As Guillem Balague says in his biography on Guardiola, Cruyff's side were: *"A collection of brilliant individual talents combined to become synonymous with beautiful yet effective, fast and free flowing football that became universally known as the Dream Team."*

However the 1994 European Cup final defeat to Fabio Capello's Milan side, a 4-0 demolition, effectively killed off the 'Dream Team'. Nonetheless, Cruyff's ideas would be laid down in the foundations of the club. Balague stated, *"Cruyff transformed the club that had, before 1992, been successful on the domestic front yet had failed to impose itself upon the European stage and established Barcelona as a genuine international power. In fact, Cruyff did more than set a unique footballing model in motion; he challenged Barcelona fans to confront their fears, to overcome the sense of victimisation that had been a constant feature of the club's identity since the beginning of the century."*

A philosophy, rather than a system

"I am who I am; confident, arrogant, dominant, honest, hard-working and innovative."
Louis van Gaal

Dutch football and its philosophy was at the epicentre of innovation and future game development come the beginning of the 1990's. Cruyff was at Camp Nou laying down his Dutch vision with Barcelona, and putting foundations in place which would last decades and produce one of the greatest sides ever seen. Sacchi was developing his own ideas taken from Rinus Michels and seeking to play Totalfootball, embracing something close to universality. His Dutch trio of Gullit, Van Basten and Rijkaard were on top of the world, European champions for Holland and back-to-back winners for Milan in 1989 and 1990.

Yet it was perhaps another Dutchman who would have a major influence on the development of the game we see now. A man who would have a major impact on two of the modern game's greatest coaches in Pep Guardiola and Jose Mourinho, as well as coach and develop players - now coaches - in Frank Rijkaard, Frank De Boer, Luis Enrique and Ronald Koeman. This was a man who would identify young potential and play a major role in bringing through and nurturing the world class creative talents of Xavi and Iniesta while at Barcelona. A man who would also lay down the ideas of Totalfootball at Bayern Munich and help build one of the most complete sides in football history.

It is fair to say that the influence of Louis van Gaal on the modern game and his vision to develop a team of universality makes him one of the future game's most important visionaries.

Ajax is a club that places value on being daring, brave, creative and ingenious. They pride themselves on developing innovative approaches rather than strictly adhering to rigid systems or physical strength. It is no surprise that players like Johan Cruyff, Dennis Bergkamp and Clarence Seedorf have come through the club's ranks and become world class players. Opinionated, intelligent and quality players – all three of them! Ajax values this type of player and it is probably why Totalfootball has been able to thrive in this environment.

Whomever is coach of the Ajax team there is a high expectation on them to deliver performances in line with their culture. In the book *The Coaching Philosophies of Louis van Gaal* the authors Kormelink and Severens state that the role of an Ajax coach is more than just to win, an Ajax coach must play: *"attacking soccer, dare to take risks, to accept nothing but the best in terms of express the philosophy on the field. And to win prizes each year."* Not an easy task. A feat that van Gaal achieved, though.

At the turn of the 1990's, van Gaal was given the reigns of the home of Totalfootball at Ajax, and when he took over the team in 1991 he inherited a young side with lots of potential. In his book *Stillness and Speed* Dennis Bergkamp discusses his time and experience with van Gaal. When van Gaal got the Ajax chief coach job: *"Everything became more intense. We talked a lot about things like taking positions, and every game was evaluated in detail afterwards. He constantly emphasised what was important, what we needed to learn and practice. He brought structure to the way we worked and gave us clarity."*

"You could sense there was a new generation emerging. Van Gaal made us even more eager and ambitious. Our game was innovative, attractive to watch and enjoyable to play. We trained meticulously. Every detail, shooting, passing, everything had to improve. And everything became more tactical. Where should you run and why? He constantly hammered home that you had to be aware of everything you were doing. Every action had to have a purpose."

Bergkamp would move to Inter Milan in 1993 for a record fee for a Dutch player, with Jari Litmanen coming in as his replacement. Litmanen's arrival, some believe, helped give Ajax the 'balance' in attack they required to become European champions. Yet van Gaal acknowledged that it was the return of Frank Rijkaard which truly stabilised his side before they went on to become European Champions in 1995.

As with his time at Milan, Rijkaard was the key piece to the team, the man who could control games. In van Gaal's 4-3-3/3-4-3 – a very fluid system – the use of a libero type playmaker in Rijkaard was fundamental to Ajax's play. As we spoke of earlier, Rijkaard's ability to play in front/beside or behind the two central defenders gave Ajax great fluidity and allowed them to dominate games.

Van Gaal would take Ajax to UEFA Cup success in 1992 and to back-to-back Champions League finals in 1995 and 1996. The young Ajax team van Gaal assembled would be regarded as Ajax's and Holland's 'Golden Generation' with a plethora of talent in the side. 11 trophies in six seasons is still seen as a very 'unique achievement' in the history of the game.

"My jaw dropped when I saw van Gaal's Ajax play," noted Pep Guardiola, *"They did everything a football team should do perfectly in my eyes."* After Ajax played Real Madrid in the November of 1995 Jorge Valdano, then coach of Real Madrid, proclaimed that: *"Ajax are not just the team of the nineties, they are approaching football Utopia."*

Ajax would reach the Champions League final again that season but could not defend their title and would lose on penalties after drawing 1-1 in 90 minutes. It was to be the end of Ajax's golden era as the game would embrace the transfer market like never before. The group of players predominately developed and produced through the club's academy would be dismantled with key players Edgar Davids and Michael Reiziger leaving for AC Milan. It was a new era for football as the newly won freedom of players to move at the end of their contract would hit Ajax hard. Injuries and issues would also cost Ajax in the coming seasons until van Gaal decided to depart in 1997 and join Barcelona.

His speech in October 1996 declaring he was to leave the club at the end of the season was a poignant reminder of his affection for the club. *"I was born here, played for Ajax myself, worked as a youth coach and assistant coach, and was given the chance, as chief coach, to change the whole structure of the club. I was able to adjust the squad of players in accordance with my own insights. I view Ajax as my life's work."*

In the book *The Coaching Philosophies of Louis van Gaal* which covered his time at Ajax, and particularly the Champions League campaign of 1995, van Gaal explained his approach to football and management. It is a fascinating insight into the mind of one of the most innovative coaches the game has seen. Van Gaal calls it a 'philosophy, rather than a system'. Regardless of the players or the formation, his teams must adhere to his fundamental ethos of total football.

His belief in the team over the individual is fundamental, *"Soccer is a team sport, its members of the team are therefore dependent on each other. If certain players do not carry out their task properly on the pitch, then their colleagues will suffer. Each player must carry out the basic tasks to the best of his ability."*

"The characteristics come back to my point on vision. You have to play as a team and not as individuals. That's why I'm always going back to the vision, then the team, and then which players fit in my system, a 1-4-3-3, because I'm always playing that. If a young player can do it, then I select him. If it's an older player, it doesn't bother me; it's not the most important factor. Age is not important."

Van Gaal sees it as his moral duty to entertain the crowd. His teams always go for possession, while they simultaneously attempt to score goals. The idea of continuous circulation of the ball - passing as a means to tire the opposition until space is found - can also be seen clearly in Pep Guardiola's approach.

Van Gaal's insistence is on fluid, interchangeable football in which players are comfortable operating in a number of positions. Explaining his success at Ajax, he said: *"I took players out of the old mould and even in the defence replaced them with others who could take initiative. Every single Ajax player is creative."*

Maarten Meijer, who studied van Gaal's career for his book: *Louis van Gaal – De Biografie*, offered more insight: *"What van Gaal was looking for was, as he put it, 'multi-functional players, players who could play with both legs, had both defensive and offensive capabilities, were physically strong, were quick starters, had the necessary tactical acumen to function smoothly in rotation football, and, above all, put their skills in service of the team effort."* That may be the best summary of universality we have seen.

The philosophy of van Gaal is what makes his system 'work', and it is perhaps the most universal approach seen among the visionary managers. As Bergkamp explained, *"All players are equal. For him there's no such thing as big names, because everyone serves the team and the system – his system."* Dennis Bergkamp, now coaching at Ajax with Frank De Boer, remembers a strong emphasis on collective responsibility – in fact *collectief* is van Gaal's favourite word.

In Chapters 6 and 7 we discussed the importance of teamwork and collectivism and van Gaal is one of the most ardent proponents of this philosophy. The key for van Gaal's philosophy to work is team-building, which for him is constructed from strong discipline and communication. He is firm in his belief that if there is no discipline off the pitch, there is none on it. As he says, *"First of all, you have to do your job, be on time, and be polite. We respect each other, we trust each other, and we are honest to each other. Within such a framework, you can fully develop your identity and creativity. Discipline is the basis for creativity."*

Van Gaal would move to Barcelona in 1997 and although his legacy at Camp Nou is somewhat misunderstood the reality is, as Guillem Balague explained, *"altogether different and, while it's true that the blueprint for the club's playing traditions was established by Johan Cruyff, it is van Gaal who deserves much of the credit for building upon those foundations and advancing the methodologies and systems upon which much of Barcelona's current success has been based."*

But perhaps it is his influence on Pep Guardiola which is his most important legacy at the club. When van Gaal arrived at Barcelona in 1997 it was a chance for Pep Guardiola as Guillem Balague explained: *"to learn from the architect of the extraordinarily successful Ajax team that he admired so much."* The pair constantly discussed football, tactics, positioning and training exercises. Balague stated that Guardiola recognized van Gaal as a *"key figure of the recent success of the side."*

The Dutchman saw in Guardiola an intelligence which he respected. As he says, *"I made Guardiola captain because he could speak about football. You could see he was a tactical player. He could speak like a coach even then, not many players can do that. He possessed an innate ability to lead a group of his peers and superiors. Pep is a very tactical guy and also a good human being and because of that he could persuade his fellow players."*

After leaving Barcelona van Gaal coached the Dutch national team as well as leading AZ Alkmaar to the Dutch championship in the 2008/2009 season - before moving to Bayern Munich. His time at Bayern almost brought treble success in his first season, but the team lost to Mourinho's Inter Milan in the Champions League final.

Although he appeared to fall out with key members of the team and board, his influence on the young players was, like at Ajax and Barcelona, impressive. Van Gaal saw in the young Thomas Müller, a player now regarded as one of the most complete forwards in world football, tremendous potential and vowed that: *"With me, Müller will always play."*

In Bastian Schweinsteiger, van Gaal saw a player whose skills were being wasted out wide as a wide midfielder. He convinced the German to develop his game as a central midfielder and we now see Schweinsteiger as one of the best midfielders of his generation, playing a man of the match performance in central midfield for Germany in the World Cup 2014 Final and helping his nation win the tournament.

The same happened with David Alaba who, for van Gaal, fitted the Dutchman's profile of left wing back. As van Gaal explained, *"I talked with Alaba about the left full-back position. He didn't want to play there. He was educated as a midfielder but I had a vacant position for him because I had injuries and thought he could do the job. After a lot of talking, in the end, he played there because he wanted to help the team. Where is he playing now? Left full-back."*

And as we've seen Alaba now has the ability and freedom under Guardiola to play as a wing back or move into central midfield positions. He is a true universal player. Yet he needed a coach who saw the game in this way. Van Gaal's influence on players, coaches, and the game itself makes him one of the most important visionaries of universality in the game. It is clear that van Gaal's insight and ability to see things in different players has truly helped the game progress.

El Loco

"A man with new ideas is mad until he succeeds." Marcelo Bielsa

Now although Totalfootball had its proponents it was clear that between 1994 and 2005 football was dominated by 'pragmatic' coaches: men who believed in fixed and rigid systems. This is not to say their approach was wrong. It is just that fluidity was not essential for coaches like Capello, Lippi, Ferguson, Hitzfeld, Mourinho and Benitez. For them it was about the use of specialists - specific players executing specific roles. In fact these coaches seemed to be moving the game towards specialism and away from fluidity altogether. However, there was a man who was seeking to advance the game, to create his 'own' game.

Marcelo Bielsa's creative football brain is different to almost all others and has earned him the nickname *El Loco*, the crazy man. Yet the tag 'crazy' comes because he does things differently. He is imaginative and sees the game in a different way. It should be no surprise that he was inspired and in awe of van Gaal's Ajax side. *"When executed properly it is winning football,"* beamed Bielsa, who has never hidden his admiration for the Dutchman.

After winning Argentinian league titles with Newell's Old Boys at the beginning of the 1990s, Bielsa was marked as one of Argentina's top young coaches. He became Argentine national boss in 1998 but his reputation took a serious knock when the team, regarded as favourites to win, were knocked out of the 2002 World Cup finals at the group stage. He resigned two years later.

The Argentinian would take over as Chile's national coach and would reach the last 16 of the 2010 World Cup only to lose to Brazil 3-0. It was a sad end for the side that captivated fans' imaginations with some wonderful attacking football. Playing his favourite 3-3-1-3 formation Bielsa made Chile a serious threat - as well as entertaining - and the loss to Brazil was disappointing and perhaps even a little surprising.

The ideas and philosophy he developed with Chile (which we saw at the 2014 World Cup as Jorge Sampaoli is a disciple of Bielsa's tactical approach) have become revolutionary and inspiring for many lovers of the game, as well as coaches. Bielsa's approach to football is one of the most intriguing and entertaining, little surprise therefore that Pep Guardiola regards Bielsa as one of his most inspirational guides. Bielsa's philosophy has helped define Guardiola's view on the modern and future game more than perhaps any other.

Now, it is important to understand that Chile are basically a 'five and six side' - the goalkeeper, three in the back line plus the holding midfielder are primarily defensive with everyone else looking to push forward. And for Bielsa the system is ultimately key. He expects movement and rotation yet there must be synchronisation in how the players move and interact. Sound familiar?

Bielsa aims to take the game to his opponents, to press and defend high up the pitch, and stretch the play as wide as possible when in possession. It is a very attacking and expansive formation which characterises Bielsa perfectly. Possession and movement are the cornerstones of Bielsa's philosophy with the ball; pressing when out of it. He hates sideways passing for the sake of it and seeks 'vertical penetration' whenever possible.

He recognizes the importance of the rapid movement of the ball from front to back to catch opponents off balance, but he also sees the value of retaining possession. In this way he needs players capable of playing transition-based counter attacking football as well as possession-based build up play. For him players need to be versatile.

Defensively, Bielsa talks about the value of squeezing the game into a 25-metre area (another Sacchian trait). He is keen to leave his back three and holding midfielder to defend - creating his desired defensive 3 +1 base, which offers the team defensive security as the three central defenders split to cover the zones left, right and central. Meanwhile, the holding midfielder plays a front sweeper role, ahead, to cut out any attacks and clear up any clearances. This defensive approach is also something which Guardiola holds key to make sure his team has a strong defensive 'balance', which is little surprise considering the impact Bielsa has had on Guardiola's philosophy.

His idea is the same as van Gaal's in terms of wanting to play the game in the opponent's half of the pitch, hold a high defensive line, and press the opposition very aggressively. The high line must always be accompanied by an intense press. The team must always have a spare man at the back. It is an attacking and very physically demanding system to employ.

Bielsa has stated that: *"Our simple ethos is this: we try and win the ball back as quickly as possible from our opponent's as far up the field as we can. And by that I mean everyone is involved in regaining the ball, from the forwards through to anyone else. Then once we have the ball, we try and find a way of getting forward as quickly as possible, in a vertical direction if you like. But we don't get frustrated if we can't get it forward immediately, we aim to be comfortable on the ball, and if it's not a case of going forward straight away, we keep it."*

The beauty of Bielsa's philosophy is that the formation changes so quickly and so significantly because a number of players can play two or even three positions. Like

Universality

Barca showed themselves capable - players could move almost seamlessly between roles and positions in order to move defenders and exploit space.

Creating overloads in specific zones has always been one of Bielsa's main priorities and the need to control the tempo of games, to control possession, and to wait to create 2v1 opportunities are a big part of his philosophy. His wing backs are effectively wingers who are given license to overload wide areas and push forward creating 2 on 1's against opposing full backs.

Interestingly, the full back is given license to go on the *inside* of the winger, something we have seen Bayern do under Guardiola. Often the wingers stay high and wide to stretch the opposition's defence creating the gaps which the wing backs, and the midfield runners from the second line, can exploit when attacking.

Bielsa's use of playmakers has similarities with Totalfootball and Arrigo Sacchi's philosophy. As we saw earlier the game is moving away from a rigid and specific Number 10, and embracing rotating playmakers - something that Bielsa implemented with Chile. The playmaking duties can be attributed to a few different players, and in that respect, Bielsa again aligns himself with the Sacchian notion of 'whoever has the ball is the playmaker'.

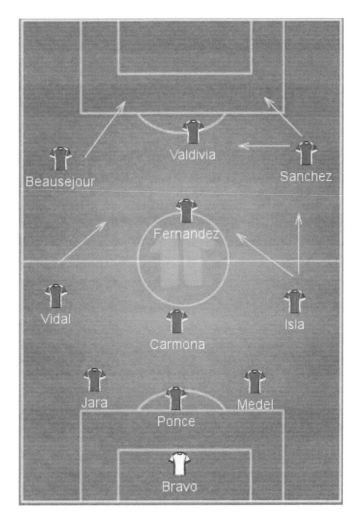

*Marcelo Bielsa's Chile playing his favoured 3-3-1-3 formation
versus Honduras in the 2010 World Cup.*

When he became coach of Athletic Bilbao in 2011 Bielsa faced a problem with his desired tactical strategy. You see he always wants an overload in his defensive line. If the opposition played with two forwards he would play with three defenders. If they played with one, he would play with two. He preferred to use a back three and implement his 3-3-1-3 formation, yet when he arrived in Spain he found almost everyone playing a 4-2-3-1. It was a single forward league. Therefore he found himself having to play the same system. Playing against a single striker, the Bielsa system needed two central defenders and, therefore, a back four was utilised.

Their two legged performance against Manchester United earlier in the Europa League had alerted many in Europe to Bielsa's young and exciting team, as well as giving the manager much earned plaudits. It was high energy, determined and skilful football. Players were moving at high speed into space, rotating positions, playing quickly. Bielsa had transformed a side from being an effective direct side to one which played attacking football akin to *Totalfootball*. And he had achieved this in a matter of months.

When Bilbao faced Barcelona in the league in 2012 Guardiola remarked on the intensity of Bilbao's play, *"We've never played against a team who were so intense, so aggressive, and has denied us so much space,"* said Guardiola. This would characterise Bilbao's approach under Bielsa, and would take the club to the Copa Del Rey final and Europa League - losing to Barcelona (Guardiola) and Atlético Madrid (Simeone) respectively.

Unfortunately Bielsa would lose Javi Martinez the following summer, a key tactical player for the side due to his ability to bring the ball out from deep and into midfield. Although many saw Martinez as a classic holding midfielder, like Busquets, Bielsa preferred a defensive-minded holding midfielder. He actually wants his ball-player in the defence because his strengths lie in playing the ball rather than winning it back.

However after the 2012/13 season it appeared Bielsa had pushed the side too far and could no longer maintain the team's intensity. It was a shame because Bilbao had produced something special during the previous season. Like van Gaal he had influenced a group of young players in Ander Iturraspe, Markel Susaeta, Ander Herrera, Oscar De Marcos and Iker Muniain as well as enhanced the talents of players like Javi Martinez and Fernando Llorente.

Bielsa has proven himself to be a man with different ideas and approaches to the game. In a similar way to Sacchi, Cruyff, and van Gaal he has developed his philosophies in line with the principles of *Totalfootball*. He has shown bravery and courage in his beliefs yet perhaps the reason his value is not seen by more people is because he has not been able to manage a club which can offer him a genuine chance of trophies. Sacchi was fortunate to attract the attention of Silvio Berlusconi; he inherited a great Milan side and a lot of money to turn his vision into success. He admits that without that investment he would probably not have won anything.

Bielsa may not have the opportunity to confirm his status as one of the best coaches in the game yet it is perhaps his influence on Pep Guardiola which could be called his greatest triumph. We now see a coach who is attempting to stretch the boundaries of the game in terms of tactics and style. We saw near perfection at Barcelona and now at Bayern we see something even more advanced, we see the future. We see a move to *universality*.

Chapter 17: The Architect

The game of the 21st century would be changed markedly by Barcelona whose philosophy and style would be built on the methods and beliefs of Rinus Michels, Johan Cruyff, and Louis van Gaal. Barcelona would embrace Totalfootball more than any other club outside Ajax. These visionaries would revolutionize the club in their image, shaping the club we see today.

After these foundations had been put in place, it would take another ex-Ajax man to push Barcelona forward into the 21st century. From 2003 Frank Rijkaard would begin to change the landscape of the club, and football itself. It would be the beginning of a major revolution for the game.

Rijkaard, as we've seen, was regarded as one of the most complete players to grace the game, a key figure for the Champions League successes of Sacchi's Milan and van Gaal's Ajax. He was a great player. And he would take this experience into his coaching. In 2003 he took over the reins at Barcelona, and the club found itself managed once more by another Dutchman ingrained in the Totalfootball philosophy.

His side would be built around the talents of Ronaldinho, Eto'o, and Deco, and would embrace the youth academy graduates Valdes, Puyol and Xavi, as well as nurture the burgeoning talents of Iniesta, Messi, and Bojan. In a few years he would take Barcelona to the top of European football with the 2006 Champions League success over Arsenal proving to be his crowning glory. However, after that success, Rijkaard could not maintain the high levels of discipline and control which had enabled the side's success. The club and the players needed someone new.

A choice which shaped the future

By the end of 2007 Barcelona had a shortlist of two names; Jose Mourinho and Pep Guardiola. Mourinho had proven his credentials as a world class coach at FC Porto and Chelsea. He would guarantee trophies and success for Barca. Guardiola, on the other hand, was working with Barcelona's 'B' side - his first experience in management. Hiring him would be appear to be a big risk.

The final decision rested largely on the coach's personalities and philosophies. Guardiola, of course, was a symbol of the club, a lasting memory of the 'Dream Team' era. He was a man who held the principles and philosophies of Cruyff and van Gaal close to him. He *was* Barcelona.

Mourinho, on the other hand, although he was assistant coach for several years with Barcelona, firstly with Bobby Robson and then Louis van Gaal from 1996-2000 - had developed his own ideas and philosophies of the game. The board had a dilemma. As well as a possible issue with Mourinho's style of play, it was his character and personality, mainly his desire to antagonise and play psychological 'games' which was not looked upon favourably by the Barca board. Ultimately they took a 'risk' on Guardiola, a gamble which paid off quite beautifully.

In choosing Guardiola over Mourinho, Barcelona not only helped themselves but helped football's future. Mourinho would have done something different in terms of the squad and playing style. Favouring physical athletes over small technicians it is probable that Barca would have become a successful yet 'normal' European side, more in line with the game at that time.

It is fair to assume that Mourinho would not have achieved what Guardiola did in terms of style, he would not have brought out the skill and quality in Messi, he would not have used a 'false nine' but more likely brought in a Didier Drogba type player to the Camp Nou. He would have embraced Yaya Toure and not seen the emerging talent of Sergio Busquets. Mourinho may have even allowed Xavi Hernandez to leave in order to have a Michael Essien or Frank Lampard come in. Just imagine that… It is not to say he wouldn't have been successful but he would not have influenced football like Guardiola did. The Barcelona board's decision changed the course of football's future and helped bring the possibility of universality into reality.

A journey of education

Although Guardiola had only experienced management for one season before he got the job as Barca's head coach, the truth is that he had been learning and preparing for life as a coach for some time. While at Barca Guardiola played beneath some of the finest football managers and coaches in the game. As a young boy at *La Masia* (Barcelona's youth academy) he learnt from the talents of Carles Rexach, and he was then taken under the wing of Johan Cruyff who educated him in his Totalfootball philosophy, where he subsequently became a crucial member of the team in the key midfield pivot role.

And while van Gaal's time at Barca from 1997 to 2000 was viewed with mixed opinions by many, his greatest achievement whilst in charge may have been the influence he had on Guardiola. Yes, van Gaal won the league twice in his time at Camp Nou but he also expressed how difficult it was to implement his football philosophy at Barcelona due to 'cultural differences', stressing that some players were unwilling to follow his lead.

After leaving Barca, Guardiola sought out coaches who he could learn from, preparing himself for a life in coaching. In Italy he moved to Brescia and worked and learnt from the legendary Carlo Mazzone. He then played for Roma under Fabio Capello in order to learn from one of the finest defensive coaches in the game. He was preparing for a future life as a coach, shaping his ideas and philosophy along the way.

He would even spend six months playing in Mexico. The reason? Because he wanted to learn from Juan Manuel Lillo, a coach he had always admired in terms of his teams' style of play. As Guardiola confessed, he *"could not retire without playing on a team coached by him."*

Lillo was the coach who many credit with the development of the 4-2-3-1, the formation we have seen that has dominated the modern game. Lillo points out that he and Guardiola share the same ideas about football, in particular an obsession with space. *"Pep and I are intent on the same thing - gaining superiority from position,"* Lillo explained. *"What use is good play between the lines if it does not take out opponents?"*

Back in 2006, before Guardiola would embark on his coaching career he took a trip to Argentina to meet Marcelo Bielsa. Guardiola travelled 11 hours to seek the wisdom of 'El Loco'. He asked Bielsa whether he should become a football manager, and then asked him: if so, how? They talked for hours, connecting on their love of football and tactics. Guardiola wanted to know more about Bielsa's football philosophy. This conversation may be the most significant on Guardiola in his development as a coach and for Bielsa he saw a man who could truly implement his ideas on the game and succeed through them.

It is evident that Guardiola learnt from so many coaches in his time as a player and on his route as a coach that these experiences, their differing and expansive knowledge, moulded the man we see today.

Not extinct, just dormant

As we've seen - the game of football is always in a state of flux. Sometimes this is slow, with a sense of calm and familiarity across the game, and then - all of a sudden - a wave of something new affects this balance and calm, a new idea or style is thrown up which poses new thinking and fresh problems. Guardiola did this at Barca; he re-shaped the modern game and asked questions of every coach, asking them to re-evaluate how they saw and played the game. This accelerated football's evolution.

His philosophy in terms of how to play the game has not changed over the course of his career. As a young player he knew his limitations and therefore embraced his attributes. He became a great pivot, capable of circulating the ball, passing with precision, making great decisions and controlling the tempo of games. He was a fundamental figure for Cruyff's vision to succeed.

And yet, in June 2001, Guardiola would leave Camp Nou. A player who - although plagued by injuries - wasn't finished at the age of 30. He was the victim of the 'changing game', and his exit was the confirmation of the end of an era, for both Barcelona and the game itself. The 21st century had given rise to a new type of midfielder, one very different to Guardiola. It was apparent that, by 2001, the game had moved on and left his type behind.

Almost a decade after the 1992 European Cup success the game now wanted more from their midfielders. Everyone, apparently, wanted physicality in their midfield; Patrick Vieira, Roy Keane, Claude Makélélé and Edgar Davids type players. The 'possession-based pivot' wasn't regarded as important anymore. The player who would sit in front of his defence and distribute the ball was no longer seen as crucial. It was the 'defensive midfielder' - the 'destroyer' - who was now in vogue.

As Guardiola said, in 2004, *"I haven't changed... my skills haven't declined. It's just that football now is different. It's played at a higher pace and it's a lot more physical. The tactics are different now, you have to be a ball-winner, a tackler, like Patrick Vieira or Edgar Davids. If you can pass too, well, that's a bonus. But the emphasis, as far as central midfielders are concerned, is all on defensive work... players like me have become extinct."*

Extinct? When we consider the importance of a Busquets, Pirlo, Carrick and even Lahm in today's game we see that the pivot is *fundamental* for top sides. And why is that? Well much of it has to do with Guardiola himself. In hiring Guardiola as their coach Barcelona were bringing back the ideas of Cruyff. The pivot was vital for the 'system' to work. Therefore Guardiola sought a player who could do what *he* did twenty years previously. In Xavi and Busquets he brought back the so-called 'extinct'-type player and made them an example of what a modern midfielder should be. He would stick with the philosophies which he embraced as a young player and, in doing so, would change the modern game. Football's cycle in action once more.

Pep Guardiola instilled his very own playing style into Barcelona. Xavi, Iniesta and Busquets, all Guardiola-type players, would tower over the game; they would be shining examples of the value of intelligent 'technicians' in midfield. A type of player and style of football, which was once considered extinct (by Guardiola himself) was now seen as the best way to play. It is not too far reaching to say that - in the space of a season - Guardiola changed how football was seen. The midfield battle became not about being 'physical' but about intelligence, movement, and possession.

It could all have been different, however, had Iniesta not scored 'that' goal at Stamford Bridge. That goal in the second leg of the Champions League semi-final against Chelsea was essential for Barca to create the 'legacy' that they have. Had Chelsea won that tie it is possible that Guardiola's style may not have become the revelation we have witnessed. It is conceivable to say that 'that' last second goal was the catalyst of change for football's future, and was the significant moment in the development of universality.

From 2009 to 2012 the 'Barcelona style' became 'the way' to play the game. Possession-based football that embraced small technicians over physical giants and

172

athletes was a dramatic change since the turn of the century. Guardiola impressively managed to change the mindset of the footballing world. 'Tiki-taka' was the model on which football's future would be built. Movement, rotation, speed of play, and tactical intelligence became synonymous with Barca and became a blueprint to replicate.

Of course Guardiola was fortunate to have conditions which were *perfect* to help him develop this style. That first season at the 'B' side was ideal for his development, it was a chance to test his beliefs and prepare him for the top job, as well as have players like Busquets and Pedro coming through at the 'right' time. There is also a feeling that had he moved to another club to 'prepare' as a manager there is a chance his philosophies would have struggled to be implemented and he may have become just another coach. However it did seem that fate was calling him. It was all a perfect mix of *timing* and *opportunity*.

As first team coach Guardiola inherited a squad of players lacking direction yet full of quality. There was a Spanish core which had been developed under the Barcelona philosophy and which had just achieved international success at the 2008 Euros. And, of course, there was the burgeoning talent of Lionel Messi, a player who was now ready to truly step up and achieve his potential. Add all this to Guardiola's methods, intensity, and work ethic and what you had was a set of fortuitous circumstances for both the coach and the players which enabled the team to become one of the greatest ever seen.

As mentioned - Pep Guardiola's philosophy - an extension of the one founded by Johan Cruyff – alongside his work ethic and tactical astuteness were essential to moulding one of the greatest club sides ever seen. And, as with van Gaal, discipline and togetherness were essential. Those days of 'playboys' like Rivaldo and Ronaldinho were banished under Guardiola. Instead, he embraced youth and sought to develop a strong core 'group'.

In his first talk with the group at the club's training camp in St Andrews, Scotland, Guardiola laid down his vision and expectations, *"This is Barça, gentlemen, this is what is asked of us and this is what I will ask of you. You have to give your all. A player on his own is no one, he needs his team-mates and colleagues around him: every one of us in this room, the people around you now."*

Guardiola built on Barca's pure football principles with near obsession and adhered to the 'tiki-taka' style. In that first meeting he also spoke of how the side would play, *"The style comes dictated by the history of this club and we will be faithful to it. When we have the ball, we can't lose it. When that happens, run and get it back. That is it, basically."* Unsurprisingly the common trend found across all the visionary coaches listed in the previous chapter is that they all believe in dominating games through possession. And, as we saw earlier, the idea of possession being the best form of defence is the hallmark of the van Gaal/Guardiola philosophy.

Guardiola's philosophy meant that Xavi was central to his vision and system. In Xavi, Guardiola had a player who was intelligent and mature, who he could trust to lead his side on the pitch. Xavi had been a key part of Barcelona's side for almost a decade yet his influence increased under both Luis Aragonés and Pep Guardiola as they saw - in him - a player who was *perfect* for the implementation and control of a possession-based game. He was the conductor on the pitch, like Guardiola had been under Cruyff.

The philosopher

Due to their success and dominance Barcelona became a blueprint for the modern game. The physicality and strength of the decade before Guardiola was now seen as slow and rigid against a style of football which was sharp, quick, and frighteningly efficient.

Guardiola had proven to be one of the most tactically astute coaches in the sport. When players talk of his coaching they talk of an educator, a man who explains 'why' in everything he does. They learn and believe in his ways because he convinces them that what he says is true. The results and performances prove how well he works his magic on the team. His sides are prepared and drilled to perfection. Every little detail matters.

His level of commitment, focus and determination transformed a group of players in that summer of 2008. A squad clearly possessing quality, yet lacking guidance and motivation, was turned into one of the greatest sides in world football, perhaps *ever*. Guardiola proved his managerial talents by taking good players and turning them into world class ones. He made Barcelona a unified team, functioning as *one*.

Germany's coach Joachim Löw, a man who has sought to embrace the philosophies of Guardiola during his time as Germany's national coach, spoke of his admiration for how Guardiola has changed the modern game, *"What Guardiola has done to some extent is challenge some of the truisms and clichés of football, such as defending is about sitting deep and denying space for teams, Barcelona have done the opposite, they've gone and looked for teams, defended with possession which teams perhaps haven't done before."*

Of course, Guardiola, like most visionaries and revolutionaries, took the philosophy to new levels and this was, maybe, too far for many of his players. He sought to push the limits and boundaries of his philosophy and of his players. He sought near complete *Totalfootball* in the look of Cruyff and van Gaal's desired 3-4-3, yet struggled to find the right 'balance' in the side. He could not perfect 'the next step', one which appeared to be his desire for universality.

His final season at Barcelona was perhaps a season too far for him, with his team evidently looking fatigued and starting to lose focus. The weight of being the best appeared to be taking its toll on them and him as a coach.

During his four years as Barca's head coach Guardiola pointed us to the future game. He spurred many coaches and players to replicate the Barca philosophy (this happened across all levels of the game from youth to senior). This is what revolutionaries achieve, they inspire and educate a new way of being and ultimately dictate where the future is going. It was a footballing revolution.

Winning everything is not enough

Guardiola's next move would become a major talking point. He was the most in-demand coach in world football. And of all the opportunities to continue his vision - Bayern Munich was the perfect fit for him. A club which, over the previous decade, had been steadily building into something unique and dominant was seeking a 'revolutionary' to take the project further.

From 2008 the club saw different coaches arrive, bringing their own philosophies to the team with them. Jürgen Klinsmann had attempted to make them more 'English' with high tempo football. Louis van Gaal had brought the Dutch attacking philosophy to the side (much in the same way that he did at Barca). Jupp Heynckes brought key defensive organisation and structure, and the addition of Matthias Sammer in the coaching team added intensity and (importantly) mindset which the players and team needed.

This gradual evolution of the side had helped to create a complete team, built over many years, mixing different ideas and styles, and comprised of home grown talent alongside some world class players. By 2013 Bayern was considered to be one of the most 'complete' sides ever seen in the game. The team looked capable of playing any style necessary in order to succeed. It was a well-planned and ultimately successful project and it was clear that Bayern were set on building a machine. They were creating the world's best side; they were looking to create a *legacy*.

After that 2012/13 season, when Bayern were so dominant and successful under Heynckes, during which the team played a style which was very much in-line with the 'modern game' (4-2-3-1 with a double pivot, inside forwards, and a strong 'complete' forward) the club now wanted to build a side for the 'future'. What the project needed was a coach to make this possible. Enter Pep Guardiola.

When Guardiola arrived in the summer of 2013 he was inheriting a side which had just conquered domestic and European football. Unlike the conditions he found in 2008 when he took over from Rijkaard at Barcelona, this was a group of players at the peak of their game. His task was to develop a team which had broken records during the previous season and which had played in a manner which many believed was 'not possible' to improve upon. It was never going to be an easy task.

The expectations on Guardiola were not only to defend the Champions League (which hadn't been done since Sacchi's Milan in 1990) but to improve on the team's performances and style. Many were sceptical of what he would do and achieve at Bayern. Many questioned how one could improve on what Heynckes had accomplished. In terms of trophies perhaps it was not possible. And the dramatic defeat in the semi-final against Real Madrid led to wide criticism regarding Guardiola's style. Some even said it was 'the death of tiki-taka.'

Bayern versus Real Madrid in the Champions League semi-final 1st leg. It was a game in which they would dominate possession yet fail to turn possession into chances and goals.

Following the defeat, accusations came thick and fast into how Guardiola's sides 'had no Plan B' and how it *"was wrong for Bayern to change their style to accommodate Pep."* This led to questions over his future and the viability of the 'project'. Had Guardiola's attempt to revolutionise Bayern (and also the game itself) been naïve? Was he seeking to embrace a style which had 'worked' in the past yet which was not suitable or sustainable in the future?

Was counter-pressing in fact the way forward? The results and successes in recent seasons had proven that it was a style which brought trophies. It was just a year earlier that Bayern had destroyed Barcelona in the same way that Real Madrid defeated Guardiola's side playing a high tempo counter-pressing 4-2-3-1 style.

Had Bayern gone backwards in their development? Had Heynckes found the 'winning formula' and had Guardiola now destroyed it? Under Heynckes, in their Champions League meeting, Bayern had dominated Barca's tiki-taka with an aggressive style of play; such an approach was dismissed by Guardiola in the aftermath of the defeat to Real Madrid. As he said, *"I did not want to have the typical German game of back and forth. I wanted a lot of possession and we managed that in parts. But we did not finish our chances well."*

He even admitted, after the game, that in terms of counter-pressing Madrid were the best, *"They are the best counter-attacking team in the world"* he claimed, yet in a sly dig he then emphasised that their strength and success came down more to physical attributes than football quality. *"They have legs, they are athletes. They are football players, but mainly athletes."* It was an interesting comment to make, seemingly implying that tiki-taka football was a more intelligent way of playing the game; but it had just been defeated 5-0. Was physicality, athleticism, and counter-attacking football the blueprint of the future game?

Although counter-pressing has proven to be effective in recent seasons, and while the loss to Madrid (and the manner of it) could be said to point to a future when counter-pressing leads the game, in truth the defeat to Madrid should be seen merely as a blip in the evolution of Bayern and football in general. The truth is that watching Bayern under Guardiola over the course of the *whole* season provided an *education* into the future game. Great sides make good teams look average and Bayern made many sides over the season look mediocre. The reason is simple (yet complex).

A move to universality

As discussed at length, Guardiola sees the game in terms of dominating possession and mastering space. For him this is the heart of football. This is why he seeks to flood and dominate his midfield areas. But it is not only a matter of numbers – it involves types of players and personalities. For him there is a *need* to be fluid in order to rotate and master space. This requires players who are adept at playing in a multitude of positions.

For Guardiola the key to his style being effective is to use players with great football *intelligence*. Hence the emergence of Philipp Lahm in the centre of midfield. For many he is the world's best full back, yet for Guardiola Lahm is a football genius, the most intelligent player he has ever worked with (some compliment when you consider he worked with Xavi, Iniesta, Busquets and Messi). Therefore why put a player with such intellect on the wings? For Guardiola Lahm is a player who *needs* to play centrally and be a nucleus to the side. And if anyone knows how to play the pivot role it is Guardiola.

Many thought it was foolish to move Lahm around; an unnecessary and problematic move. Yet for Guardiola, it was not foolish but *logical*. What Guardiola is really teaching us is that the future game is *all* about intelligence. Reactive players will not work in the future, the skills of anticipation and perception as well as mastering space and time will become the hallmark of football's future.

The project at Barcelona was magnificent yet perhaps fell short of Guardiola's overall vision. At Bayern he has been given another chance with arguably a greater, more *varied* side. Bayern personify a mix of physical athletes with strength, skill, speed and intelligence. It is a 'perfect mix'. Bayern's owners appear to have got what they wished for, not only positive results but a man who will make them 'iconic', who will create the aforementioned 'legacy'.

Looking at his setup it is clear that Guardiola sees the game going to where many have prophesied before; a 2-8-0 formation, where eight players are free to roam and move into space. It is positional freedom yet structured in terms of *where* the eight should be positioned.

The positions of the centre backs are relatively fixed (though expect forward runs from central defenders as they embrace the libero role) as, too, is the single pivot in midfield who can move between a sweeper in defence to a holding midfielder ahead (similar to what Rijkaard offered van Gaal for Ajax).

In front of this defensive triangle (diamond if you count the keeper) the game is fluid and universal. Out wide are modern 'wing backs' that rotate. Like Sacchi and Bielsa, Guardiola wishes to have two players wide at all times, yet 'who' they are is not important. The midfield is in constant flux which makes it almost impossible to track. The set-up is, at times, reminiscent of Marcelo Bielsa's 3-3-1-3.

Now to play a universal type game requires players who can retain possession with quick combination play. For Guardiola, controlling the ball, seeking to find overloads and pressing high in transition underpin his system. Creating overloads is a primary focus and the circulation of the ball is employed to find 2v1 or 3v2 situations. Why? The answer is space. Guardiola is obsessed with it, how to find it and how to exploit it on the pitch. And finding ways to use the space effectively is where coaches focus most of their efforts.

Quick ball circulation sees the ball move quickly to open areas seeking to expose spaces between and around defensive blocks. With players constantly moving - the opposition struggles to defend as they see a constantly shifting landscape in front of them.

Defensively, the advantage of a short passing game enables a team to have several players around the ball while dominating possession; if possession is lost there are four or five players who are capable of pressing and closing a player and ball down immediately, suffocating the opposition. This style overwhelms and stifles the opposition making it extremely difficult to find spaces in which to play. It ends up reducing good teams into being rushed and mediocre ones. Like 'good' sides did against Barca they often end up hitting hopeful long balls to their forwards in fits of desperation, which often means Guardiola's teams regain possession quickly and effectively.

Bayern's play under Guardiola could be said to rival that of his Barca side. Yet, at the same time, his Bayern squad can be argued to be faster, more physical, and more universal than even Barca were.

Writing the future

It is not inconceivable to say that Pep Guardiola is the most visionary coach and thinker of his generation. His education in football as a player and coach has given him the cultural exposure and understanding to become the new (revolutionary) master of the Totalfootball philosophy.

Guardiola continually seeks to evolve his style and team to remain ahead of the rest, looking to find new ways to counteract defensive setups which seek to stifle his approach (as we have seen with the rise and success of counter-pressing). As Jonathan Wilson proclaims, *"What marks Guardiola out is his awareness of the future…in terms of understanding the sweep of history, of recognising that what is good now will not necessarily be good in a year or two's time…that awareness marks Guardiola as a true dynastician."*

However, it also seems that Guardiola is seeking to achieve more than just success. Like Sacchi he has spoken about the obligation to 'entertain' the fans. And it does appear that, like van Gaal, he is in search of multi-functional players who can play in multiple positions. Surely a clear sign that he is in search of universality? Through Guardiola, and other progressive coaches, the game is moving to where Arrigo Sacchi prophesised.

Modern progressive coaches see the potential that the modern player provides. They see that positional fluidity and versatility not only help their sides to succeed and entertain, but also to push the boundaries of the game. What Guardiola and other visionaries, such as Marco Bielsa and van Gaal are showing us, as coaches and students of the game, is that the future of football is not fixed but fluid. These coaches have shown us new tactical concepts and are now leading us into a new and exciting period of style and formations. It is evident that a world of universality beckons.

For fans of the game who love being entertained as much as winning – the future appears exhilarating, bold, and one of innovation. And, of course, the beauty of football also means that as these new styles and approaches are developed – there will be coaches across the globe urgently looking to thwart them! Football as 'athletic chess' is alive and kicking. Viva la revolution!

Chapter 18: Universality

Arrigo Sacchi has suggested that the game of the future will not just be a team-centred game but a *universal* game. The game of the future will require positional *freedom* and *variability*, with interchangeable footballers capable of operating *wherever* required.

Now the concept of universality has been around for decades. It's simple really; everyone has the same responsibility, to attack and defend. Players should be capable of fitting into different positions and carrying out that specific job. The basis for each player is the same, to be part of the team at all times and to fit into any position which is required of them.

However with coaches like Guardiola, van Gaal (at Manchester United) and Bielsa (at Marseille) influencing players as well as future coaches it appears that we may be witnessing a genuine era of universality. With the level of athleticism, the quality of pitches, and an ever-growing intelligence from players and coaches - universality really *can* become a reality.

This trend did not look likely during the 2000's, when the game became obsessed with 'specialists'. At this time the game was looking rigid and inflexible. It had evolved *against* Sacchi's philosophy and vision. Yet the game has changed. And this is in part thanks to what happens at youth levels. Like Sacchi says, what happens at youth level is fundamental for success at the top, *"In the end the national team is only ever the last beneficiary of whatever work has been done at the outset. If something starts badly, it will not end well."*

While Director of Football for Real Madrid in 2004 (a position which left him frustrated both in terms of the transfer policy at Madrid as well as the evolution of the game) he observed the development of players in the youth system at the club. He found that: *"We had some who were very good footballers. They had technique, they had athleticism, they had drive, they were hungry. But they lacked what I call knowing-how-to-play-football. They lacked decision making. They lacked positioning. They didn't have the subtle sensitivity of football: how a player should move within the collective. And for many, I wasn't sure they were going to learn. You see, strength, passion, technique, athleticism, all of these are very important. But they are a means to an end, not an end in itself."*

In Sacchi's opinion a willingness to learn, allied with an intelligence of understanding the game, were the main requirements to becoming and succeeding as a footballer. Something which he felt youth academies failed to develop. Sacchi also felt that players were being brought up as *specialists* at far too early an age.

In 2011 he was asked to oversee an overhaul of Italy's youth sector, while his former star player Roberto Baggio was given similar responsibility for reinvigorating the famous coaching school at *Coverciano*.

Sacchi was not pleased with what he found, *"I see kids who are 14 or 15 years old who are already specialists. But football is not a sport of specialists,"* he said. *"I was watching the under-15s the other day – 14-year-old boys – and the central defenders arrived and all they did was mark their man. They took themselves out of the game. This is suffering, this is not joy, this is not football. If someone does just one thing over and over, they will get better at that thing. But is football just one thing?"*

Although Sacchi found the 21st century a frustrating time, as his philosophy was seemingly ignored in favour of the specialist, the truth is that his beliefs now define the modern game, and importantly appear to be the blueprint of the future. In turn, the emergence of Guardiola's philosophy along with an evident shift in the development of more universal-type players through European youth academies points to the possibility that (with the right coach and players) universality could become a realistic achievement.

Redundant systems

Joachim Löw had evidently been influenced by the work of Guardiola and moved away from 'fixed' systems at the 2014 World Cup- embracing different formations and seeking positional movement and rotation. Germany's success gives us the first lesson for the future game. Positional freedom and fluid systems.

Now, of course, there will still be many coaches who seek to use fixed positions for players across the pitch - it is easier for them to control and prepare players in this way, and they may seek individuals who are still 'specialists'. The Champions League in recent years has shown that strict and rigid tactical systems *can* nullify the opposition and bring success. It is not always pretty but a strong defensive base can be difficult to break down.

Yet this is a strategy which limits creativity. These strong defensive sides have got to a level where it is reasonably easy to defend against them and their players. It is therefore important for fluid and flexible systems to replace these rigid units to cause greater problems for the opposition.

On our journey across football's evolution over the past two decades we have seen many formations which have risen and brought success. We have covered the evolution of formations and systems, and the key formations which most sides have used in recent years have been: 4-4-2, 3-5-2, 4-2-3-1, 4-3-3. Within these frameworks coaches have moved players to suit their needs.

Recently, Atlético Madrid embraced the 4-4-2 and went on to become one of Europe's strongest sides. Their defensive pressing was a mix of high pressing and a deep compact block; they attacked and defended in 'waves'. Mourinho's return to

Chelsea pointed to a similar tactical plan, building on a deep compact block into a higher pressing side. Both coaches focused on the counter attack to expose sides.

However, when we talk about 'systems' of play we need to understand that modern teams rarely play to a *defined* formation. There are many different distinct moments in the game when a variety of strategies, formations, or tactics will be used. And the higher the level, the more complex and detailed these differences are.

Strategies when the team have the ball and when they don't, or a strategy to exploit a weak area of the opposition. Perhaps a certain time in the game... like at the World Cup in Brazil where (because of the climatic conditions) coaches set out different strategies for the first half compared to the second as a way to save energy. Sometimes changes happen because of the scoreline, being 1-0 up or 1-0 down can affect how a team plays.

A snapshot of a game often looks chaotic and random, yet formations are given to us as things of simplicity. But the truth is that these 'formations' are not really there. As Slaven Bilic said, *"Systems are dying, it's about the movement of 10 players now."* This is a perfect summary of football's future.

Having a framework and formational basis is important as a starting point, but it should not be rigid. You will see a more defined formation when a side is out of possession yet in possession the key is to exploit space and the more 'loose' a side is, the easier it can be to find space and lose markers.

So, is the time for formations over? Should we not be looking at the philosophy over the system? Ultimately every formation can be played in a different way; it is based on the philosophy of the coach and how attacking, defensive-minded, controlling or risky he wishes to be. As van Gaal has made clear, look at 'his philosophy' rather than the system.

Andy Roxburgh, former UEFA technical director, prophesised that the game was heading towards 4-6-0 where there are four defined defenders and in front of them six midfield players all of whom can rotate, attack and defend. It was, to him, the start of universality as all those six players would need to attack, run, and defend all over the pitch.

Some coaches, like Craig Levein at Scotland, used a 4-6-0 formation as a negative defensive approach yet Spain under Del Bosque won the European Championships in 2012 by using a false nine to create one of the most fluid 4-6-0s seen. This play has been seen in the style of Barcelona and Spain in players like Iniesta, Fàbregas and Messi. These are universal type players who could play anywhere in the attacking system and be capable of performing. This is also a reason why perhaps the classic centre forward has not worked for these sides. One-dimensional play is not suited to fluid football.

Roxburgh's vision has been moved even further ahead as we see what Guardiola is doing at Bayern. The coach is breaking new ground in terms of preparing for the future of football. There is a fixed goalkeeper and two central defenders, yet ahead of them are eight players all moving and rotating. A 1-2-8-0?

Now to say eight players can go anywhere is not the case. In my opinion the future game will require *strict* tactical systems where the players are free to move and rotate *between* certain structures. Importantly, and this is what Barcelona and Bayern have excelled at, they perform all this inside a very well organized, disciplined, and synchronised system. As Sacchi has said, *"Many believe that football is about the players expressing themselves, but that's not the case. Or, rather, it's not the case in and of itself. The player needs to express himself within the parameters laid out by the manager."*

Guardiola's wish to develop his side with a Bielsa-type 3-3-1-3 is evident; he asks more of this wing backs to vary between playing wide and moving infield to become central midfielders. He has taken this formation and suited it to his needs, he seeks total domination of the ball and does not wish to give up possession cheaply.

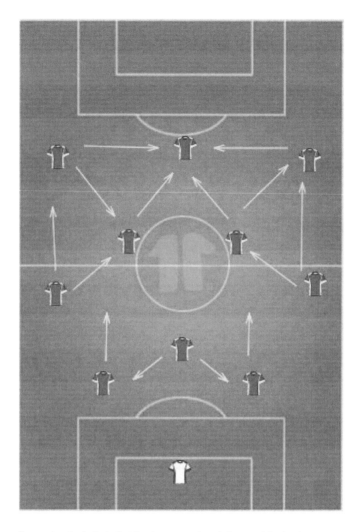

Football's future formation? A 3-2-2-3? A triangular defensive block that can rotate and ahead of them a structured tactical setup yet which allows rotation and fluidity.

Universal players

"How can you talk about 'total football' if your players don't understand the game from every point of view? You have to be able to read each situation not only from your position but from that of your colleagues. Each pass of the ball by your team, or by the opposition, changes the situation."
Johan Cruyff

If we consider what a universal type player needs to be able to perform in a number of positions then we should look at who we have at this time. In the past decade players such as Didier Drogba, Steven Gerrard, Wayne Rooney and Yaya Toure have been regarded as the most complete and universal type of players due to their physical capabilities and ability to play in almost any position (and perform their roles well). Their strength, however, lies in their physical attributes of size and strength.

Are the players mentioned above dynamic enough for the modern game, though? In players like Arturo Vidal, Luka Modric, Philipp Lahm, Gerard Pique, Javi Martinez, Bastian Schweinsteiger and David Luiz we see genuine universal-type players who are excelling in contemporary football. These players can play in a multitude of positions, they can drop back into defence or move into midfield and are able to fulfil defensive or attacking roles. They can deal with the demands of the game as they possess complete attributes. They are not 'specialists' but universal players.

Philipp Lahm's emergence as a central midfielder points to his universal capabilities, a small player yet one who possesses the key physical attributes of endurance, speed and agility which are necessary for his role as a wing back or midfielder. Allied with his decision making and technical skill and it is no surprise Guardiola has seen in him a player who fits his universal type profile.

In terms of attacking forward players we see a clear rise in the complete forward. If we take the present universal players in the game we can argue that Cristiano Ronaldo and Lionel Messi are the most complete forwards in the sport. Ronaldo has the physical attributes necessary to play in a variety of positions across the forward line. He is a winger and a centre forward in one. He has speed, strength, power, spring and agility.

In Messi we see perhaps the *most* complete player in the game today. He can play wide, up front, as a 10, or in the midfield. He is everything in one. His vision, intelligence, and decision making is unrivalled. His ability lies in his technical skill, his excellent decision making, and his physical agility. His explosive speed is incredible. Messi can be deemed the perfect specimen of a universal player.

Along with Ronaldo and Messi we are witnessing this type of player becoming more prominent. In Luis Suárez we see another player who can be regarded as one of the most universal forward players in the game at this present time. His ability with the ball and versatility to play in different areas and positions makes him extremely hard to play against and helps his side unlock defences. Meanwhile, his Barcelona teammates Neymar and Andrés Iniesta have the technical and tactical versatility to play in almost any position in midfield or attack.

Mario Götze, a player who will become a central part of Guardiola's tactical evolution at Bayern is (like Messi) capable of playing in a multitude of positions and importantly able to do so with the highest of quality. He is Germany's most complete forward. And there is also Marco Reus, Alexis Sanchez, Karim Benzema, Gareth Bale and James Rodriquez who all are complete forwards capable of taking up positions in different forward areas and being effective. English football is seeing the emergence of Raheem Sterling and Alex Oxlade-Chamberlain who both possess the attributes of a complete forward. England's future may rest on these young men.

Above all, however, the key trait which has become essential for the modern game is *intelligence*. If Spain and Germany have taught us anything it is that the future game will need clever players and coaches as the game itself becomes more intelligent. In order to develop teams who can rotate and play fluid football, coaches must seek to develop game intelligence.

Possessing a football brain is important because, as the speed of football gets ever quicker, it requires players who have the ability to read the play and anticipate it at ever faster rates. The modern player needs to be an excellent decision maker and a great learner - tactical nous is becoming a pre-requisite not a bonus.

Germany's emergence as a developer of great players and teams is in part because of the country's development of tactical intelligence. They have always had strong defences, which is why they are always challenging in major tournaments, yet now they have a model of development which creates complete players who possess the skills required for the game of today and tomorrow.

Universal athleticism

Roberto Mancini said, at a conference several years ago, that the evolution of football will be more to do with improved physical preparation than with tactical development. In his opinion it will be the physical elements of players which will take the game forward. When we consider this in relation to universality then it makes sense. The game has become faster, with players being quicker and more explosive. The game has become about athletes, which is why individuals like Riquelme have lost their place in the game.

Now there are many who believe that 'position-specific fitness' will become vital in the development of elite players for the future. It is a valid argument, each position has different needs and requirements and it has always been puzzling to think that every member of the squad should perform the same physical workout plans when their role requires different skills (e.g. distance covered for midfielders, speed endurance for wingers and full backs, and explosive sprints for forwards). Every position will need a different physical requirement.

The future game will see a significant enhancement in the athletic capabilities of players and coaches should be aware of this. There will be increased physical demands in the future due to a higher tempo of ball movement and faster oppositions will mean a side's speed and endurance will be paramount. As the ball is kept in play more often, and games are longer, players will cover greater distances. Greater distances and higher speeds mean more sprints at higher intensities. The game will lead to players needing to cover between 12 and 15 kilometres a match, at different speeds and directions.

In fact, the most crucial aspect underpinning the game's progress is that of *speed*. Technical speed will continue to get quicker. In turn, mental speed will need to increase; the speed of reactions, vision, and tactical decision making. This, accordingly, will put more demands on the intelligence and speed of thought of players.

Developing the future

In order to meet the game's changes, coaches - especially those who coach young players - need to develop players who *understand* how and when to change roles and positions. But are our coaches (of both young and senior players) *willing* to allow their players and teams to experiment and be creative? Or, will they find it safer to keep fixed formations and pigeon hole players as this is 'easier' to coach'?

We have to ask if a 'fixed developmental approach' will help develop smart, intelligent players capable of playing in the future. Will these players have the skills and adaptability to play in numerous positions and systems? The answer is *no*. To prepare for the future game we need to develop players capable of dealing with the demands of the game. Fixed and rigid coaching and training is *not* the answer.

The game of the future will favour versatile players; players with all-round technical skills, who have no fixed position. They will have the ability to move constantly and become the playmaker at any time. They will have less time to operate and therefore need to be excellent decision makers capable of playing a variety of positions on the pitch. This will put a lot of demand on their development as a young player.

Technical excellence will not be important but essential. Players will be expected to be dribblers and carry the ball when required. Without question 1v1 ability will be fundamental for every player. And the need for one touch play will increase as game tempo will increase.

If we agree that the future player needs to have the necessary all-round capabilities then what will define the best? There will be many who will argue that technical excellence is the main defining element for world class players. And this is correct. Technique, speed, and tactical execution *are* crucial components of football, but it is *mental toughness* that marks out the very best players.

The very best have mastered the skill of mental toughness and have a strong football mind. Top players and coaches understand the importance of sport psychology in football and this needs to be embraced and pushed at all levels. When you listen to the world's best players at this time, Messi and Ronaldo for example, talk is always about their need to improve further, to keep honing their skills, the constant striving to be better. They never seem to be content and thus continue to improve and be the best. They have the *mindset* of a champion.

Being able to train the mind and work on improving a player's mindset has become an important tool in developing top level players. The psychology of footballers can be argued to be the single most important factor in turning a good player into an elite one. Therefore being able to train the mind to become the best it can be is fundamental to success in the future game.

The rise of universality

Barcelona's rise allowed us to see what universality *could* look like. A team that comprised of technically excellent players, playing as one whole, was breath-taking and the accolades of the 'best team ever' were warranted and deserved. From the goalkeeper to the forwards Barca possessed superb footballers, and there was no weak link. Defensively Guardiola had perfected the pressing game which gave the side defensive cover as they stifled the opposition. They had achieved perfect balance between attack, defence and transition. It was as near to complete the game had seen.

And then we witnessed the next step in the evolution of the game, this time in Germany. Bayern's emergence as a serious challenger for world dominance has shown us a *new* version of what a complete team can produce. This is not just a side who play one way but a side that can do it *all*.

Bayern have players who are capable of operating in a multitude of positions and systems, who can rotate and interchange when necessary. Furthermore, at the international level, Germany's success at the World Cup has also heralded a revised world order. After several years of semi-final exits in major international tournaments German national coach Joachim Löw finally found the balance and quality required to take Germany to the top of the international game.

A German midfield of players like Bastian Schweinsteiger, Sami Khedira, Philipp Lahm, Mesut Özil, Thomas Müller, Mario Götze and Toni Kroos has enabled Löw to allow his side to rotate with each other and different systems in the game. These players' versatility in terms of technical and tactical ability as well as their intelligence and physicality means they can all operate in different areas of the midfield effectively, allowing for the creation of time and space on the pitch.

Löw varied his approach throughout the tournament, using a false nine with Mario Götze in some games, or playing the German 4-2-3-1 in others. It was a sign that German football had a group of players who could implement various systems and positions. They proved, not just in their success but in their style, that Germany's football was the most advanced and progressive in the world when it came to developing players and teams for the future game.

Like Spain in 2010 it is no surprise that Germany succeeded in winning the World Cup in Brazil. Theirs was the most *complete* squad at the tournament, perfectly suited to the needs of the modern game. Germany were quite simply on another level to the opposition. They were more fluid, flexible, and intelligent.

Now there is no doubt that the influence of Pep Guardiola helped Germany to succeed. His arrival at Bayern in 2013 and the implementation of new ideas have certainly enhanced the development of the German players in the side. Lahm's tactical shift has brought out more from this exceptional individual. And it is not just those in outfield positions who have been enhanced. Manuel Neuer's 'sweeper' role has been enriched by Guardiola's philosophy. Not only is Neuer regarded as the best keeper in world football now, but some believe *ever*.

Guardiola's ideas on the game have taken football forward more than any other coach. His success has helped this become a reality as success often breeds replication. His philosophy is simple; he wants his team to exploit space on the pitch to have near complete domination of possession, always seeking to overload key areas. The importance of movement and positional interchange is what counts. And he has taken rotation even further. It's not just in midfield where players move. He has his wing backs rotate and move centrally, he has his centre forward switch with his midfield and wingers.

Guardiola's first season at Bayern brought football which was as beautiful a vision as Sacchi and Bielsa could have hoped to imagine. The building blocks through the season pointed to something special from Guardiola - a new model for football based on the philosophy of Totalfootball and universality. The following years will give him the platform (and a means) to build a team which not only dominates Europe but which can rewrite how the game is played.

The future game

On this book's journey into football's development we have seen that *every* position has evolved and been enhanced. The game has become faster, with skill levels rising and tactical intelligence and mindset becoming fundamental. We have seen tactical evolutions and revolutions with football's 'cycle' in full force.

The game itself has become more in-depth, studied to a greater degree, and this has meant a higher level of detail in preparation, analysis, and planning. The game has become more creative as progressive, intelligent coaches seek to find new and innovative ways to stay ahead of the rest.

As well as this, youth development across the world is becoming more professional and detailed which is seeing a greater number of young quality players being produced. The demand for quality has never been greater and young players are battling with peers *across the globe* to become a professional. And this competition is driving much of the change we are seeing.

Football's future can be summarised as being more intelligent, athletic and technical than ever before. As coaching becomes more detailed and intellectual the tactical elements of the game will become enhanced too. And *everything* points to why universal players capable of *adapting* to these tactical changes is paramount. One-dimension football will not work as the game evolves.

The game has evolved from the need to dominate *possession* to dominating *space*. Space is what the game is about, the ability to master and exploit it. Because of this a shorter passing game has taken hold for many coaches who strive to keep possession and dominate games. Yet we have also seen the rise of verticality, of quick, direct transition-based football which seeks to exploit the space differently. Without question transition has become one of the most important elements for achieving success.

Defensively, teams know how and when to press high and when to drop deep. The development of defensive 'blocks' and 'triggers' have become central to the sport. Knowing how to defend later has become a key element of the game and will continue to be. Space behind an opposition's defence is what coaches seek and with enhancements in speed and the modern offside rule - deep runs behind a defence are more problematic to defend against, and more conducive for attacking success.

Ultimately the future game will be one of *tactical variation*. This was illustrated by Bayern in 2012/13 where they were able to play a variable style of football as well as vary the tempo to suit the needs of the game and to exploit opposition weaknesses. Their ability to play a longer vertical game as well as building up play through the thirds centrally and wide drove their success. This was allied to their ability to break at speed, and be ruthless on the counter attack!

Pep Guardiola he has taken his Bayern squad and moved them forward. He is embracing the philosophy of universality. Above all it is Guardiola who has the potential to take the game further than any others because he not only has the willingness and creative brain to achieve it, but he also has the players to make it a reality. He has sought to fuse the philosophies of Spain and Germany together to produce a style of football which is complete and dominant.

Football's future will be defined thanks to the visionaries and risk takers who seek to try new things and experiment with the game. This is how anything evolves, change through trial and error. We may just be on the cusp of something very special in the history of football. The vision of many progressive coaches has been to master

Universality

universality and, finally, it appears that we are one the cusp of this becoming actuality.

Bibliography

Introduction

LMA (2004) Part 2 of the interview with Arsene Wenger
http://www.leaguemanagers.com/news/news-4853.html

Wilson, J (2010) The Question: Why is the modern offside law a work of genius?
The Guardian. http://www.theguardian.com/sport/blog/2010/apr/13/the-
question-why-is-offside-law-genius

Chapter 1

Hayward, B (2013) The transfer that changed football - how Ronaldinho's switch
from PSG to Barcelona sparked a revolution. Goal.com.
http://www.goal.com/en/news/1717/editorial/2013/04/02/3870186/the-transfer-
that-changed-football-how-ronaldinhos-switch

Iyer, V (2012) Claude Makelele – The Position, The Player And The Man The Hard
Tackle http://www.thehardtackle.com/2012/claude-makelele-%E2%80%93-the-
position-the-player-and-the-man/

BBC Sport (2003) Man Utd sign Ronaldo bbc.co.uk.
http://news.bbc.co.uk/sport1/hi/football/teams/m/man_utd/3142959.stm

Chapter 2

Winter, H (2001) Arsenal sign Wenger with expert timing. The Telegraph.
http://www.telegraph.co.uk/sport/football/teams/arsenal/3018234/Arsenal-sign-
Wenger-with-expert-timing.html?mobile=basic

Auclair, P (2013) Thierry Henry: Lonely at the Top. Macmillan.

Chapter 3

Jenson, P (2011) Xavi: Paul Scholes is the best midfield player of the last 20 years...
He would have been valued more if he was. Spanish Mail Online.
http://www.dailymail.co.uk/sport/football/article-1355726/Xavi-interview-Paul-
Scholes-best-midfielder-20-years.html

Williams, R (2008) Only Cole demurs as Chelsea cheer Makelele mastery. The
Guardian.
http://www.theguardian.com/sport/blog/2008/may/20/onlycoledemursaschelseac
h

FourFourTwo (2012) Inside the mind of Pep Guardiola.
http://www.fourfourtwo.com/features/inside-mind-pep-guardiola

Lowe, S (2009) Pep Guardiola reaps reward of hard work and high style. The Guardian. http://www.theguardian.com/football/blog/2009/may/28/pep-guardiola-barcelona-champions-league

Arsenal Column (2009) Use of wing backs will only put teams in a flap. https://arsenalcolumn.wordpress.com/tag/full-backs/

Chapter 4

UEFA.com (2013) Heynckes hails exceptional Bayern. http://www.uefa.com/uefachampionsleague/season=2013/matches/round=2000351/match=2009612/postmatch/quotes/index.html

James, S (2013) How Germany went from bust to boom on the talent production line. The Guardian. http://www.theguardian.com/football/2013/may/23/germany-bust-boom-talent

Lowe, S (2013) Barcelona's crushing blow at Bayern feels like a changing of the guard. The Guardian. http://www.theguardian.com/football/2013/apr/24/barcelona-bayern-changing-guard

Chapter 5

Wilson, J (2008) The Question: why has 4-4-2 been superseded by 4-2-3-1? The Guardian. http://www.theguardian.com/football/blog/2008/dec/18/4231-442-tactics-jonathan-wilson

Smyth, R (2013) Alex Ferguson will bring tactical nous as well as motivation to Madrid. The Guardian. http://www.theguardian.com/football/blog/2013/feb/11/sir-alex-ferguson-tactical-nous-madrid

Wilson, J (2013) The Question: Has 4-2-3-1 lost its gloss? The Guardian. http://www.theguardian.com/sport/blog/2013/jan/15/the-question-4231-football-tactics

Cox, M (2010) Teams of the Decade #11: Valencia 2001-04. zonalmarking.com. http://www.zonalmarking.net/2010/01/29/teams-of-the-decade-11-valencia-2001-04/

Wilson, J (2010) The Question: Is television holding back the evolution of football? The Guardian. http://www.theguardian.com/sport/blog/2010/jan/05/is-television-holding-back-football-evolution

Chapter 6

Van der Does, R (2011) Champions League Final: Breathtaking Barça Leave Ferguson In Awe. Footy Matters. http://www.footymatters.com/european-football/champions-league-articles/champions-league-final-breathtaking-barcelona-leave-manchester-unitedferguson-in-awe/

Richards, A (2012) 'Nobody can be happy with the outcome of the Champions League final' - Johan Cruyff. Goal.com. http://www.goal.com/en-india/news/221/champions-league/2012/05/22/3118178/nobody-can-be-happy-with-the-outcome-of-the-champions-league

Chapter 7

Balague, G (2013) Pep Guardiola: Another Way of Winning: The Biography. Orion.

Jackson, P (2006) Sacred Hoops: Spiritual Lessons as a Hardwood Warrior. Hyperion; Reissue edition.

Bayern,com (2013) Heynckes: it's down to fantastic teamwork. http://www.fcbayern.de/en/news/news/2013/41842.php

Bandini, P (2011) Arrigo Sacchi, the magician of Milan, begins to build a new Italy. The Guardian. http://www.theguardian.com/football/2011/nov/22/arrigo-sacchi-milan-italy

Corrigan, D (2014) Ancelotti praised as Real record nears. ESPNFC.com. http://www.espnfc.com/story/1726297

McRae (2013) Jürgen Klopp rallies neutrals to support 'special' Borussia Dortmund. The Guardian. http://www.theguardian.com/football/2013/may/21/jurgen-klopp-borussia-dortmund-champions-league

The Telegraph (2014) Arsenal v Bayern Munich: Arsène Wenger says Barcelona sides under Pep Guardiola were stronger than Bayern. http://www.telegraph.co.uk/sport/football/teams/arsenal/10647638/Arsenal-v-Bayern-Munich-Arsene-Wenger-says-Barcelona-sides-under-Pep-Guardiola-were-stronger-than-Bayern.html

Chapter 8

The Goalie Is The Game Decider, That's how the modern goalie plays. Soccerpilot.com. http://m.soccerpilot.com/magazine/how_the_modern_goalie_plays.html

Sportsmail (2011) Dutch of class: Swansea boss Rodgers hails arrival of new keeper Vorm. http://www.dailymail.co.uk/sport/football/article-2025197/Michel-Vorm-hailed-Brendan-Rodgers.html

Golriz, B (2012) Is Spain's Number 1 also Spain's Best Goalkeeper? Not Just the Bottom Line. http://notbottomline.wordpress.com/2012/02/08/is-spains-number-1-also-spains-best-goalkeeper/

Chapter 11

Sports Analysis (2012) Doing the dirty work: the holding midfielder. http://analysesport.wordpress.com/tag/midfield/

The Arsenal Column (2012) Sergio Busquets: Re-inventing the midfield pivot role. http://arsenalcolumn.co.uk/2012/07/21/sergio-busquets-re-inventing-the-midfield-pivot-role/

Quixano, J (2012) Euro 2012: Spain profile – Sergio Busquets. The Guardian. http://www.theguardian.com/football/blog/2012/jun/04/euro-2012-spain-sergio-busquets

Lowe, S (2011) Sergio Busquets: Barcelona's best supporting actor sets the stage. The Guardian. http://www.theguardian.com/football/blog/2011/may/27/sergio-busquets-barcelona

Chapter 12

Ferguson, A (2013) Alex Ferguson : My Autobiography. Hodder & Stoughton.

Metro (2006) Rafa: I'll get the best from Gerrard. http://metro.co.uk/2006/10/24/rafa-ill-get-the-best-from-gerrard-299690/

Chapter 13

Vickery, T (2008) Riquelme - one of a dying breed. bbc.co.uk. http://www.bbc.co.uk/blogs/legacy/timvickery/2008/10/riquelme_one_of_a_dying_breed.html?postid=69857579

Chapter 14

Doyle, M (2013) Low labels Ribery Bundesliga's best. Goal.com. http://www.goal.com/en/news/15/germany/2013/07/20/4130257/low-labels-ribery-bundesligas-best

Chapter 15

Delaney, M (2011) The 100 greatest players of all time. The Football Pantheon. http://footballpantheon.com/2011/09/the-100-greatest-players-of-all-time/5/

Chapter 16

Wilson, J (2009) Inverting the Pyramid: The History of Football Tactics. Orion.

Sky Sports Football's Greatest Teams : Milan

Hindley, M (July 2014) The Revolutionary Genius of Johann Cruyff. Champions Matchday.

McNulty, P (2014) Man Utd: Louis van Gaal is 'arrogant, dominant and honest'. bbc.co.uk. http://www.bbc.co.uk/sport/0/football/27301473

Bergkamp, D (2013) Stillness and Speed: My Story. Simon & Schuster UK

Defending with the ball (2014) Louis Van Gaal Tactical Philosophy. http://defendingwiththeball.wordpress.com/tag/ajax/

Kormelink, H & Seeverens, T (2003) The Coaching Philosophies of Louis Van Gaal and the Ajax Coaches. Reedswain Incorporated.

Meijer, M (2014) Louis van Gaal: The Biography. Ebury Press.

Robson, J (2014) Van Gaal has totalfootball masterplan for United Manchester. Evening News. http://www.manchestereveningnews.co.uk/sport/louis-van-gaal-total-football-7146779

FIFA.com (2013) Van Gaal : Age is not important. http://www.fifa.com/worldcup/news/y=2013/m=12/news=van-gaal-age-not-important-2244745.html

Lowe, S (2012) Athletic Bilbao's Bielsa – obsessive and dangerous for United's chances. The Guardian. http://www.theguardian.com/football/blog/2012/mar/07/marcelo-bielsa-athletic-bilbao-manchester-united

Chalk on the boots (2013) Keep Pressing Forward. https://chalkontheboots.wordpress.com/category/in-depth/

Cox, M (2011) Athletic 2-2 Barcelona: Bielsa stifles Barca by telling his players to stick tightly to opponents. zonalmarking.com. http://www.zonalmarking.net/2011/11/07/athletic-bilbao-2-2-barcelona-bielsa-guardiola-tactics/

Chapter 17

Cox, M (2012) How the 2000s changed tactics #1: The fall and rise of the passing midfielder. zonalmarking.com. http://www.zonalmarking.net/2012/04/24/how-the-2000s-changed-tactics-1-the-fall-and-rise-of-the-passing-midfielder/

Balague, G (2012) How Pep Guardiola got the Barcelona players on his side to halt team's decline into decadence. The Telegraph. http://www.telegraph.co.uk/sport/football/teams/barcelona/9683924/How-Pep-Guardiola-got-the-Barcelona-players-on-his-side-to-halt-teams-decline-into-decadence.html

Murphy, C (2012) Reinventing the wheel: How Guardiola revolutionized football. CNN. http://edition.cnn.com/2012/05/28/sport/football/football-guardiola-barcelona-messi/

SkySports.com (2014) Pep Guardiola defends Bayern Munich possession tactics after defeat at Real Madrid. SkySports.com. http://www1.skysports.com/football/news/11890/9280482/champions-league-pep-guardiola-defends-bayern-munich-possession-tactics-after-defeat-at-real-madrid

Wilson, J (2012) The Question: what marks Pep Guardiola out as a great coach? The Guardian. http://www.theguardian.com/sport/blog/2012/apr/04/the-question-pep-guardiola-barcelona

Chapter 18

Whittall, R (2013) The Skeptical Tactician: Is non-adaptability of players like Rooney a product of over-specialization in development? http://blogs.thescore.com/counterattack/category/tactics/page/2/

Bate, D "The Future Game" Presentation. http://www.ldcunited.com/downloadfiles/32914371_Dick_Bate's_English_F_A__Presentation.pdf

The Way Forward: Solutions to England's Football Failings

by Matthew Whitehouse

English football is in a state of crisis. It has been almost 50 years since England made the final of a major championship and the national sides, at all levels, continue to disappoint and underperform. Yet no-one appears to know how to improve the situation.

In his acclaimed book, The Way Forward, football coach Matthew Whitehouse examines the causes of English football's decline and offers a number of areas where change and improvement need to be implemented immediately. With a keen focus and passion for youth development and improved coaching he explains that no single fix can overcome current difficulties and that a multi-pronged strategy is needed. If we wish to improve the standards of players in England then we must address the issues in schools, the grassroots, and academies, as well as looking at the constraints of the Premier League and English FA.

"Whitehouse, while still relatively unknown, has written a masterpiece. Young, forward thinking and passionate about the English game, this is a book you'll be hearing a lot more about over the coming years as England aim recover their respected standing in world football both in terms of the national side and the players coming through the ranks."

These Football Times

4.9 out of 5 stars

5 star		52
4 star		5
3 star		0
2 star		0
1 star		0

September 2014
57 Amazon.co.uk reviews

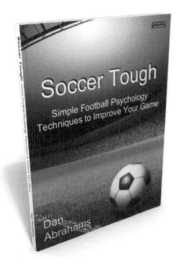

★★★★★ ▾ (57)

(Amazon.co.uk Sep 2014)

Soccer Tough by Dan Abrahams

"Take a minute to slip into the mind of one of the world's greatest soccer players and imagine a stadium around you. Picture a performance under the lights and mentally play the perfect game."

Technique, speed and tactical execution are crucial components of winning soccer, but it is mental toughness that marks out the very best players – the ability to play when pressure is highest, the opposition is strongest, and fear is greatest. Top players and coaches understand the importance of sport psychology in soccer but how do you actually train your mind to become the best player you can be?

Soccer Tough demystifies this crucial side of the game and offers practical techniques that will enable soccer players of all abilities to actively develop focus, energy, and confidence. Soccer Tough will help banish the fear, mistakes, and mental limits that holds players back.

★★★★★ ▾ (4)

(Amazon.co.uk Sep 2014)

Scientific Approaches to Goalkeeping in Football: A practical perspective on the most unique position in sport
by Andy Elleray

Do you coach goalkeepers and want to help them realise their fullest potential? Are you a goalkeeper looking to reach the top of your game? Then search no further and dive into this dedicated goalkeeping resource. Written by goalkeeping guru Andy Elleray this book offers a fresh and innovative approach to goalkeeping in football. With a particular emphasis on the development of young goalkeepers, it sheds light on training, player development, match performances, and player analysis. Utilising his own experiences Andy shows the reader various approaches, systems and exercises that will enable goalkeepers to train effectively and appropriately to bring out the very best in them.

★★★★★ ▾ (2)

(Amazon.co.uk Sep 2014)

Small Time: A Life in the Football Wilderness by Justin Bryant

In 1988, 23-year-old American goalkeeper Justin Bryant thought a glorious career in professional football awaited him. He had just saved two penalties for his American club - the Orlando Lions - against Scotland's Dunfermline Athletic, to help claim the first piece of silverware in their history. He was young, strong, healthy, and confident.

Small Time is the story of a life spent mostly in the backwaters of the game. As Justin negotiated the Non-League pitches of the Vauxhall-Opel League, and the many failed professional leagues of the U.S. in the 1980s and 90s - Football, he learned, is 95% blood, sweat, and tears; but if you love it enough, the other 5% makes up for it.

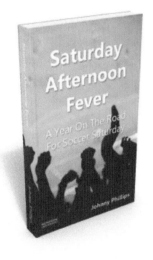

★★★★★ ▾ (9)

(Amazon.co.uk Sep 2014)

Saturday Afternoon Fever: A Year On The Road For Soccer Saturday
by Johnny Phillips

You might already know Johnny Phillips. He is a football reporter for Sky Sports' Soccer Saturday programme and a man who gets beamed into the homes of fans across the country every weekend.

For the 2012/13 season, Johnny decided to do something different. He wanted to look beneath the veneer of household-name superstars and back-page glamour to chronicle a different side to our national sport. As Johnny travelled the country, he found a game that he loved even more, where the unheralded stars were not only driven by a desire to succeed but also told stories of bravery and overcoming adversity, often to be plucked from obscurity into the spotlight… and sometimes dropped back into obscurity again. Football stories that rarely see the limelight but have a value all fans can readily identify with.

★★★★☆ ▾ (4)

(Amazon.co.uk Sep 2014)

Jose Mourinho by Ciaran Kelly

From growing up in a Portugal emerging from dictatorship, and struggling to live up to his father's legacy as an international goalkeeper, the book details José Mourinho's extraordinary journey: the trophies, tragedies and, of course, the fall-outs. Starting out as a translator for the late Sir Bobby Robson, Mourinho has come to define a new breed of manager, with his unrivalled use of psychology, exhaustive research, and man management providing ample compensation for an unremarkable playing career. Mourinho has gone on to become one of the greatest managers of all-time.

From Porto to Chelsea, and Inter to Real Madrid – the Mourinho story is as intriguing as the man himself. Now, a new challenge awaits at Stamford Bridge. Covering the Mourinho story to October 2013 and featuring numerous exclusive interviews with figures not synonymous with the traditional Mourinho narrative.

Making The Ball Roll: A Complete Guide to Youth Football for the Aspiring Soccer Coach by Ray Power

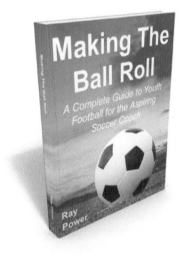

★★★★★ ▾ (18)

(Amazon.co.uk Sep 2014)

Making the Ball Roll is the ultimate complete guide to coaching youth soccer.

This focused and easy-to-understand book details training practices and tactics, and goes on to show you how to help young players achieve peak performance through tactical preparation, communication, psychology, and age-specific considerations. Each chapter covers, in detail, a separate aspect of coaching to give you, the football coach, a broad understanding of youth soccer development. Each topic is brought to life by the stories of real coaches working with real players. Never before has such a comprehensive guide to coaching soccer been found in the one place. If you are a new coach, or just trying to improve your work with players - and looking to invest in your future - this is a must-read book!

★★★★★ ▾ (5)

(Amazon.co.uk Sep 2014)

The Footballer's Journey: real-world advice on becoming and remaining a professional footballer by Dean Caslake and Guy Branston

Many youngsters dream of becoming a professional footballer. But football is a highly competitive world where only a handful will succeed. Many aspiring soccer players don't know exactly what to expect, or what is required, to make the transition from the amateur world to the 'bright lights' in front of thousands of fans.

The Footballer's Journey maps out the footballer's path with candid insight and no-nonsense advice. It examines the reality of becoming a footballer including the odds of 'making it', how academies really work, the importance of attitude and mindset, and even the value of having a backup plan if things don't quite work out.

★★★★★ ▾ (2)

(Amazon.co.uk Sep 2014)

Conference Season
by Steve Leach

Disillusioned with the corporate ownership, mega-bucks culture, and overpaid prima donnas, of the Premiership, Steve Leach embarked on a journey to rediscover the soul of professional football. His journey, over the 2012/13 season, took him to twenty-four different Football Conference towns and fixtures, visiting venues as diverse as the Impact Arena in Alfreton, Stonebridge Road in Ebbsfleet, and Luton's Kenilworth Road.

Encountering dancing bears at Nuneaton, demented screamers at Barrow, and 'badger pasties' at rural Forest Green – Steve unearthed the stories behind the places and people – it was a journey that showed just how football and communities intertwine, and mean something.

Conference Season is a warm and discerning celebration of the diversity of towns and clubs which feature in the Conference, and of the supporters who turn up week-after-week to cheer their teams on.

Other Recent and Forthcoming Books from Bennion Kearny

★★★★★ ▾ (6)
(Amazon.co.uk Sep 2014)

What Business Can Learn From Sport Psychology
by Dr Martin Turner & Dr Jamie Barker

★★★★⯨ ▾ (7)
(Amazon.co.uk Sep 2014)

The 7 Master Moves of Success
by Jag Shoker

Soccer Tactics 2014: What The World Cup Taught Us
by Ray Power

What is Tactical Periodization?
by Xavier Tamarit

CPSIA information can be obtained at www.ICGtesting.com
Printed in the USA
LVOW01s1243220914

3711LVUK00004B/4/P